THE CIVILIZATION OF THE AMERICAN INDIAN SERIES

THE PHOENIX
OF THE
WESTERN WORLD

QUETZALCOATL
AND THE
SKY RELIGION

Sarcophagus lid from Palenque

THE PHOENIX OF THE WESTERN WORLD

QUETZALCOATL AND THE SKY RELIGION

BY
BURR CARTWRIGHT BRUNDAGE

DRAWINGS BY JEANNE MEINKE

UNIVERSITY OF OKLAHOMA PRESS
NORMAN

By Burr Cartwright Brundage

The Juniper Palace (New York, 1951)
Empire of the Inca (Norman, 1963)
Lords of Cuzco: A History and Description of the Inca People in Their Final Days (Norman, 1967)
A Rain of Darts: The Mexica Aztecs (Austin, 1972)
No Chance Encounter (St. Petersburg, 1974)
Two Earths, Two Heavens: A Comparison of Inca and Aztec Cultures (Albuquerque, 1975)
Gian Carlo (St. Petersburg, 1975)
The Fifth Sun (Austin, 1979)
The Phoenix of the Western World: Quetzalcoatl and the Sky Religion (Norman, 1981)

Library of Congress Cataloging in Publication Data

Brundage, Burr Cartwright, 1912–
    The phoenix of the Western world.

    (The Civilization of the American Indian series; no. 160)
    Bibliography: p. 325.
    Includes index.
        1. Aztecs—Religion and mythology.   2. Indians of Mexico—Religion and mythology.   3. Quetzalcoatl.   I. Title.
    II. Series.
    F1219.76.R45B78   299'.78   81–40278
                                        AACR2

DEDICATION

At some time in the latter part of the seventeenth century in the Viceroyalty of New Spain there was produced a manuscript that bore the name "The Phoenix of the Western World" ("El Fenix del Occidente"). So far as is known, this manuscript was never published and has since disappeared. Undoubtedly the great Mexican savant Don Carlos de Sigüenza y Góngora was the author—or if it was not he, it is at least certain that he was somehow importantly implicated in it. This was the first monograph that we know to have been composed on the subject of the Aztec god Quetzalcoatl and to have been based on sufficient knowledge.

To honor Don Carlos and to keep his memory green, I have here ventured to resurrect the title of his manuscript, applying it to the present work, which also investigates the god Quetzalcoatl.

CONTENTS

CONTENTS

ILLUSTRATIONS

(See "Descriptions of Illustrations" at the end of this book.)

MAP

PREFACE

In a work of synthesis such as this one the problem of organization loomed large, but even more difficult of solution was the question of a style of presentation that would be personal and attractive. I finally chose to do the book as an extended essay rather than as a monograph. In other words, it is aimed at the reader of literature as well as the scholar. The late Sir. J. Eric S. Thompson would have approved of this style, I believe.

Learning has become pretentious and has put itself in danger of forgetting the color and excitement of knowledge. The act of acquiring knowledge is ultimately of as much worth as the knowledge gained, for the latter is in any case tomorrow surpassed. The Aztecs may seem a strange, perhaps unprofitable, people to ruminate on. Certainly Tenochtitlán was no Camelot. But the love of learning has no rules, and an acorn is as good as an elephant to start with. My compeers will recognize in this book the delight of asking questions, though they will without doubt suggest other answers than those I have given.

The god who is at the center of this book, Quetzalcoatl, is viewed as he appeared in late Aztec times, but I have made some attempt to account for him as he appears in other Mesoamerican cultures and in earlier periods. The main thrust of the book is descriptive and synthetic; it seeks to understand Quetzalcoatl as he stands in the heavens in the company of other gods. A definitive study of Quetzalcoatl in all his ramifications would have required volumes, and I had no such gigantic project in mind.

I present the book specifically as an addition to the field of the history of religions—more broadly, as a work in the humanities, where the mystery of the Divine and the tale of men's relations to Him is always central.

The book owes its visual appeal to Jeanne Meinke, who did the line drawings to my specifications but with her own meticulous touch. There were many other calls upon her time. Jean Cobb Schultz typed the major parts of the manuscript with admirable neatness and dispatch. To these two persons I am most grateful. The book is to some extent theirs.

Last but not least I owe a debt to Doris Heyden for her graciousness in supplying me with material and answers from Mexico when they were unavailable to me here.

St. Petersburg, Florida   BURR CARTWRIGHT BRUNDAGE

THE PHOENIX
OF THE
WESTERN WORLD

QUETZALCOATL
AND THE
SKY RELIGION

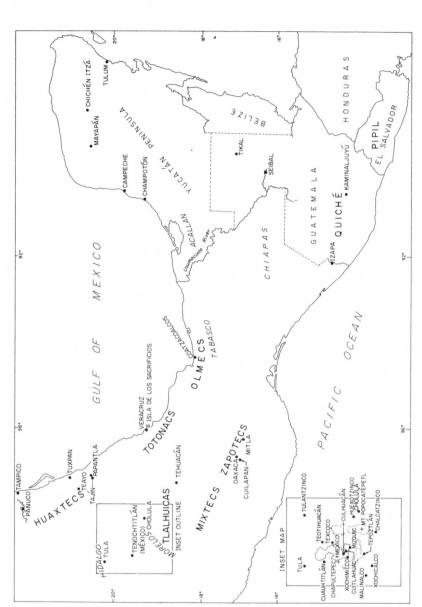

Mesoamerica—place-names mentioned in the text

INTRODUCTION

After some contemplation of Aztec religion I have found in it what appear to be four nuclear emphases. For simplicity's sake I shall refer to them as religions. These four religions are easily distinguished in terms of the god or gods who stand in their centers and who define their general orientations. For the purpose of rendering them easily recognizable, it is certainly permissible to put them in separate categories as I do here; yet they tend constantly to bleed into one another, to call upon the others' gods, even to share in their rituals. Such a network is natural to the preliterate mind, which eschews categories and accepts the universe as a whole.

The four religions, in a rough chronology of their probable first appearances are (1) the religion of fire, (2) that of earth, (3) that of sky, and (4) that of Tezcatlipoca. This book is concerned only with the sky religion and will attempt a definition of it, but a word must first be said about the three others if we are to assess correctly the sky religion within the complex whole.

The religion of fire pivots exclusively around the god Xiuhteuctli. There are fire goddesses in his pantheon, but none even remotely affects the whole picture as he does. His name can be translated either as Lord of the Years, or Lord of the Jewel, where *jewel* refers to the fire. Mesoamericans agreed that Xiuhteuctli was the first of the gods. He particularly displayed the quality of venerability in his avatar as Huehueteotl (the Old God), and from this primacy came his designations as the Father of All the Gods and the

3

All-Father. The Coras and the Huichols even today know him as the Grandfather. He had several other avatars, not noticeably different, and one important embodiment as a fire dragon, the Xiuhcoatl, which monster performed also in the sky religion.

Xiuhteuctli lived underground. His essential fires, hidden under the earth, were reflected in the sky that glowed at dusk and dawning. Or they might be seen escaping through volcanic vents among the mountains. Out of the basically terrestrial derivation of fire the priests of the sky religion were to extract a contradictory myth, namely, that fire was celestial in origin because of its close association with the sun and the dawn.

All of this can be duplicated among preliterate peoples in many parts of the world. What is impressive here is that the fire religion provided what the other three did not, an anatomy of the cosmos. In one of his avatars Xiuhteuctli was the Lord of the Four Directions. As such he gave to men a solid basis for knowing where they stood on the earth, where the center was, and what were the symbols that contained the meanings of the four cardinal directions. He was also the genius of time. He gave to men the periods in the coursing of time without which a sense of endings and renewals was not possible. Thus the fire religion gave support to the other three religions, providing them with a constitution that they could know to be reliable.

There was another and more familiar sense of belonging that this religion gave to men. In the home the hearth was modeled on that divine hearth that burned day and night in front of the house of Earth Mother in Tenochtitlán. That eternal flame gave validity to the domestic hearth and sanctified it. Consequently the family saw its service to the Old God as an original obligation to be zealously honored. The offering to him of the first scraps of food and the first drink, like baptism when the new infant was passed through the

4

flames, were undoubtedly to the Mesoamerican peoples comforting and congenial religious exercises.

The fire religion had a pronounced ancestral orientation. The religion held that the essence of all life was igneous. As the Grandfather, fire was acknowledged to be the head of the lineage. The Otomí tribes, for instance, honored him as Otonteuctli, their progenitor or totem. Appropriately the month of the fire god was the last one of the solar year or the first one, depending on how one wished to view the hiatus between endings and renewals. Every fourth year during that initiatory month adults danced hand in hand with children to become new again. And at that time the young were ceremoniously introduced to their true parent, fire.

The religion of fire was the ground upon which two of the other three religions rested. In the form of light fire was prominently featured in the mythologies of both earth and sky; in their rituals fire was a sine qua non. The religion of fire gave to men what safety there was in life, and with it light and warmth. As such it stood in opposition to the cult of Tezcatlipoca, which was dire, pessimistic, and full of cruel chances. But even the latter religion had to accept a pyrogenous and a fivefold world—the world as described by the religion of fire.

Very different was the earth religion. In it the earth was not understood structurally, as I have shown above. Rather it was understood as an amorphous and sluggish power. It taught the Mesoamericans to see the world in terms of an endless career of issuance, growth, and decay. As key concepts in this ponderous faith Mesoamerican man used three passages connected with the human species: birth, burial, and the mating of male and female. By casting earth as woman, he made a fateful decision, for he thereby gave to earth, which was a cosmic entity, something of the same aura of disguised hostility and irritability with which he clothed the woman. Burial was of course a ritual part of this religion and was the resting place of all man's nightmares, an unwanted return to the cavernous mother. The religion of earth obviously did not encourage contemplation. On the contrary it blocked thought, perhaps therapeutically, and substituted for it a kind of torpid fascination. In it apparitions were formalized and the dead frozen.

There was a supremely important male god in the earth religion whom one might at first glance take to be a rival to the Earth Mother—this was Tlaloc. Both he and the Mother could appear as mountains. Yet Tlaloc was the mountain only as it conjured up thoughts of the waters reputedly stored within it and waiting release as clouds of rain. The Earth Mother literally *was* the mountain; the mountain was her body and flesh. Tlaloc lived inside the mountain, but the Mother was the numinous and granite core, the very roots of the mountain. Tlaloc sent the rain forth from caves in the mountain, but he did not produce men, plants, and animals out of his bowels as did the Mother. So in a sense he was not a rival. Indeed, he can be looked on as one of her avatars.

Earth has, of course, many avatars, and to mention even the chief ones here would be tedious. She ranges in her appearances from the spirit of salt to that of the sweat bath. At her prettiest she is a lovely Aphrodite-like Xochiquetzal; at her worst she is the skeletal Lady of the Dead. Whatever the earth can suggest to man could become one of her avatars.

In one instance the Mother seems to escape from the purely terrestrial and to make an exceptional leap into the skies, thus defying our categories. As the old goddess Starskirt she is the Milky Way and the mother of all the gods, each of whom is thereby a star. As Tlazolteotl (Huaxtec) or Ixchel (Maya) or Coyolxauhqui (Aztec) she can also be the moon. These avatars appear to contradict her telluric character. But we can recover the logic of this slippage of hers, and we can see that it represents hardly any change for her at all. Moon and Milky Way are plainly produced in the womb of earth and are born from her as night begins—so they are her daughters and can be classed as avatars. These specialized avatars were absorbed into the sky religion (permanently in the case of Starskirt), where in some cases they became indispensable in its mythology. The moon, however, remained basically terrestrial.

There were no Eleusinian Mysteries solemnized in the Mesoamerican earth religion in which a celebrant could be moved to a higher plane of comprehension and instilled with a sense of mystic relatedness to the Mother and her goodness. The Mesoamerican approached her only when abundance, issue and death were in question, not ecstasy. Thus he could approach her only in social groups, and not as an individual. He could never forget that first and foremost the Mother was a monster, that one of her basic characteristics was hunger, and that, as the spouse of the Lord of the Land of the Dead, she eventually cannibalized all her children. Her voracity was not to be taken as a kenning for some deeper and more humane attachment, but as a simple and irrefutable fact of nature.

If repetition of rituals is the touchstone for spotting religious significance, then we may state that the earth religion was the foremost of the four. Of the eighteen months of the Aztec year, ten specifically celebrated the principle of earth, its fruits, and its powers. That is more than any of the other three religions can claim. We would expect this of a world that has left hunting and gathering as a way of life to till the soil. Still we must not think that the Earth Mother appeared only with the beginnings of peasant communities, for, as one formulation of the supernatural, she must be almost as old as man himself.

The religion of Tezcatlipoca is the only one of the four

7

with a truly universal extension, and in that respect it can show a faint resemblance to the biblical religion. It is circumscribed by nothing.

Tezcatlipoca does not belong to the priests as does Quetzalcoatl. He affects men at all levels, and they can experience him in their capacities as individuals. Or again, whole communities can suffer or be carried to prestigious heights because of him. All of mankind is subject to his caprices.

He is a far greater god than was Jupiter—with whom Bernardino de Sahagún compares him. Alone of the gods he can flout the *tonalpohualli*, the Aztec equivalent of fate. He is outside all restraints. No decalogue applies to him. In his final formulation he is not a nature god, and therefore no relationship to nature can restrain his actions. He delights in his own unpredictability. He is thus as majestic and "other" as is the biblical God, except that he is lawless. To men he is their ultimate enemy; to the gods he is an outlaw—or better still, a scofflaw.

Tezcatlipoca was thought to be the youngest of all the gods, being described as an eternal youth. Perhaps that is why his religion has so small a part to play in the Aztec solar calendar. And yet, although his religion may have evolved late in time, he was certainly modeled upon the shaman, the most primitive religious practitioner of them all and one who long preceded the priests of Quetzalcoatl. Although only one of the eighteen months of the ceremonial calendar was alloted to Tezcatlipoca, that one, called Toxcatl (Drought?) was generally considered to surpass all the others in importance.

Tezcatlipoca has many avatars, most of whom are built on the pattern of the boisterous and the untrammeled. In brief his religion is an attempt to codify the amoral and the unforeseen as an important part of the human experience. The reverse of this coin is that the religion of Tezcatlipoca institutionalizes man's apprehension of his own littleness and his crucial lack of security. The religion is clear and unequivocal on this point. It has an even sharper focus than the fire religion, which is almost its exact opposite. Tezcatlipoca is cast as pitiless supernatural power. The Preacher of Ecclesiastes would have felt on familiar ground with him. Tezcatlipoca straddles both earth and sky and is as easily at home in the one as in the other. One of his best-known avatars is Tepeyollotli, generally depicted as a jaguar, who is the god of dark caves in the earth. Again, Tezcatlipoca was said to have been cast out of the heavens for his sins— or to have descended therefrom on a cobweb. He fathered avatars for both the earth and the sky religions, yet he remains always circumjacent to both.

In my consideration of the sky religion I shall be dealing at some length with this god, but I must emphasize that, however active he may be in the mythology of the sky religion, he does not thereby become one of its pantheon. As an incorporeal and uncreated spirit of the universe, he remains truly outside nature. He would in fact be fate itself, except that he can be appealed to.

Thus what differentiates the religion of Tezcatlipoca most clearly from the other three is its almost complete indifference to nature. One cannot point to sky, earth, fire, water, space, or any other category of nature and say, "Here is that upon which the religion stands, and here is the element necessary for its understanding." Tezcatlipoca's religion begins nowhere, embodies a god who is a necromancer, and then ends nowhere. The other three religions have definite orientations. Undoubtedly the religion of Tezcatlipoca had the potential to develop into a monotheism, but only the religion of the sky could have completed such a work by equipping him with an inner law. And that did not happen. Mention of this unachieved potential of the religion of Tezcatlipoca now brings us to the sky religion.

It must be understood that when I talk in this book of the Aztec sky religion I am not talking about a strictly delimited

9

church that insists upon its own gods and cult performances and no others. I have said above that it could and did mingle with the other three religions. Its ceremonies formed elements in the festivities of the other religions, and in fact could be supportive of them. It could borrow deities from the other religions or lend them on occasion. There were no such persons who were specifically "sky priests," and indeed there was no single term that meant "sky religion." By what right then do I devote an entire work to such an inexact concept?

When I began this work, my objective was to present only the god Quetzalcoatl, the Feathered Serpent, to the reader. I soon found that, even more than most of the other Mesoamerican gods known to us, Quetzalcoatl kept vanishing into the images of the other gods, and those gods into others, and so on in an extensible line. As an example, Quetzalcoatl could become Xolotl, who could become Nanahuatl, who could then become the fifth sun, and so on. My control of this difficult material faltered until I suddenly realized that the concentric circles of godhead forming and reforming outward from Quetzalcoatl were in toto the picture of a complete religion and that the Feathered Serpent was a center point—or, better still, the symbol of an undifferentiated numen at the center point. I then shifted the approach from research on a single god to that on a religion whose limits could be set by the outer fringes of the several series of avatars of Quetzalcoatl. With this came the realization that Quetzalcoatl was far more than the protean god I had thought him—he was emblematic of a whole religion. And this religion, however much it may have touched earth, fire, and the underworld, remained always, and centrally, celestial.

There is a serious chronological problem in all this, however, which effectively prevents any clear-cut presentation. We do not know how deep down in Mesoamerican time are buried the roots of the sky religion, nor for that matter do we know how old are the other three. Did one of them precede the other three? Did they appear in bits and pieces, yet simultaneously? Is what we have of their mythologies representative only of the Postclassic period? And can we assume that the symbols used in the first stages of the religion carried the same meanings that they were to do later among the Aztecs and the Quichés, for instance? Having no real answers to these questions, I have arbitrarily assumed that they appeared in the order I have offered above (fire, earth, sky, and Tezcatlipoca), but there is no evidence to support this assumption. It is a useful thesis by which to organize the material, but nothing more.

The sky religion appears in art as early as the middle of the second millennium B.C. Signs or glyphs representing the heavenly bodies (sun, moon, the planet Venus, and probably sky itself) appear first among the Olmecs. These were transmitted to the Mayas, who developed them further. The sky religion arose to a commanding position in the halcyon days of Teotihuacán and Xochicalco, and was slowly retreating in importance at the time of the Spanish entry. If one includes his many avatars, Quetzalcoatl is depicted more often in Mesoamerican art than is any other deity.

About the meaning of the Mesoamerican religious complex in general (in which the sky religion was embedded), opinions will surely differ. I see its beginnings characterized by a feeling for the Divine realized as a set of vast, numinous powers, powers that were somewhat later expressed emblematically as dragons—a sky dragon or dragons, an earth dragon, a fire dragon, and so forth. They were all of them chimeras made up of parts of animals, each part standing for that characteristic attributed to the possessing animal.

Along with these draconian beginnings went the animation of specific things, in other words, the attribution of will and supernatural energy to the many parts of the extra-human world. This animism, which pointed only to the discrete, bled constantly into the draconian categories and in doing so produced gods. When visualized, these gods were the analogues of shamans and priests. The later god level, however, did not displace the draconian level. Along with both animistic perceptions and true gods, the above-mentioned dragons, which were large agglomerations of power, continued to inform the universe. This threefold layering was certainly the situation in Aztec times, when, we find, Quetzalcoatl was not only a dragon of celestial scope as well as the wind but at the same time an anthropomorphically conceived god, an archetypal priest.

Among the many changes that occurred in Mesoamerican religion was a real though tardy refinement of the concept of the Divine. We note this especially in the Aztec sky religion and in the cult of Tezcatlipoca. Certain members of the priesthood, as well as leaders of such preeminence as Nezahualcoyotl, were moving, though awkwardly, in that direction when they talked about a god called Yohualli Ehecatl (with whom I shall be dealing later in the book). The Spanish conquest, however, brought any such tentatives to a grinding halt. In particular the sky religion, none too homogeneous to begin with, evaporated overnight and disappeared from history.

In the course of this book I shall use the name Quetzalcoatl to refer to a concept of the god either when I do not care to define him closely or when I am treating him as the sum of all his avatars. Specific avatars (such as Ehecatl or Ce Acatl) will be named where needed, but a "Quetzalcoatl" must be understood to stand before most of such names and to qualify them. Quetzalcoatl is certainly wind, he is the morning star, he is the priest par excellence, he is a power for generation, he is a patron of lineage, and so forth—or he can be combinations of any of these and more. We are thus dealing with a god who developed multidirectionally and who consequently does not wield a single over-

whelming power as does Tezcatlipoca. It may be that Quetzalcoatl was indeed conceived as sovereign by his own
priests in their more speculative moments, but we have no
hard evidence for it. My use of the name Quetzalcoatl is
therefore a confession of my inability to discover a homogeneity about him. Quetzalcoatl is an enclosure name for the
pivotal deity of the Aztec sky religion.

That of course is what makes him interesting. The fact
that he who is wind is also the morning star, who is also a
warrior god, who is also a royal mascot, and so forth, presents us with a being of rainbow colors, a deity who is a
master of kinetics. He raises innumerable problems and
presents us with a dilemma. Can a god who is always found
in parts and categories be a single god? Should we not treat
him as many gods and let the matter drop there? Is a god
who can be approached and petitioned by the devout so far
particularized that his *mana* has disappeared? Is he in brief a
living god, a tandem of gods, a mere concept, or the symbol
of a force?

Whatever and whoever he is, Quetzalcoatl stands at the
center of a belief that the sky was one of the faces of God.
He represents at the very least "that majestical roof fretted
with golden fire," which at the same time could be, as the
world's best poet says, "a foul and pestilent congregation of
vapours."

The scope of my subject is daunting. To capture the true
sense of a religion is in any case difficult. I have had to write
the book mainly from the Aztec point of view, and most of
the statements herein are based on data from late Aztec or
Mixtec sources. But I have allowed myself additionally to
wander at random in and out of other Mesoamerican cultures and chronologies. Data will occasionally be drawn
from the Olmecs, Mayas, Tarascans, Huaxtecs, even the
Huichols. For such leeway I offer no apologies. But I do not
wish to give the impression that I am trying to exhaust the
subject in the manner of an encyclopedia. After all, this

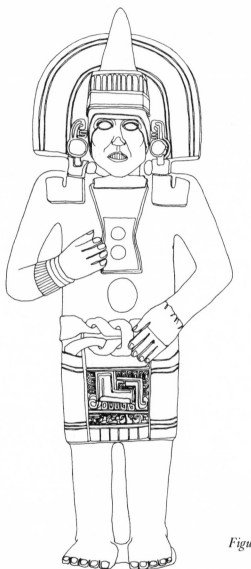

Figure 1

book is as much a series of ruminations as it is a defensible treatise. I have wanted to contemplate Quetzalcoatl rather than to prove points about him, and in the process I have offered several reconstructions.

Before I begin, let us consider one concrete example of the Mesoamerican's thoughts about this god who was in the sky. From the Huaxtec area comes a statue of Quetzalcoatl that visually explicates, as nothing else does, the god's layered nature (fig. 1). This statue is meant to be viewed from both the front and the back, and the two views speak of different natures. Seen frontally, the statue is that of a youth tatooed on most of his body and wearing only a kilt and a pointed Huaxtec cap. There is no doubt about his identity, for he wears the back-curved shell eardrops peculiar to Quetzalcoatl. Surrounding his head is an aureole engraved with stylized dragons in a semicircular arch over his head. The whole means that he is the sky.

Walking around the statue, the viewer sees that the back of the aureole is as before fan-shaped but is now engraved with striations emanating from the head (fig. 31). The back of the head has become a skull, while a small skeleton hangs down from it like a wizened cape reaching to the statue's thighs. This skeletal alter ego also wears the Huaxtec cap and a kilt decorated much like that on the front figure. The feet and hands of the gruesome creature are not bony, however, as we might expect, but are clawed. Around the neck hangs a pectoral edged with signs denoting the planet Venus. There can be no doubt that the backpiece represents that avatar of the god known as Xolotl, an essential underworld being in the sky religion, the evening star.

From the front the statue has an undeniable presence. The impassivity of the face is noteworthy, while the richly engraved surface of the limbs, body, and kilt contrasts with the smooth modeling of the face. The stance is quiet and gives the impression that the god is holding his breath, that in fact he represents the abeyant. There is no denying the formal power of the piece.

Compared with the simplicity of the frontal side, the back is emphatic and complicated, for the inertness of the puppetlike body speaks against the more lifelike human back upon which it hangs. It does not command respect as the frontal figure does. It is ominous and stirs up the turbulence of thought. Both the frontal and the dorsal figures, sky and evening star respectively, were authentically the god Quetzalcoatl. The artist here successfully interpreted the nature of the old sky religion and its central god, Quetzalcoatl. Through the language of art a whole statement has been made about the divinity in the sky.

ONE
THE SKY

In the Introduction I presented the four major categories in Aztec religious thought, those expressive of fire, sky, earth, and Tezcatlipoca. I have chosen the second of these concepts as the subject matter of this book. Inasmuch as the god Quetzalcoatl most nearly represents the sky, he appears therefore as the thematic figure in all that follows. The sky is defined as a dragon, his several appearances are discussed, and the geographical spread of his religion is briefly noted. There follows a contrast between the sky and the earth religions, with something on the ambiguous connections between the two. I point up the latter in the paradisean figure of Xochiquetzal, a mother goddess placed in the sky. The position of the sun god Tonatiuh is treated to clarify his relationship with Quetzalcoatl. Myths of the creation of the sky follow, together with a list of all the significant celestial beings and finally the sky religion is summarized under thirteen headings that are diagnostic.

The Sky as a Dragon

For Mesoamerican man "sky" integrated a number of items that we today would compartmentalize, manifestations such as wind, clouds, rain, hail, sun, moon, stars, night, day, comets, and thunder. We are appalled by the illogic of creating such a catchall rubric, but to the native of Mesoamerica sky was less a result of diverse powers than a theater of the supernatural in motion, far more dramatic than the placidity of the earth. As such it could be one thing. Sky was man's earliest book of tales, a single volume.

Sky bound together day and night, but was more imposing conceptually than either of them; witness the extraction from it of the idea of time. Time, or at least periodicity, could be conjured out of the heavens, whereas earth was inert, responding but not activating. This distinction was very clearly felt. Naturally there was an attempt to see a male-female relationship between sky and earth, but it never went so far as to become anthropomorphic only. Basically it remained conceptual.

The word for "sky" in Nahuatl is *ilhuicatl*, a compound form containing the word *ilhuitl* ("day") plus a gentilic ending,[1] a possible translation being "the one who is habitually in the day," where day is thought of as a habitation. In Aztec religion I know of no god expressly referred to as unmodified "sky."[2] There is to be sure an avatar of Huitzilopochtli called Blue Sky in which only the sky of full daylight is referred to.[3] He is thus not the over-all numen we are looking for, but he illustrates that at least the Nahua-speaking peoples of Mesoamerica could and did deify a part of "sky."

In Mesoamerican thought sky was not, therefore, Father

19

Sky as opposed to Mother Earth. Earth was indeed Mother, but the Mesoamerican cultures saw both sky and earth as dragons.

The dragon is the product of the common imagination of mankind and is found in diverse cultures. In Mesoamerica his most common name was Quetzalcoatl, and he was a near-replica of the European dragon in whom we delighted as children. Our own dragon had a serpent's scaly body, a crested head, forelimbs equipped with frightening talons, and wings that carried him through the air. This is a good description of the Mesoamerican sky dragon, excepting only that he is not generally shown with wings; he flies by virtue of the fact that his body is covered with feathers. Dragons appeared as armorial bearings on French, Spanish, and English shields of the late Middle Ages and on Aztec shields of exactly the same centuries. In Renaissance art Saints Michael and George were appointed to be the slayers of these monsters, but there is no comparable slaying in Mesoamerican annals. A Mesoamerican dragon stood for a numen sovereign in its own sphere, a being against whom none could come; it did not, in other words, stand for the leviathanic enemy of God, of the wicked versus the good. Sky had no enemies.

The question that arises for us at this point is whether the Mesoamerican sky dragon was a true chimera emblematically crafted of equal parts of several creatures or whether he was basically evolved from one animal. In the case of the earth dragon we know that the animal model was the caiman, or crocodile.

Two animals, bird and serpent, were basic to the sky dragon's ultimate design, both being epitomes of motion, but of the two the serpent was probably the fundamental one. The motility represented by the serpent appears to have been particularly suggestive in the shaping of the dragon. It is also suggestive that, in Nahuatl, compound words for dragons of various sorts have *coatl* ("snake") as a matrix, never *tototl*, the word for bird. The coilings and windings of a snake symbolize perfectly the nimbleness and sinuosity of water, the uncurling of smoke in the still air, the flailing waterspout, or the dust devil sweeping over the land—all of them functions of the air. Among the Huichols, whom we may consider as modern-day representatives of the ancient Mesoamericans, rain clouds are thought of as winged snakes.[4] Indeed, almost everything in the air—smoke rising from burning fields, lightning, even fire itself—was thought to be serpents inhabiting the atmosphere. The sky dragon was thus the end representation of a long appreciation of the part played in the universe by motion, and we must keep this in mind if we are to understand the several avatars that he produced.

For one who wishes to clarify further the meaning of the dragon, the question of the specific genus of serpent that models for him naturally arises. Five genera of serpents could have been involved: the rattlesnake, the coral snake, the bushmaster, the fer-de-lance, and the boa.[5] All but the last are venomous and highly dangerous to man, and all but the first are confined to the southern and lowland parts of Mesoamerica. The rattlesnake alone was familiar to all the Mesoamerican peoples, whether they came from the watery inlets of Quintana Roo or from the cool highlands of Zacatecas. He exists in several highland species as well as in one extensive tropical species (*durissus durissus*) found in southern Mexico and Guatemala. Thus Maya, Veracruz, and highland cultures could have built their concepts of the dragon on the rattlesnake alone. And in the main that is what seems to have happened; from Olmec times down to the coming of the Spaniards the dragon was generally distinguished by rattles.

In the Maya area, however, the boa shared honors with the rattlesnake as contributing to the formulation of the dragon. There the sky dragon was patterned on a boa constrictor, and at such times he was associated with Chac, the

Maya rain god.[6] This is an easily understandable application of a water principle to the sky iconography, for the boa was a snake with a distinct aquatic preference.

In the late period the coral snake is closely associated with the goddess Tlazolteotl as an emblem of sexual sin, and very seldom in the codices does it assume the proportions of a dragon. Nor does it have any overt associations with Quetzalcoatl with which I am familiar. The other two, the fer-de-lance and the bushmaster, undoubtedly are somehow involved, but the evidence for this involvement is clouded.

I have said that the generalized concept of "snake" evoked coextensive concepts of motility and renewal in the Mesoamerican cultures. The narrower concept of "rattlesnake" added the idea of the atrocious. Thus the fully evolved sky dragon spelled out a conjunction of motion, of apotheosis, and of danger. The regenerative quality of snakes, who slough their skins to become new again, seemed to be, like the dawn, the reappearance of a familiar god. Their slipperiness and their coiling were like the smooth flight of the stars. Mixed in with it all was the hazard in the sudden strike of the rattlesnake. This latter characteristic displayed the quality that the Mesoamericans believed to be most indicative of the sky—peril.

Added to this prototypal serpent dragon were important elements taken from the quetzal bird, its crest, tail, hooked beak, and, at least later, the color of its plumage. The quetzal is a shy, beautiful trogon of the cloud forests with an altitudinal range of four to six thousand feet in Central America. Formerly it was prevalent in Chiapas but probably never extended very far west of Tehuantepec. The quetzal wedded to the rattlesnake was the preferred model for the sky dragon. Its rattles were the thunder, its feathers the rain, and its gaping mouth the wind.

This sounds as though the origins of the Mesoamerican sky dragon have been solved, but such is not the case. Jaguar, fish, crocodile, and even human traits occasionally appear in the depictions of the monster. Even the rattlesnake is not the sole ophidian donor to the dragon, for the bushmaster and probably the boa constrictor were also contributory, the latter particularly in the role of custodian of waters. In other words, there were other heraldic interpretations of the celestial monster in Mesoamerican teratology besides the one modeled on the quetzal-serpent motif, and we shall consider them briefly. Nevertheless the bird-serpent dragon is the only one of the several varieties of dragons who became in time a leading deity. We call him Quetzalcoatl, which literally means Green-feathered Serpent.

The first dragons depicted in the archaeological record come from the Olmec culture (1300–700 B.C.) on the southern arc of the coast of the Gulf of Mexico where the habitats of rattlesnake and the quetzal overlapped. An imposing representation of this creature is to be seen on a well-known monument from La Venta.[7] Here the dragon rears and coils behind a personage who is obviously a priest, inasmuch as he wears a replica of the dragon's head as his *nahualli* headpiece (fig. 2). The dragon is shown as a thick but well-formed rattlesnake, except for his head. The head has an exaggerated, beaklike snout and a pronounced crest, both characteristics of the quetzal. The brows are developed backward in a fashion that was to appear constantly throughout the succeeding centuries. No feathers are discernible on the body, however. The priest is sitting slumped over with his legs outstretched and holding an incense bag. From his position we infer that the dragon has either engorged him or in some sense struck him down. Above the priest appears an apron or loin cloth with a symbol resembling the Saint Andrew's Cross on the belt, no doubt a priestly garment.

At Chalcatzinco, an Olmec site in the highlands, a dragon, again with the Saint Andrew's Cross and with crocodilian dentition, appears to be in the act of destroying a man.[8] Billowing clouds, or perhaps winds, issue from him. Else-

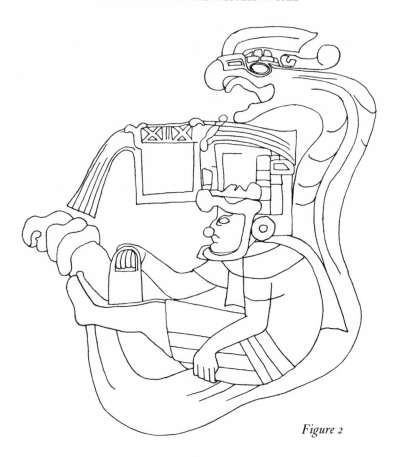

Figure 2

where in Olmec art the dragon is shown with forked tongue
and feathers. Usually these dragons are connected with
caves, or with rain and water symbols.

It has been thought that the Olmec dragon was iconographically suggested in the beginning by a series of cloud
or wind volutes surrounding or attached to a masklike face.
There are indeed some remarkable depictions of storms
from the Olmec culture, one, for example, showing a sea-

scape with turbulent winds and clouds, over which scene broods the great frontal face of a masked god, undoubtedly the storm king himself (fig. 7). Winds issue from his grotesque mouth, and human figures appear and then are carried away and overthrown by the blasts.

What is of interest in such fragments is the explicitness of the phenomenon depicted, for there can be no doubt about the subject matter—it is a hurricane. Whoever the god in the center may be, we can surely identify him as a predecessor of Quetzalcoatl. There is no suggestion of fertility or the growth of plants in such a representation, which would of course more closely suggest the god Tlaloc.

In the following centuries artists interpreting this creature would have seen the separate volutes as sequentially arranged to form a serpent's body with projecting wind scrolls, after which the curls adorning the body were thought of as feathers. When he appears somewhat later in Izapan art, the sky dragon has become even more fanciful.[9] He has in fact become amphibaenic, having a head at both ends of his serpentine body (fig. 3). In this guise he represents the overarching sky, probably in its east-west orientation. If this is so, then we can read into it a further reference, namely that of an oceanic entryway and a corresponding place of exit for the sun as he moves relative to the earth. Sky thus disgorges the sun in the east and engulfs him in the west. One would normally think of this disposal and release of the sun as being a function of earth, but as the Izapan peoples on the shores of the Pacific saw it, the solar and stellar bodies subsided into great waters that appeared to be connected with the sky. This double-headed dragon lasted throughout all of Mesoamerican art, not disappearing until the end of the Aztec culture.

The celestial numen with the single head became the dragon familiar to us at Teotihuacán, Xochicalco, and Chichén Itzá and in the Aztec codices and sculptures. Here the bifid tongue of the serpent is stressed, and the feathers are

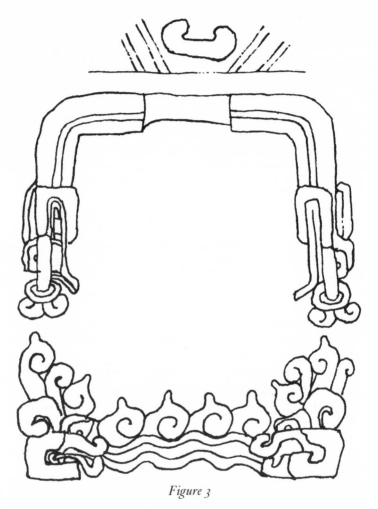

Figure 3

specified to be the blue-green tail feathers of the quetzal
trogon. The dragon is bearded, and he spews forth destructive winds and clouds. Crocodilian characteristics are lacking, and he is presented as a rattlesnake. In fact, so outstanding is his ophidian character that he can be suggested

simply by a stone pillar carved into the likeness of a vertically piled-up set of rattles.

The heterogeneity of the elements of the sky was accurately reflected in the number of beings that could go into the making of this the greatest of all Mesoamerican chimeras, and yet his basic unity as a snake was preserved. What he evoked in the Mesoamerican imagination was probably threefold: a great celestial rundle that flies unseen above one's head except when it blows forth clouds, a convolute pathway for all stellar objects, and finally the home of hurricanes and darkest night. Its potentially lethal quality was stressed from the earliest times.

Such in brief was the Mesoamerican sky dragon in his several forms, a veritable basilisk with shining eyes who was both night and day.

Some Varieties of Dragons

The *quetzalcoatl* form of the dragon mentioned above is the one that will interest us particularly in this book, but we must note that the Mesoamerican imagination went far beyond this construction. Many other dragons were created, and some were to become important in iconography and myth, almost all being classed as serpents—that is to say, the word *coatl* ("serpent") formed the last element in their names. When thus modified with a preceding word, the word *coatl* took on the meaning of "dragon." For the most part these chimeras were creatures of the sky, and the original ones continued to exist alongside later, derivative forms; the plumed serpent, for example, and the bicephalic dragon can be shown in the same codex.

There was a form more generically conceived than the *quetzalcoatl*. This was the "cloud dragon," or *mixcoatl*. If we think of the slow uncoiling and mushrooming of cumulus clouds in the summertime, we can see how the concepts of serpent and cloud could easily interpenetrate to create a new way of thinking about the sky. Indeed, it seems to me possible that the *mixcoatl*, the sky serpent whose body was suggested by boiling clouds, was antecedent to the less naturalistic *quetzalcoatl*.

The word *mixcoatl* means "tornado" or "whirlwind" in exactly the same sense as does *quetzalcoatl*.[10] It is perhaps even possible that the original name for the boreal god was Mixcoatl, the name Quetzalcoatl coming later. The development from one to the other could have been brought about by the artists who early depicted the sky dragon.

We have already seen that in the earliest depictions of the sky dragon the clouds were symbolized by volutes attached to and running the length of his body—in some depictions they were shown as segments of his body scarcely connected. To the artist these may have called to mind feathers, as indeed would be plausible when a serpent who flew through the air was in question. Inasmuch as the long green tail feathers of the quetzal trogon were precious articles everywhere in Mesoamerica and symbolized water, the artist would accordingly have thought of them first as being the particular feathers represented. Cloud and feather thus became one and the same insofar as the sky was concerned in Mesoamerican thought. Only later did a separation appear as two deities emerged, the original cloud-flecked dragon, and his later avatar, the dragon with feathers. The early identity was never forgotten, however. I believe that Mixcoatl was the fundamental hypostasis; this would follow from the fact that the Feathered Serpent in mythology was to become his son, Ce Acatl.[11]

Next in importance was the *xiuhcoatl*. The word is difficult to translate because the first element can mean either "year" or "turquoise" (which carries the secondary meaning of "precious"). The meaning is generally taken to be the latter one. Xiuhcoatl appears in mythology and cult as the fire-breathing dragon that Huitzilopochtli can hurl as a weapon at his enemies, for which reason the name is sometimes loosely translated as Fire Snake. This dragon is closely connected with the sun. Symbolizing the light in the sky or the sun's rays, he carries the sun on his back throughout his daylight journey. He is the course or path of the sun through the void. In art he generally has two forelimbs ending as talons. In some depictions flames lick round his body, which is made up of a short series of encasing segments. His tail never shows rattles but ends in a very distinctive solar ray or flint knife, both of which characteristics differentiate him from the *quetzalcoatl*. His snout is adorned with a back-curved horn edged with stars. Alternately he—or a dragon like him—can have the body of a turtle, the carapace being easily distinguished.[12]

There were also four directional sky dragons[13] who sometimes doubled as the Atlantes that held up the sky, one at each of the four cardinal points. The best known of these quadruplicate dragons from Aztec culture is the *itzcoatl*, shown with obsidian knives set along his back as hackles.[14] Among the Mayas the four world-directional dragons were the *chicchan*, who lived in caves and water holes and brought rain. They can have human forms from the waist up, but below they appear as feathered serpents.[15]

Indeed sky dragons of all varieties stalked over the land. That stretch of coast running from the home of the Totonacs to Campeche (the old Olmec heartland) was known by the Aztecs as the original breeding ground of the *quetzalcoatl* dragons, most of them being associated with high winds.[16] In fact the great city along that coast in Aztec times was Coatzacoalco, the Place of the Dragon Pyramid. Farther inland the dragons were known as *quetzalcuitlachtli*, flying griffons, the noise of whose wings was deafening.[17] So horrendous were the latter that they finally succeeded in depopulating one of the valleys in the Tehuacán region.[18] As late as 1529 one appeared in the northwest warning the tribes there of the approach of the infamous Nuño Beltrán de Guzmán.[19] Dragons existed everywhere, and in one of the codices at least fourteen minor variants are depicted side by side.

So pervasive was the idea of the chimera in Mesoamerican iconography that it would have been strange if bird and serpent were the only prototypes used in their construction. There was another dragon built with saurian armature and often depicted, like the iguana or crocodile, with four legs and the typical horny hide of the latter. If the serpent was translated into the sky to produce the celestial dragon just considered, the caiman, or American crocodile, primarily represented the waters of the earth—and by extension the earth itself. The creature was known in Nahuatl as the *cipactli.*

The *cipactli* is not particularly close to the concept of the dragon discussed above, for he was strictly terrestrial. Yet he must be mentioned here because on occasion he seems to merge with the celestial dragon. The reason for such a conflation is that both dragons were symbols of water, the sky dragon as the rain-swollen clouds and the earth dragon as the crocodile wallowing about in the rivers and swamps and suggesting the primeval mire thrust up when time began. Thus the waters that were held in the heavens were symbolized differently from those held within the earth, ophidian in the one case, saurian in the other. Yet the distinction was not neat. In Chiapas the feathered serpent was "he who went about in the water,"[20] and in the codices he is shown inhabiting deep lakes along with the *cipactli.*[21]

The best-known example of the interpenetration of the two dragons sky and earth is certainly Itzamna, the Maya god. There is still uncertainty regarding this deity; I offer here only the few facts that seem to be commonly accepted.[22] The name Itzamna means Iguana House. This deity can appear as a true chimera in the sky pouring water down on the earth. He is probably an iguana but can still

Figure 4

have serpent, crocodile and even deer attributes. He is sky
and earth together. As a quintuplicate monster he formed
the four sides of the sky, overarched and meeting above,
plus the earth as a floor below. Thus he accounted for both
sources of water, celestial and terrestrial. He is painted
blue, his elongated body is divided segmentally into sky
glyphs, and he may have a mouth at both ends. He is not
shown plumed, and he never has an avian head. In other
words, he is not a *quetzalcoatl*. Obviously he is elaborately
conceived, but we know him in his Late Classic form, and
what his predecessor may have been is unclear.

Among the more graphic of the many versions of the sky
dragon is another one favored by the Maya artist. He is
often bicephalic, and his body is a long joined band of
glyph boxes, each box referring to an aspect of the sky.
Each box contains a glyph, one for night, one for the planet
Venus, one for the sun, one for the moon, and so forth. Few
of the glyphs can be read with certainty, yet enough can be
made out to see that this presentation of the dragon is something like our zodiac. In some instances in the center of the
band—the position that would correspond to the zenith—
the mythical Moan bird stares out at the beholder. Or the
center may be taken up by the head of the Cauac dragon
seen *en face*, he being the thunderous numen of the sky
(fig. 4).

As a visual statement this dragon stands at the end of
centuries of observation and speculation and implies a
highly institutionalized religion. The Aztecs had nothing

31

like this in their iconography. Many of the arts from the earlier levels of the sky religion did not come down to them, at least not in forms that found expression in their art.

Along with its heraldic derivatives the serpent is found everywhere in Mesoamerican iconography. It is the commonest of themes, and it interpenetrates all art forms. When one today walks through the splendid Aztec Hall of the Museo Nacional, the serpent and the dragon overwhelm one in their abundance and allusiveness. The power inherent in the draconian symbol was such that new forms and avatars were constantly spilling out of the pristine mold. Our own European dragon came to his floruit just as the time became ripe for him to retire to fairyland and the nursery. That was because by then he was no longer symbolically conceived. No religious meaning of any consequence supported him. The Mesoamerican dragon, on the contrary, was the central figure in the sky religion as well as an important embodiment of earth. As the sky the dragon continued to fascinate the Mesoamericans down to the time of the destruction of their cultures by the Spaniards.

At this point I must mention an important variation, or rather an extension, of the meaning of the dragon. One of the commonest icons in Mesoamerican art is the god within the dragon's maw. Its antecedents are seen as far back as Olmec times. Some—perhaps many—of this kind of dragon encasement can be interpreted as earth entrances or caves, but the one that particularly interests us here I would prefer to call the dawn-dusk dragon. This chimera is to be thought of as determinedly ambiguous while still remaining celestial. The face in the gaping jaws represents the ingestion, the indwelling, and the spewing forth of a god—any one or all of these meanings. If the god in question is the sun, he can be either the sun consumed by night or the emergent morning sun. If it is the planet Venus that is in question, then only the context tells us whether the evening or the morning star is meant.

The ambiguity was designed to extend also to the dragon within whose jaws the god appears. We ask ourselves, generally in vain, whether he equates with the western or the eastern portals of the sky, or possibly with the consuming and ejecting earth. Or can he be exclusively the sky in the underworld as it is entered and abandoned by stellar beings? We are probably correct in saying that it is impossible to separate these identities and that what is intended is an inclusive idea enlarged to cosmic proportions—a situation wherein it is irrelevant to inquire whether the dragon is the last celestial fire in the western sky or the western hills waiting to swallow the sun.

In Mesoamerican thought the dynamics of the dragon are basically celestial, best seen in the planet Venus (Ce Acatl), which is a notorious wanderer, a creature of constant motion. Earth supplies us with several forms of the dragon: Cipactli, the Cauac monster, Tlalteuctli, and others. But the inert Cipactli, who is the most representative of these earth dragons is not polymorphic—he is always and only the crocodile or the caiman. On the contrary, Tlalteuctli is truly a dragon of the earth, but she (or it) is a dragon only for the purpose of devouring life. She is neither feathered nor winged, but is mainly depicted as a toad *en face*, or merely as a dark maw gaping upward. Nowhere to my knowledge does this dragon appear with a face within its jaws, however often it is shown engulfing men and gods. In other words, there is no ambiguous slippage of meaning between Tlalteuctli and her victims. She is monolithic and rigidly defined and evokes only one reaction.

The celestial dragon, however, particularly the one with the god's face within its jaws, is kaleidoscopic and elastic in meaning, for it can stand for the falling down of the sun into a sacrificial pit or its reawakening out of the night sky. Dusk and dawn mingle their crepuscular lights in the icon of the sky dragon with the god's face within. Yet however fluid the meaning is, it remains celestial. It certainly may refer to the sky of daylight, but more generally it evokes the two terminals of the night, dusk and dawn, and in that sense it implies "night" as a place of death and probable rebirth. Occasionally the god within the dragon's jaws is shown with closed eyes, as if he were the dead or not yet awakened Piltzinteuctli, the sun god who will emerge in the east. When that is the case, the dragon is incontestably the nocturnal sky.

The dawn-dusk dragon marks a departure from the unalloyed concept of sky. It takes into account the presence of a god with very specific, not numinous, attributes. These attributes can be one or more of the following: warlikeness, computational and augural skill, culture patronage, lineage protection, or sacrifice. The face in the maw is thus a mythical extension into specificity of an originally numinous being.

Sky versus Earth

I have posited the existence of a sky religion in Mesoamerica that is most easily grasped in the ubiquity of the dragon in art; it is also roughly presented in several cosmogonic myths. Inasmuch as this religion must be at least as old as the Olmecs, whose archaeology is still only in its beginning, I am not sure of myself in describing its origins. What follows, therefore, is only one possible reconstruction.

Out of the concept of the sky as a vast unresolved numen were finally to be extracted the symbols needed for the further elaboration of the religion. These symbols were at first mainly dragons, as we have seen. Then, as chiefdoms finally arose, the new elite class associated with them endowed a subgroup, the priesthood, with the responsibility of placating, aggrandizing, and utilizing the dragons and their congeries. Not that there were no other deities—there undoubtedly were—indeed there were probably many, among them the corn spirit, the genius of wild animals, Earth Mother, the storm king in his mountain, and the patron of fire who lived in the volcano. The sky dragon, however, held out possibilities denied to the other nature gods. At no period was the sky as concretely imagined as was the earth, for it had been first a bundle of concepts rather than a formed and adequately visualized god. Earth, the lumplike mother, terrible in her hugeness and in her deathly appetites, was felt, it is true, to be an integral being, but she was stiff and inflexible. Because of her clay-and-stone nature she could not be developed as easily into more spiritual forms.

Most of the nature gods had severe limitations imposed upon them. In general they did not move out of the initial area of activity in nature that had been assigned to them. Sky was different in that it invited manipulation, being itself shapeless. The manipulators were the priests, the new subclass differently organized from the earlier sorcerers or shamans. They were petitioners, not ecstatics and coercers, and through the pleadings and argumentation in their psalms they became the first intellectuals in those early societies.

I have stated the above narrowly. The idea of a priesthood, once produced, would naturally be adopted by many important deities. It would have been instantly appreciated by all that priests were useful middlemen in cultures of growing specialization. Depending on the nature of its particular god, a priesthood could be assigned to other than the basic cult activities; some priests, for instance, could be allotted to mythopoeic invention, or they could become involved in the formulation of specific religious claims as over against other cults. They could even expand the god through new and exciting theatrical effects. Those of the sky persuasion were par excellence scholar-priests, and they were powerfully supported by the new ruling elite, who expected in return a religious validation of their social position.

The details of the above reconstruction cannot all be true, but there is a likelihood that the framework will stand. If so, then we can understand why the elite first settled upon the sky as the numinous source of its prerogatives. The sky was protean and impalpable, and therefore could be easily shaped.

The colors of the sky change with startling rapidity. The sky empties itself of clouds and then like an arcane receptacle fills up again to repletion. The sky suffers the parturition of sun, moon, and stars. It stretches overhead in two opposed forms, night and day. Rainbows and comets invade it. Birds spiral up into it, and fires glow in it at dawn and dusk. A tree or a mountain can pierce it. The tree particularly, with its apical ascent of branches, easily suggested to the priestly mind levels of heaven, thirteen in all and each populated. But because inconstancy and variety of forms also characterized the sky, its priesthood was not likely ever to reduce it to an easy unity.

Owing to its profusion of aspects and eerie movements the sky did not play the same kind of role in Mesoamerican religion as did the earth. Earth was changeless, and concepts of time could not be brought into association with it, whereas in the sky moving creatures, such as stars and clouds, had wills and moved according to their whims or to their failures of energy. Earth was first and foremost a locus: it had no part in the gyrations of things.

Earth could not, however, escape a certain celestial influence. The great Earth Mother, the engulfer and the womb of renewal, was often identified with the moon, with the Milky Way, or with mountains that invaded the sky and gave rain. These were extensions of the earth concept that gave rise to such great avatars as Tlazolteotl or Citlalinicue, moon and the Milky Way, respectively.

If earth thus suffered some permutations because of the influence of the sky, in reverse the sky was affected by the earth. The periodic transformation of the celestial vault from day into night suggested it. In Mesoamerica the interior of the earth, which was symbolized by the jaguar, called forth infinite speculation. It was exactly this arcane interior, entered only through caves and fissures in the rock, that was the home and birthplace of the stars. Also it was the wandering place of the sun after its setting. Such a nocturnal hiatus cried out for an explanation. It could be interpreted in two ways: visually, as a projection under the earth of the night sky overhead, or conceptually, as the region of underearth out of which marched the stars and into which dropped the sun. It was, in other words, a baleful but still a partly renovative world. As a chthonic region the underworld was Mictlan (Xibalba), the land of the dead. As a celestial region the underworld was simply a translation of the night sky into other and even darker terms.

The Sky as Tamoanchan and the Role of Xochiquetzal

We have seen that the sky as a sliding dome over one's head had as its most inclusive emblem the feathered serpent or dragon. This was the sky that was crowded with clouds, demons, and divine fires, all in motion. When the sky was considered as a place, however, it could be thought of as Tamoanchan, a paradise of sensual delights. The word Tamoanchan is Mayan and comes to us from the southern part of the central Mexican massif. It was an undoubtedly early designation of the sky as a land of Cockaigne, but the designation had almost disappeared by Aztec times, having been replaced by Tlalocan ("the abode of the god Tlaloc"). I shall comment later on Tamoanchan; all I need do here is give the accepted translation of the word, Place of the Moan-Bird Serpent. In the preceding sections I have presented the dragon as basically ophidian; here, as an emblem of

37

Figure 5

Tamoanchan, serpent and bird are equally involved. The resulting chimera thus becomes a kind of basilisk rather than the dragon as I have described him up to now.

From Teotihuacán comes a most interesting representation of this creature as it is descending from the skies, half bird, half deity (fig. 5). Its outspread wings show wind jewels, quetzal-bird heads, and of course feathers. The body is designed to represent clouds but also shows wind jewels, which, as we know, are the particular symbol of the god of the air. The tail and legs of the creature are also marked with quetzal-bird heads to signify the waters of the sky. The creature's two hands are scattering flowers, and the face within the open beak of the bird is identified by its mouth painting as that of the goddess Xochiquetzal.

It is not generally recognized that the male quetzal trogon, famous for its emerald coloration, shows on its breast an equally striking area of a bright crimson that is almost a violet. This latter coloration in fact must have been especially apparent to the hunter looking upward into the high foliage of the rain forest—more apparent than the emerald of the bird's back and tail feathers. What more impressive symbol of the sky as a whole than this most beautiful of birds—a bird whose plumage could symbolize not only the waters in the sky but also the great shining light that punctuated it, the sun. The quetzal bird thus represented the widest possible range of celestial phenomena and can be adjudged to be a proper symbol of the sky. The bird also represented beauty, however, and as such it was emblematic of the goddess Xochiquetzal, in Teoti-huacán art being worn in her hair as an ornament. This apparent shift to the feminine needs to be explained, for up to now I have given the impression that throughout Meso-america the sky was thought of as masculine.

First it must be said that Xochiquetzal is not the sky and is not—as was Quetzalcoatl—an expression of the numen of the sky. She is rather the goddess who inhabits Tamoan-chan, the upper level of the sky. She represents not the sky itself but the flowers that the sky with its fertilizing rain and warm sunshine calls up out of the earth below. In this sense she is still the Great Mother, specialized in a floral guise, who has been taken out of the earth and etherialized as a queen of beauty in an upper element that is not hers at all.

Tamoanchan is an unlikely home for this goddess—unlikely because as one of the basic forms of the Earth Mother she belongs below, ponderous and terrestrial. There is, however, a logic in her being in the sky. The stairway by which she ascended into the heavens was the *xochitlicacan*, the world tree with its thirteen branching levels thrusting upward into the heavens, the topmost of which bloomed with eternal blossoms.[23] Such a rarefied level had to be by definition a paradise and accordingly called for a sovereign who could accord with its floral atmosphere. Thus Xochiquetzal.

Mesoamerica was not backward in its knowledge of the many stages of sophistication that could be attained in the sexual arts, and it had early created an Aphrodite to symbolize them.[24] The Nahuas called this goddess Xochiquetzal, or Precious Flower. They lifted her out of the soil and rock of her real home and placed her, as here, in the summit of the heavens, exactly as the quetzal bird in art perches on the top branch of the flowering world tree. She personified the life of sensuality that the human mind imagines as a possibility but never commands in reality. The sky was a possible habitat for a goddess who was an avatar distilled out of the numen of the earth, carrying with her the perfume and beauty of flowers.

Yet in a strange way this queen of love always remained an alien in the sky. Even though she reigned there as the paragon of sex, womanhood, and beauty, she could never quite tear her roots out of the earth. As proof of this her mythology has this to say about her:

Because she was earth in its floral exuberance, we have seen that Xochiquetzal legitimately lived in Tamoanchan, the garden of delights, where all was feasting, sexual joy, song, and overflowing abundance. Two high gods, however, had attached a taboo to the flowering tree that stood in the center of the garden.[25] The goddess disobeyed this injunction and tore off a floral spray. Thus she ceased to be Ichpochtli, the Virgin.[26] The tree itself cracked and bled and thus forever lost its pristine health. For this sin the goddess was cast out of Tamoanchan to descend to the earth.[27] Some said that she descended as a demon. Or, as a variant has it, the goddess was seduced into sin by Tezcatlipoca and then carried off as a punishment into the underworld by Xolotl.[28] Whichever version we care to read, the core myth remains: an ancient sexual admonition was flouted and with it paradise lost. And so the goddess returned to her more congenial home, the earth. Depictions of Xochiquetzal in the codices can show a coral snake (lust), a scorpion (punishment), and a Xolotl creature (the underworld personified) all peeping out from under her royal throne. She was said to be the first female to sin, and she was accordingly viewed by the early friars as the Mesoamerican Eve.[29]

We are thus allowed to interpret the descending bird from Teotihuacán, which I described at the beginning of this section, as perhaps an avatar of the goddess. The bird appears in many forms and places.

In Palenque, as a type site, we see the bird standing on the pinnacle of the blossoming world tree.[30] It is obviously the quetzal bird, but it has some hints of the dragon, for its beak and wings are derived from that creature, and it is adorned with the wind jewel. The bird of the sky in fact cannot really be separated from the cosmic tree and is simply a statement of its apical essence in the topmost heaven (see frontispiece).

The Mayas were intimately acquainted with the quetzal trogon, which they called *kuk*. As an emblem of the sky this bird assumed for them a semidraconian form as the Moan bird.[31] The Maya word *moan* means drizzle or cloudy and thus can have reference to the sky waters. It is also the Maya word for the screech owl—which gave the Maya mythographers the right to create the chimera of the sky on an avian model. Such puns are common stimuli for the human imagination.

The Feathered Serpent as an emblem of the sky in its totality had been fully evolved in Teotihuacán. But now we find that there is also a sky bird. We may properly ask whether this second avatar of the sky embodies a different emphasis in the iconography.

In the art of Palenque we have seen the bird as the spirit of the world tree, placed in its top branches. It can also be drawn as a bird's head *en face* and placed in the middle of the sky band. There is then no apparent connection with a female deity such as Xochiquetzal. The sky band is always divided into glyphic sections, each box indicating a feature of the sky, sun, moon, the planet Venus, night, and so on. The band as a whole is treated as though it were the elongated body of the dragon. From this we must assume that the bird of the sky signified exactly the same thing as did the feathered serpent—namely, the totality of the items in the sky, but perhaps with a slight emphasis on the life-giving rains. Tamoanchan, the Abode of the Moan-Bird Serpent, can thus be loosely translated as Cloudland. For the sky as the habitation of gods we have two names. Omeyocan was the thirteenth and highest level of the heavens and was the seat of the two high gods, who sent souls down to earth for their incarnations, whereas Tamoanchan was, as we have seen, the upper level of the sky viewed as a paradise ruled over by Xochiquetzal. The first was a primum mobile and the authoritative source of all the vitalities in the world—a needed philosophical basis for the works of creation. The second was the crystallization of man's expression of himself, his needs and desires. Tamoanchan was built around a cosmic concept, namely, the world tree, but its flavor was in every sense worldly.

The difference between the two can be even more easily captured in the divine descents that were made from each of these two heavens. It was the god Quetzalcoatl who came down from Omeyocan to bring culture and an awareness of structures to men. From Tamoanchan it was the goddess Xochiquetzal who descended, bringing sensual delights, symbolized by flowers. The difference is underlined when we recall that the purveyor of culture was the god of air or sky whereas desire was brought by an avatar of the earth.

In the last analysis sky remained masculine.

Some Speculations on Tonatiuh's Lapse

The unquestioned paladin in the sky was, or should have been, Tonatiuh, the sun god. He is described as residing in his glorious abode surrounded by beautiful birds that once were redoubtable warriors.[32] He is there the summa of masculinity, the iron-hearted *tiacauh*, or "hero." His mythology speaks of him as the creator of all things[33] as well as the giver of victory on the battlefield. He can be referred to as the *tlatoani*, as if he were "king" of the gods;[34] or Ilhuicahua, the "possessor of the sky,"[35] or even as *icel teotl*, the "unique god."[36] In view of this preeminence of his, it is surprising that he is not portrayed in the likeness of a dragon, as is the morning star. The art of the Postclassic period can portray the sun being carried across the daytime sky on the back of a firedragon,[37] but the two, hero and dragon, do not merge. Like the other gods the sun can take on different figurations. He can be Tloque Nahuaque, an overgod who is so vague as to seem little more than a cosmic abstraction.[38] He can be the most powerful of the gods in Teotihuacán, or he can be Huitzilopochtli, the parochial god of one tribe. Such a wide range should have made Tonatiuh, rather than Quetzalcoatl, the central figure in the sky religion. Yet, except on occasion, he fails to achieve such status in the Aztec period. His regalia reflect this, for it is simple and undeveloped, even unimaginative.

Xipe—another sun god—is far more universal than is Tonatiuh. He personifies the warmth of springtime, the new verdure, and the birth of the young of men and animals; at the same time he stands for vigor and the skills of war. Why in the instance of the god Tonatiuh did such a spread of qualities narrow down to the martial alone? He should have been the touchstone of all celestial meaning. Why, in the religion of the Aztecs, was Tonatiuh solely a warrior? The answer must be—Quetzalcoatl.

After all, heroism is a narrowly conceived aptitude. When Mesoamerican societies began slipping under the domination of warrior lodges, when the role of the *tlatoani* no longer was propitiation only but was concentrated even more on the feeding of the gods—at that point the sun god was shorn of his wider effulgence. As his worship was concentrated in the hands of one part of the society, namely, the warriors, his ability to interpenetrate all aspects of society disappeared.

All religions show a centripetal tendency that is basically

rational. That is to say, the need to explain things and to allocate responsibility in the heavens in turn will demand an increasing cohesion in the mythology. Usually this need is satisfied by giving to one god a veto power over the others or by setting up one god as an Olympian ruler or as a senior in age and wisdom—there are many ways to embody this in myth and doctrine. Besides Tonatiuh there were other sun gods and avatars of sun gods in Mesoamerican religion, but in the late period in the central highlands we hear of none, after the narrowing of Tonatiuh, whose powers were augmented so that they filled a central position. Instead it was the sky that, in the person of Quetzalcoatl, was augmented. But we know the sky to have been diffuse and many-faceted, joining in itself wind, planets, stars, rain, and even the sun. Yet while Quetzalcoatl invaded and usurped some of the sun's mythology, he was never called the Unique God. Thus when Tonatiuh failed, it was not a simple substitution of one god for another which occurred in this long quest for religious unity. As it turned out, Quetzalcoatl also was blocked from acquiring the sovereignty when, as legend has it, he was successfully attacked by Tezcatlipoca in Tula. Few gods of the Postclassic period, however, matched Quetzalcoatl in the varied character of his celestial jurisdiction.

Little or nothing is really known about the course of Tonatiuh's failure—if it was a failure. It seems that the warrior caste must have increasingly defined his cult as one of sacrifice after battle rather than as seasonal sacrifices for sunshine and well-being—thus substituting death for life as the orientation of his worship. Naturally this would have been not an oscillation from pure white to pure black but a change in emphasis only. It was enough, however, to free and intensify Quetzalcoatl's ability to assume new avatars. In other words, as the sun (Tonatiuh) was increasingly commandeered by the warriors, so the sky (Quetzalcoatl) was stretched to fill out some of the interstices resulting from that shrinkage.

One of the solar niches into which Quetzalcoatl and his avatars entered—and indeed almost usurped—was the realm of Yohualtonatiuh, the night sun. Many ancient mythologies, such as the ancient Egyptian, have typically viewed the sun's progress through the underworld as a heroic enterprise, a successful foray against subterranean enemies. Most of the Mesoamerican peoples did not see it in this fashion, however. Instead, by increasing the powers of the evening star, who was the god Xolotl and Quetzalcoatl's twin, they arrived at a belief in the capture of the sun in the underworld and his death on the sacrificial stone at midnight. Even when reborn in the underworld the sun was not able to reenter the daytime world unopposed. To ensure his rising, he still had to engage the morning star in a duel to the death—and only then was he finally proved heroic.

To explicate this depreciatory view, the myth of the sun was reworked. The hitherto "sole god" was now absorbed into the deathly persons of two deities of the night sky; that is to say, he became deathly himself. In Maya lore the sun was specifically the Lord of Xibalba, the underworld.[39] This situation is tantamount to the destruction of the sun's independence by the evening star and the morning star, who hem him in. The concept will be expanded later in this book.

This recasting of elements of sun worship by the Quetzalcoatl priesthood is well displayed in the story of the fifth sun. He is presented as an avatar of the god Nanahuatl, who is a form of the evening star, who in turn is Quetzalcoatl's twin. In brief, Quetzalcoatl has succeeded in a roundabout way in actually *becoming* the sun.

We cannot, therefore, see the Mesoamerican sun god as the always joyous and intrepid adventurer of the skies, for he turns out to be simply one of the celestial beings highly susceptible to contamination and weakness. Once he slips below the horizon, the sun is forced to come to terms with the greater mythology of Quetzalcoatl.

Quetzalcoatl as the Night Sky

The night sky was identified with the jaguar not only because of the animal's nocturnal habits but also because his spotted pelt could be seen as a reverse picture of the star-studded night. But an even more fundamental identification of the night sky was made with the Feathered Serpent. And the night sky, as we also know, was a kenning for the underworld.[40] They were two sides of the same coin.

In this primitive understanding of the night sky, the stars and constellations had to be explained. By Aztec times at least five major explanations had been offered: (1) that the stars were unblinking eyes peering down through the night, (2) that they were the dead, unnamed and sometimes hostile,[41] (3) that they were the souls of the ancestors, (4) that each one was a god's avatar or was his seat in the empyrean, and (5) that they were the *tzitzimime*, demons of indiscriminate menace often thought of as female.[42] The first four were not so far apart as to give rise to separate systems of thought. They were all set against a background feeling of inquietude, a situation in which ancestral ghosts easily became pseudo-divinities, vividly experienced in the unsettling gaze of evil eyes in the heavens. The fifth interpretation, however, imputes a total malevolence to the hosts of the night sky, and on the basis of it the Nahuas fashioned Tzitzimitl, a great goddess of the night sky and the very compendium of horrors. These were popular readings of the stars, and they had some importance also to the priests as over the centuries the sky religion developed. But the dynamic center of the priestly religion was not the stars (which, after all, were only items) but first the sky itself, the dragon, and in particular that dragon known as Quetzalcoatl.

As a celestial being, Quetzalcoatl had two appearances and, therefore, two habitats. In the one his place of origin, as befitted the deified sky, was the topmost, or thirteenth, heaven, Omeyocan. There he lived with the two high gods, and from there in anthropomorphic form he descended to earth on his various missions. We can call this form of the god Ehecatl, Air or Wind. He was thus already partly abstracted from the sky and had a form as culture hero and progenitor. Otherwise he was specifically the night sky, and his dwelling place was the Milky Way.[43] This second Quetzalcoatl was a demiurge whose role was cosmic. It is the latter nocturnal aspect of the god that we are considering here.

The Quetzalcoatl who represents the night sky can be shown as a vast feathered serpent coiled in a circle around a rabbit who represents the moon.[44] It is this Quetzalcoatl, barely moved down in status from an all-encompassing numen, who in myth participated in the great ordering of the universe. In one version of the myth the old celestial god Citlalatonac created Quetzalcoatl by breathing on him, whereupon Quetzalcoatl, thus revivified, alone and unaided formed all things.[45] Or again, the Old God informed the Earth Mother that she would conceive without sexual intercourse, whereat she did and bore Quetzalcoatl.[46]

The more widespread version of the creation myth has the high god install both Quetzalcoatl and Tezcatlipoca as lords of the night sky, and it is they who set about creating all things.[47] It must be noted here that Tezcatlipoca, whose animal was the jaguar, was also a god of the night and the interior of the earth, a situation roughly parallel to the identification of Quetzalcoatl with the night sky. Demiurgic action thus resulted first from a celestial decision on high that designated the two actors, both identified with the night, who were called to perform the great task. When the Milky Way was made, both Quetzalcoatl and Tezcatlipoca were then assigned as its custodians. There is an interesting gloss to this myth, namely, that the latter god after the creation changed his name to Mixcoatl.[48] And Mixcoatl is really only another form of the sky dragon, in the same manner as was Quetzalcoatl. Thus we light on the very ancient concept of the sky as a double dragon, and the myth that we have been considering suggests that Quetzalcoatl, when seen as a demiurge, should definitely be thought of as nocturnal rather than diurnal.

What we then have is a Mesoamerican belief in the sky as at first regnant (in the persons of the two high gods) and only then as creative (through the persons of Quetzalcoatl and Tezcatlipoca). Both decision and action are attributed to the sky, with contrasting pairs of deities representing each. The pairing goes back at least to Izapan iconography, wherein the sky is shown either as two dragons, heads down in the east and west, or as a single dragon with a head at each end.

The reason for preferring night to day as the template upon which to form a model sky says much about the human imagination—or at least about the Mesoamerican imagination. One might think that the sky of day, filled with moving cloud shapes and colors, would have been assigned the primacy in this regard. The human imagination, however, is the child of mystery and the slave of the unknown; that is to say, it is stirred more by the sense of the secrecy and impenetrability of darkness—which may yet be illuminated—than by the glorious light, which is so obviously fulfilled in every way. More specifically, however, there is the fact already noted that what was overhead was thought by the Mesoamerican people to be a coiling and twisting serpent, whether single or double, and added to this was the knowledge that the serpent casts his skin and is renewed. Day is renewed from the cast skin of night, not the reverse.

The Mesoamerican imagination in many ways depicted the firmament of night as the primate sky. Later in this book I will have occasion to introduce that avatar of Quetzalcoatl known as Xolotl. Looking ahead, I shall here simply place in the record the fact that on each of the nine steps of the underworld (that is, the night sky) Quetzalcoatl sacrifices a divine being called Yohualteuctli. This being, the Lord of the Night, stands for the corpse of the sun, which must be revived.[49] And Quetzalcoatl is that spirit in the night sky who by sacrifice brings about this regeneration of light. He performs each one of the successive nine sacrificial acts in the person of a different avatar. Together they represent the mystery of the night sky.

The Provenience and Spread of the Sky Religion

The fact that this religion was wholly in the hands of a class of disciplined priestly experts encouraged them to seize all opportunities for expanding it. Just because it was not geared solely to subsistence activities, the religion early established an essentially urban outlook. It preempted great centers such as Cholula, Xochicalco, and Chichén Itzá.

Later in this book I shall deal with the ball court, the *tlachco*. Here I need just mention that in the archaeological record the ball court is diagnostic of the cult connected with the Feathered Serpent; it is certainly evidence for the exportation of ideas that had been originally developed within the context of the sky religion. I do not intend a survey of the spread of Quetzalcoatl motifs—that would be a book in itself—which inevitably in the vast distances between Costa Rica and the Mississippi Valley would have changed their meanings to some extent. What I am rather emphasizing is the power in the religion that enabled it to attain such a geographical spread. No other Mesoamerican god traveled as far.

Perhaps the most interesting examples of the spread of the religion are to be found in the great spaces of northwestern Mexico, extending all the way up into the American Southwest. At Casas Grandes ball courts appeared soon after the first appearance there of the plumed serpent.[50] Then at some time after A.D. 600 the Hohokam peoples of what is today southern Arizona were integrating ball courts into their irrigation-oriented culture. They suddenly appear with a set of symbols that include horned bird serpents and double-headed dragons overspanning the earth and marked with sun and star signs.[51] Later in time the Hopi, Zuñi, and Pueblo peoples became familiar with the sky dragon.[52] In Zuñi, for example, the sky dragon is Kolowisi; he has goggle eyes (like Tlaloc), a curved horn (like the Xiuhcoatl), and a feathered crest.[53] These are admittedly isolated examples and are mentioned only to show the unusual integrity of the image as it passed over successive frontiers. Much more certainly remains to be done with the Feathered Serpent as he moved into the cultures of the northern lands.

We are guessing that Quetzalcoatl came originally from the lowlands along the Gulf of Mexico, and we have arbitrarily given his name to the Olmec dragon. In the Aztec texts that have survived, Quetzalcoatl is said to have appeared first in the Huaxteca, that northwestern extension of the Olmec coastal strip running roughly from Nautla up to Tampico. In myth the earliest memory of him went as follows:[54]

The first ancestors appeared out of the waters of the Gulf and landed on the coast near Papantla. No one could say whence they came. They were led by certain learned priests who had charge of the sacred writings and who carried their god Quetzalcoatl with them as a bundle. But contention grew up among the people, and as a consequence the wise men took the god and disappeared with him into the east. They left the prophecy that he would return at the end of time, when troubles should have humbled the ungrateful tribes. The place where the people were at the time when the wise men left was called Tamoanchan. Another version of the legend has it that from the coast Quetzalcoatl directed his steps onto the central plateau, while a gloss on this connects Quetzalcoatl specifically with Tulantzinco, a city guarding the route between Teotihuacán, the great center in the highlands, and the coast of the Huaxteca.[55]

When we consider that in iconography the regalia worn by Ehecatl (the wind, or the priestly avatar of Quetzalcoatl) are wholly Huaxtec, we cannot fail to see him as native to those parts, his earliest appearance there having been, as we have already seen, the Olmec dragon. Nor were his coastal origins ever forgotten even after his cult had spread to distant parts. At the time of the Spanish entry the old coastal provinces of Tuxpan and Atlan (parts of the Huaxteca) regularly supplied as tribute to Mexico blankets featuring Quetzalcoatl's wind jewel as well as conch shells with extended wings.[56] Few other provinces in the empire of the Three Cities featured such symbols of the sky religion.

The ruins of Tajín, near Papantla, corroborate the connections mentioned above in the legend of the first landing. Tajín reached its peak in the period A.D. 600 to 900 but had been a holy site far earlier. If the Totonac word *tajín* means "lightning, thunder, or hurricane" as the *Official Guide* to the site assures us, then the city may indeed have been sacred to Quetzalcoatl, god of the windstorm. Representations of Quetzalcoatl, both as dragon and as priest, are prominently displayed in the ball courts of Tajín.

I mention Tajín here as possibly a holy city of Quetzalcoatl because it is the capital site from which the ancient road ran westward over the lowlands to the escarpment and then up to Tulantzinco, which commanded the vital passes, as noted above. Myth clearly connects the god with this city. From Tulantzinco it is only a short move to Teotihuacán. This axial road between the Huaxteca and the great urban center Teotihuacán is important in explaining the appearance of Quetzalcoatl in the highlands, but there were other routes as well—a notable one passed through Chalcatzinco.

The Role of Sky in the Creation

The paleology of the sky was known to the Aztecs in two myths, the first the myth of creation and the second the myth of the sky's collapse and subsequent reinstatement. These two cannot be logically linked together, for they were designed by the priests with different ends in view. In the first myth the interest centers in the architecture of the universe and the vital role of the two demiurgic gods. This myth is a kind of magnificat, remote and antique. The second myth is more urgent, almost ominous, describing a juncture in time when history began to emerge from nature and to complicate it.

In the creation myth matter first existed as a cosmic disconformity called Tlalteuctli, or Earth Lord. Two gods, Tezcatlipoca and Quetzalcoatl, were assigned to the task of creation, and they performed it through a process of separation, for they split the great mass in two, raising the upper part to become the sky and leaving the earth as the form below. And just as under the earth there exist the tellurian waters, so above and within the sky there exist the celestial waters. These hidden reservoirs possessed both fructifying and destructive powers. The sky, however, was an entity that was precariously balanced and in need of support. Four supernaturals were accordingly designated to hold it up, one at each of the sides, or cardinal directions.[57] With the cosmic structure thus readied, the two celestial high gods,

Citlalinicue (feminine) and Citlalatonac (masculine), next
fixed the stars in their places and appointed the two demiurges to opposing custodial positions in the sky. The Milky
Way was to become the track through the sky that the two
demiurges traveled. Night itself was a supernatural and
came into being through the promptings of Yohualteuctli
(Night Lord) and his avatar Yacahuitztli (Sharp Nose).[58] As
an ultimate support for the sky Tezcatlipoca changed himself into a world tree, the Tree of Mirrors, while Quetzalcoatl did similarly, becoming the cosmic Green Willow.
Thus one can think of the sky as supported either by four
Atlantes or by two trees acting as end posts.

The myth of the sky's collapse was glossed by the mythographers as having been that catastrophe which ended the
aeon (or sun) of the water goddess Chalchiuhtlicue. In
the series of aeons or suns it was variously the first or the
fourth. Either way the fit is not a bad one, but there can be
no doubt that the tale once stood alone and was not integrated into a series. It reflected man's early and common
concern that the sky was basically unstable and could someday fall. Many cultures have reflected this great fear.

What interests us here is the appended flood story. In the
version in which the event takes place at the end of the first
sun, the sky came crashing down, killing all the giants who
then inhabited the world, but no flood followed. The other
version is more explicit: when the sky, which was basically
the bed of an ocean of waters overhead, collapsed, it let
loose devastating floods. This scenario gave the mythographers an opportunity to introduce speculation concerning
early man. If one told it as the tale of one of the five world
cataclysms, then all the men of that age were drowned or
became fish or mermen living in the ocean.[59] On the other
hand, if one told the tale as folklore, then it concerned Tata
and Nene, the first human pair.[60] Alone of mankind this
pair was saved by Tezcatlipoca, who instructed them to
climb into one of the great world trees or hollow it out as a

53

vessel. They were thus saved from the flood, but because they learned at that time to handle fire, which was strictly a celestial prerogative, the gods punished them by changing them into dogs. A more history-minded version has seven human beings saved from the flood, the ancestors of the seven tribes who issued out of Chicomoztoc, a cluster of ancestral holes in the ground.

In this second tale the sky is the home of authority as well as the seat of avenging deities. Fire was generally assigned by the Aztecs to the earth's center, but here, consonant with the dogma of the sky as primary, fire is seen to be celestial in origin.

The Quiché Mayas told a better-organized tale of creation.[61] Sky is only one of the elements in the story, though it is stated to have been the preexistent element. At first, sky and silence made up the totality of things. Under the sky the flat ocean stretched out endlessly; it incorporated the two demiurges Tepeu (Tezcatlipoca) and Gukumatz (Quetzalcoatl). Earth was created by bringing mountains up from the abyss and thus draining away the waters. The Mixtecs, like the Aztecs, began with a pair of high gods living in the sky, which is supported on the point of a sacred mountain.[62] These two first gods of the Mixtecs are once shown wearing Quetzalcoatl's regalia, attesting to the sky's primacy.

Present in the above myths is the sky as the initial scenery against which creation takes place. Either the sky is the numinous all-precursor that needs no explanation, or it is symbolized by Quetzalcoatl, who is the sky and its inhabiting winds. Such myths prove that the Mesoamerican sky religion was not formulated as one term of a dualism of sky versus earth. The sky religion, through the active imaginings of its priests, simply presented itself as intellectually necessary in any attempt to understand the cosmos.

There exists one more myth, almost biblical, alluding to the creation of the sky.[63] The great god, high in the heavens, who is called either Tonacateuctli or Citlalatonac, his nocturnal counterpart, sent a messenger down to Chimalma, the earth goddess in Tula, informing her that she would bear a son who would be lord of the air. Tonacateuctli performed this miracle "with his breath alone," so that the goddess remained a virgin. In other words, Tonacateuctli blew on the earth and produced sky. How seriously we are to take the tale, which comes to us from devout Christian friars, is debatable.

The Shape of the Sky and Its Denizens

Thus far we have discussed sky as a dragon or dragons, and we have viewed these beings as essentially animations of a place. However bizarre it may seem to us, the Mesoamericans found it congenial to endow the sky with animal movement and vitality. But they could also view the sky in terms of a structured abode, a mansion of many rooms sculptured out of immaterial air and inhabited by various gods, bogeys, and powers—it all depended on whether one was talking about the sky as a *place* or as a *being*.

They could express this architecturally. In Teotihuacán the temple of Quetzalcoatl had six superimposed levels. If for the moment we can assume that that was deliberate, then we can see in it a model for ascent from the eastern horizon to the firmament with a subsequent descent into the west. The whole number of steps will then equal twelve, which when capped by the shrine on top, the heaven of heavens, gives thirteen. In Aztec lore there were thirteen heavenly levels, and they were probably read in the manner suggested above—as though the sky were a six-terraced mountain. But they were also read in ladder fashion as if only ascent were in question with the descent omitted— thus the summit was not the seventh but the thirteenth level, called Omeyocan, the Place of the Two.

When Omeyocan is defined qualitatively, it becomes

Tamoanchan. We have already run across Tamoanchan as the high heaven wherein the world tree flowered. This tree was essential, as we now know, to the world view of the Aztecs in the sense that it served to define for them what sin was and what was its occasion.

There was a well-known myth—a doublet of the Xochiquetzal myth—that the first sin was committed at the beginning of things when seven gods who lived by right in the heavens defied the taboo against touching the tree.[64] For this Tonacateuctli expelled the seven from their celestial home. They descended to take up lesser stances in the air, earth, and underworld, where they thenceforth operated and became known to men.

This is the story of the loss of paradise, a loss incurred not by mortals but by gods, and it therefore presents sin as being a corruption in the very center of the sky religion. The list of the culpable seven varies slightly, but all are sky-connected; Quetzalcoatl, Tezcatlipoca, Tlahuizcalpanteuctli, and Itzpapalotl are prominently mentioned. It has been suggested that the seven represent the seven planets, and indeed the tracing of the seven planets across the dark field of the stars might well have brought to mind a fall or an erring of seven celestial deities. For the Aztecs the thought of original sin as a defect of the divine must have created intellectual problems. At the very least it blurred the historical record. If the functioning of the world was the sum of the activity of truncated gods, there could then have been no possibility of paradise regained and certainly no eschatology. Such thinking of course need not have affected any of the other three religions. The myth we have been considering, however, does present one god in the sky religion as somewhat ambivalent. This god is Tonacateuctli.

In Aztec mythology there were four sets of paired high gods, male and female, respectively: Ometeuctli and Omecihuatl, Tonacateuctli and Tonacacihuatl, Citlalatonac and

Citlalinicue, and, finally, Cipactonal and Oxomoco. All of them are celestial and are never found in any place but the sky. There, sitting at the apex of the heavens, they act as ultimate authorities. There are, of course, some differences in their respective mythologies, but basically they are all formed on the same pattern, crypto-numinous beings who are sexually differentiated to explain the fact of progeny. They are, in fact, the first pair, and were occasionally referred to by the friars as Adam and Eve. Thus the home of insemination and parturition is seated in the sky. Earth also displayed this power of procreation but did so with more physiological directness—in that view men issued from the Seven Caves, which was the primeval womb. The production of offspring by the celestial high gods by contrast was on a more conceptual level, for the spirits of the unborn were assigned in Omeyocan to certain earthly parents only by their divine command.

Tonacateuctli is the most interesting of the male high gods.[65] While his name means Lord of Our Substance (that is, maize), he is in reality the first known sun god, a god so old by the time of the Aztecs that his cult had ceased and only his antiquity was remembered. He was the heat, light, or fire in the sky that is essential to life.[66] He wears the fire dragon on his brow as befits the supreme sky god. He waves a fan of quetzal feathers that symbolize sky, and in all things else he is shown to be an imperial figure.[67] In the most refined myth of creation coming down to us from ancient Mexico, Tonacateuctli was said to have divided the waters of earth from the waters of the sky by blowing on them—that is to say, by inserting the air between them.[68] When we are further told that he created Quetzalcoatl, god of the air, by his breath alone, then we realize that in Tonacateuctli we have pretty well identified that god who first was crystallized out of the numen of the sky. Though his date name was Seven Flower, which identifies him as the sun, Tonacateuctli was still a god of the whole sky, whether diurnal or nocturnal. An avatar of his, Citlalatonac, was the Milky Way and the lord of the night sky. The levels in the sky below Omeyocan were thought of as the domiciles of various gods and powers.[69] The order of these beings fluctuates according to which of our sources we use. Some fill the levels with the thirteen greatest gods, others with items that logically can be considered celestial in origin, such as dust, winds, stars, and birds. Both kinds of lists, however, culminate with the paired high gods in Omeyocan. In other words, the priests could use the levels either for god ratings of their own or for popular etiological purposes.

Besides being structured in levels, the sky had another and probably basic form, that of a firmament upheld by four Atlantes, each one named and each one additionally resident in a well-known constellation of stars. These four supporting beings are of interest because of their demonic character and also because they had counterparts in the Stygian sky below this world.[70] They are the Tzitzimime (plural), who in a final destruction at the end of time will shrug off the firmament and let it come crashing down upon the earth. The four are avatars or emanations of a single female apparition of the night sky named Tzitzimitl.[71] I have mentioned her before. Folklore made much of this giantess in the heavens. I have previously noted that a deification of *ilhuicatl*, the sky, was most closely approached in the persons of Quetzalcoatl or Tonacateuctli, yet even they do not perfectly express the sky as a single entity. But if there was no divinity who embodied perfectly the day sky, there did exist this specific deity who summed up the frightfulness of the night sky, the Gorgonian Tzitzimitl. We can see now that when one considered sky in terms of thirteen levels the concept suggested the sky of day. On the other hand, if the sky was thought of as having supporting pillars, the tendency was to apply that concept to the night sky.

Tzitzimitl is the demonic counterpart of the high goddess Citlalinicue, who was the Great Mother embodied in the Milky Way. Tzitzimitl is depicted as a skeleton equipped with talons for hands and feet and having a long penis hanging down between her legs in the form of a rattlesnake.[72] She is closely connected with the stars, which can be thought of as *tzitzimime* waiting for that fateful time when they too will descend on the races of men and annihilate them. In such a mythic view the whole field of the stars becomes malevolent.

One could imagine the stars in another fashion, however, namely, as *mimixcoa*.[73] The word for them is the plural form of the name Mixcoatl, Cloud Serpent, and they were thought to be either the souls of dead warriors or evil sorcerers. When contemplated in their myriads, the stars were the Four Hundred, which is a way of saying Innumerable Ones. When given specific names, however, there were five of them, titans out of the early levels of Mesoamerican religion who acknowledged Mixcoatl as their leader. Their father was the sun, and their mother was that avatar of earth who disgorged the underground waters, spilling them out of springs and caves. The *mimixcoa* were said to have emerged out of the womb of earth through the Seven Caves,[74] from which series of fissures the Aztecs themselves also claimed to have come.

But the *mimixcoa* were even more closely identified than this. They were the ancestral dead, those who had slipped away into namelessness but who now, as a kind of larval mass, lived in far-northern skies.[75] Specifically the "cloud-serpent" forefathers were the circumpolar stars that, during the wheeling of the night sky, did not drop below the horizon. All other stars, which visibly weakened and fell into the earth before the dawn, were known as the Four Hundred Southerners. When depicted in art, stars were shown as wide-open eyes peering down through the curtain of the sky. The ancestors, in other words, did not sleep.

There was a counter population among these conspic-
uous tenants of the skies. These were the *ilhuicapipiltin*, or
"sky children," the as-yet-unborn who were to enter into
their human bodies through the wombs of women and who
were sent down from Omeyocan by the two high gods.[76]
Thus there existed the concept of mankind as owning both
a past and a future that were rendered visible in the night
sky. Only the present generation of men was missing from
this huge celestial mural. Such a conjoined stellar mythology and eschatology differs radically from the science of
beginnings and endings in the earth religion, in which men
simply appear from out of the ground and return thereunto.

As stars the ancestors had a semidivine status that in later
speculation moved toward full divinization. Because the
gods lived an empyreal life, it was only natural that the
priests assigned to each one a constellation or a bright star.
Quetzalcoatl as the morning star is merely the best known
of these assignments. The question whether there were
thirteen of these constellations (emblems of the thirteen
gods?) that formed a Mesoamerican zodiac through which
the sun or moon traveled has remained unproved up to
now. It is possible, however, that something like the zodiac
did exist, at least in the Maya area.[77]

One of the gaps in our understanding of the Aztecs is the
extent of their astronomical knowledge. Lunar and Venusian counts are attested from Maya sources—and even
eclipse tables. These presuppose advanced celestial observation techniques and records that in turn presuppose the
charting and naming of many stars and planets. Only piti-
ful fragments of such a stellar corpus remain to us from our
Aztec sources, nor do we know how much they remembered from earlier and richer times. We do know that they
designated certain stars and constellations to represent the
four compass points and the center. The Little Bear was
seen by the Aztecs as the baton that Quetzalcoatl held in his
hand, the *xonecuilli*, and this stood for the north. The

Pleiades were referred to as the Crowd or the Market Place, and they undoubtedly represented the zenith or center direction. The other constellations (the Face of the Scorpion, the Fire Drill, and what may be translated as the Night Carrier) cannot positively be assigned to the three remaining directions, though the Fire Drill (the Sword and Belt of Orion?) is a good candidate for the east.[78] We are cautioned however, against assuming that the Aztecs saw the night sky as we do, purely as a field of objects. Rather to them it was a manual of ineffable symbols, a Sibylline leaf, and an encyclopedia. Also it was a thing of terror.

Up to now I have studiously avoided reference to "astrology" in this book, a word that refers to occult influences exercised over people by the set of the night sky and the position of the planets at the moment of their birth. This hoary fallacy, still living among us today, had its counterpart among the Mesoamericans—an artificial set of juxtapositions that was carefully worked out and recorded in the *Tonalamatl*, or *Book of Destiny Days*. Instead of astrologers, however, the Aztecs produced the *tonalpouhque*, "ones skilled in the count of destiny days." Like the European astrologers they too needed to know the hour and day of a child's birth to read his horoscope, but they found that information in the *Tonalamatl*, not in the position or conjunction of certain stars.

The *Tonalamatl* and the arts of its interpretation were attributed to Quetzalcoatl.[79] It was this sacred writ that kept securely within the ambient of the sky religion the science of forecasting the future, which prerogative gave to that religion and to Quetzalcoatl an inestimable prestige. Long after the warlike character of Quetzalcoatl as Ce Acatl had weakened under the challenge of other gods, his priestly and cryptic powers continued without diminution. None of the other three religions had such easy access to the arcane.

Nevertheless we can only believe—because of the Mesoamerican's abiding interest in the stars—that planetary and lunar conjunctions were somehow important to him and formed a part of his augural skills. A kind of astrology there may have been, though Sahagún says no.[80]

Sun and moon completed the astral population, each being allotted a specific level in the sky. The beliefs about these two were so various that it is impossible to assemble them into one pattern. The best-known assemblage myth, in which all the inhabitants of the sky are worked into a single narrative, is in the Aztec gigantomachy. In that myth, moon is the leader of the evil and titanic *mimixcoa*. Earth is inert and acts only as the womb from which springs the sun, who defeats the moon and her starry host. The weapon that he uses to achieve victory is the fire dragon.

Last there was air itself, but inasmuch as this was the god Ehecatl Quetzalcoatl, who is the matter of most of this book, I will not expatiate on it here. Rainbows, waterspouts, comets, and the haze from brushfires were assembled into the inventory of the sky, all thereby receiving their status in the world of things.

The Place of the Sky Religion Among Other Cults

Let us now specify the characteristics of this ancient sky religion. Inasmuch as I am looking ahead to some of the matter taken up in more detailed fashion later, there is no need to provide the reader here with more than a sketch of what he will find in succeeding chapters. The items that occur to me are as follows:

1. The dragon was an emblem of the sky as a homogeneous segment of nature. It also prefigured the sky as a set of disparate concepts concerned with celestial activity in which the actors, whether stellar, lunar, solar, or hyperborean, display various kinds of movement.

2. The sky religion was nonagricultural in spite of its connections with water. Quetzalcoatl was indeed closely related to Tlaloc, but there was never the slightest confusion between the two. Quetzalcoatl was not a farmer's god. And the interest of the sky religion in water was directed not toward its uses in human culture but toward its fundamentally draconian nature.

3. The sky religion did concern itself necessarily with fertility, but again not always with reference to agriculture. Much of the time it concentrated on human procreation. Thus a phallic cult became part of the religion. The patronage of the god Quetzalcoatl over the founding and maintenance of noble lineages, which we shall be discussing later, followed from this.

4. The religion was explicated in terms of an archetypal myth wherein Quetzalcoatl was said to be the son of the dawn (masculine) and the earth (feminine), as well as the killer, sacrificer, and awakener (or avenger) of the light.

5. The multiplicity of avatars that the religion delighted in revolved around the figure of Quetzalcoatl, who is thus on the one hand the sum of all of them and on the other a discrete deity himself.

6. The religion created a distinctive sense of time. In this construct time was seen as being compounded of (*a*) the daily and the seasonal swing of the sun, (*b*) the revolution of the planet Venus, (*c*) an arcane numerology meshed with symbols, namely the *tonalpohualli*, and (*d*) the five aeons of cosmic time. It did not, however, succeed in reducing all of them into one inclusive formulation.

7. The ball game was the central cult act in the religion, though its importance fluctuated with the passage of the centuries. This sports arena featured that avatar of Quetzalcoatl who was the evening star. The death of light is celebrated in it, and possibilities of rejuvenation are hinted at.

8. The myth of the victory of the sun over the morning star sets forth a dogma of the sky religion contrasting with

the above but evolving from it. In it the rebirth of light is celebrated.

9. The use of twinning, iconographically and in the mythology, was central in the structuring of the divine world as seen by the sky religion. The dragon was often by nature twofold or two-headed. The night scene itself was twofold, and a reading of it depended on which aegis it was under, that of the morning or that of the evening star.

10. The sky religion provided a reasoned cosmography showing the heavens structured in thirteen levels.

11. The sky religion considered the night sky as dominant over the day sky. It therefore demanded a significant cult elaboration for the former. The ball game was developed in conformity with this emphasis.

12. The religion evoked the idea that ultimate authority must always be celestial, and to this end it deified a pair of high gods, the linch pins of the religion. They were admitted to be abstractions and were not worshiped. Only in the context of these two could creative activity take place.

13. The religion preempted the concept of the priesthood, perhaps even originated it, and gave to it a permanent sacrificial orientation.

A word of caution here. The sky religion interpenetrated other aspects of Mesoamerican religion so subtly that it is difficult to grasp it as a thing apart. Yet if we do not make the distinction, we cannot see Quetzalcoatl clearly—he remains an unexplained deity among other unexplained deities. We certainly cannot prove or disprove that the people of Mesoamerica strictly detached a sky religion from the whole matrix of their religious beliefs and practices, but it is probable that the priesthood of Quetzalcoatl appreciated the uniqueness of their worship. In any case the concept of a sky religion is a tool that enables us to discuss Quetzalcoatl intelligibly.

Again, I do not wish to give the impression that the sky religion represents the acme of Mesoamerican religion. It was one among four, all making up that greater mélange mentioned above. There was the agricultural and burial complex that we call the religion of the earth. Because of its heavy concentration on the production of food, this religion never came into conflict with the sky religion. In fact, in ways it complemented it. The religion of the fire god was no doubt the most venerable of all, and many of its observances were domestic and remained domestic, as we might expect. To the other religions it contributed fire as an ultimate offering; thus the fire religion acted as a cement binding them all together. The religion of Tezcatlipoca most nearly resembles biblical religion, and its vision of the oneness of the god and of his untrammeled will is worth noting. We shall consider the clash between this religion and that of the sky in the closing pages of this book.

The sky religion was not as clearly defined as any of the other three religions. Its forte lay in its ability to interpenetrate them or to attract their central deities into its orbit. As one of the four it was thus unique in its scope.

One can imagine a situation in which the sky religion might have acted as a catalyst in organizing the mass of Mesoamerican cults into a larger religion maintained by a single celestial dogma. For reasons that will become clear later on, it never did. It moved outward from its coastal homeland with a missionizing vigor denied to the other cults, but it had no call to eliminate its competitors. It was an elite religion, while the others, two of them nature religions, were the possessions of the people.

In summary it can be seen that the sky was the home of the worst and the best in the Mesoamerican's imaginings. If the three other religions were jointly the Mesoamerican's acceptance of reality and his distillation of it, the sky religion encouraged him to pronounce—as over and against them—his more important obiter dicta. For him the sky religion presented above all the occasion to think, to tell stories, and to verbally wonder.

We could go on differentiating the sky religion from the others of Mesoamerica. It stood out by reason of its intellectually and socially conscious orientation. The *amoxtlacuilo* ("painter of books") who produced such magnificent visual records of Mesoamerica was a man of Quetzalcoatl and skilled in his arts. It was he who knew that the sky had been created on the date 1-reed (Ce Acatl).[81] This memorable point in the past was also the birth date, and therefore the name, of the god Quetzalcoatl, who stood at the center of the sky religion.

TWO
THE POLYMORPHOUS GOD: DEMIURGE, CULTURE HERO, AND ANCESTOR

This chapter begins the discussion of Quetzalcoatl's many avatars, and in particular of the wind, Ehecatl, which seems to have been the earliest. Ehecatl is described in some detail with special reference to his buccal mask and his curious celestial baton. Next I touch on an aspect of the god's uniqueness in considering his patronage of circular temples as opposed to those with a square base. I emphasize his closeness to man in his capacity as a culture hero. The elements in man's culture that were of the god's doing are then listed and analyzed, particularly his curious connection with maize. Two other important offices of his are also noted, those relating to human fecundity and to lineage. In the latter capacity the god was connected to every royal house. A portion of the Selden Roll *is commented on in this instance of the god's ancestral guardianship. Finally I describe the god and his cult in the holy city of Cholula.*

The Centrality of Quetzalcoatl

In the religion of the sky were many gods and demons. Of these there are few who may not be considered in some way or other either avatars of Quetzalcoatl in the first or second degree or alternate patrons of realms generally ascribed to him. Such demons as Tzitzimitl, the gods Xipe and Huitzilopochtli, and a few other members of the sky religion are alone exempt from his influence and do not share in his mythology. His pivotal position in this religion is broken only at the point where he becomes a spiritualized instrument in the hands of a high god. I have reported that Tonacateuctli, here a creator resident in the depths of the Milky Way, engendered Quetzalcoatl with his breath so that he might go down among men to bring them guidance.[1]

As the élan vital of the sky, the Feathered Serpent properly provided such a focus to the pantheon. Whether we are dealing with an aspect of the planet Venus, with divine sanctions for rule, or with cloudbursts and waterspouts, all are derived from that single concept of sky as kinetic to the nth degree—which is a definition of Quetzalcoatl. In illustration of this I present a résumé of certain pertinent pages of the *Codex Vienna*, a Mixtec document.[2]

The passage begins with a scene in the heavens in which inchoate principles and night alone are shown as existing. Two high gods then put in their appearance; they are defined for us in terms of air or wind, for both of them wear as a casque Ehecatl's buccal mask. Air (or sky) in other words is already posited to exist even before the full creation. After this, assorted demons and dragons are produced, which initial burst of creativity culminates when the two high gods evoke the sacrificial knife as the primordial principle. This instrument in turn gives birth to Quetzalcoatl in his avatar as Nine Wind. He surrounds himself with sixteen subsidiary avatars, each distinctive. All of this takes place in the sky, and it is there that we see Nine Wind finally being given the various items of his regalia that will identify him henceforth as Ehecatl.

Equipped in this characteristic fashion, the god now descends to earth carrying the staff of the planet Venus. Among the deities who greet him on his arrival on earth is a pair of his Xolotl avatars, one of them turquoise, the other gold. They control the entrances and exits to the underworld and are obviously of great importance inasmuch as they are shown to have been in existence before Nine Wind himself. The activities of Nine Wind include shouldering up the sky, so that it and the ocean of waters that it contains may be adequately supported. In this he performs of course as the wind god, Ehecatl.[3] Only then can the organization of the world below follow, as well as the naming of the elements of nature. After this, in his role of patron of lineages, he arranges a marriage involving the god Five Wind, a celestial avatar of himself, thus beginning the royal line of Mixtec ancestral deities and totemic beings. He then proceeds to designate the role and insignia of each of the great gods, in which office he is acting as a priest organizing the pantheon. And finally as master of omens he brings the narcotic mushroom into the lives of the gods, thus indicating his prophetic powers.

The above is not an exhaustive list of the appearances of Quetzalcoatl in the *Codex Vienna*, but it is enough to illustrate my contention that Quetzalcoatl was a god who in his multifaceted person dominated the sky religion. He was a god who manifested himself only in such theophanies as could be derived from a source in the sky, and in all such instances he was a central figure.

The extraordinary ubiquity of Quetzalcoatl in the mythical record derives from the simple fact that only the sky spans up and down, rising and falling, night and day, light and darkness. Earth cannot be so divided or twinned. Earth is a dead, unmoving center. Sky is circumambient, and it is in motion. It is nowhere, yet it leads everywhere.

Quetzalcoatl as Wind

If we take the name Quetzalcoatl to designate the god in his draconian form, namely as sky both generalized and unspecified, then the god's first avatar out of this numinous continuum will be as Ehecatl, the wind. Ehecatl is that one of the several names given to the god that has the most immediate reference to nature. All of his other names stem from aspects of human culture, such as sacrifice, the augural almanac, commerce, and so forth.

Wind is an indefinable force, walking in restless ways and appearing at times as a demonic presence. In their mythologies many people have separated sky from wind (or air) and cast the latter in the role of a supporter or stay for the former. Ehecatl was no exception to this. He was known to support the sky, when it was considered as the shell of the firmament; so we have the sky, who was Quetzalcoatl, shored up by his most active avatar, Ehecatl, the wind.

At the topmost level of the sky lived Ometeuctli and Omecihuatl, Two Lord and Two Lady. The name of this celestial region was appropriately known as Omeyocan, the Place of Twoness or Coupling. In Aztec mythology Quetzalcoatl came from Omeyocan, and this high derivation etherialized his nature as wind or air. It is almost certain that Ehecatl was looked upon by priests as the "breath" of Tonacateuctli, another form of Two Lord. It is this spiritualized avatar of Quetzalcoatl who acts as demiurge or activator.

The word for "air" or "breeze" in Nahuatl is *ecatl*, which when reduplicated as *ehecatl* takes on the stronger meaning "wind." While the word could be used to describe breath in certain combinations (as in *ehecayotica*, "breathing"), it is to be distinguished from the customary word for "breath." *Ehecatl*, therefore, is the word that designates one of the more common features of the natural world, the wind. By adding increasing violence to the concept of wind, we can derive squalls, tempests, and hurricanes.

At least as far back as Izapan times wind was depicted as a human figure plunging down from the sky (shown as a double-headed dragon) to whip up the waters below.[4] Wind could also be understood as a human figure wearing a buccal mask of the Olmec type and a beard, holding up the sky.[5] His body was also shown as a curled cloud, and his belt of dangling heads (the stars) stood for the overarching sky.[6] By Izapan times wind is clearly distinguished from sky (fig. 6).

We have been slow in our understanding of the god Ehecatl as a voice as well as a power.[7] Previously I noted the mystery and the violence of the wind as being of his essence. The latter concept was derived from periodic cyclonic invasions of the coastal lands out of the Gulf and Caribbean waters—a hurricane or a twister once experienced can never be forgotten. The Mesoamericans built Ehecatl on that model, and they were not slow, therefore, in stressing his stentorian voice.

In Teotihuacán times the feathered conch-shell trumpet was made into a pseudo-divinity itself, mellow and oracular. The ancient buccal mask belonging to Quetzalcoatl is surely connected with wind conceived of as a *voice*, as against wind conceived of as *motion*. Certain drums also spoke for him.[8] Some cities in Mesoamerica regulated their life with the morning and evening drums sounded by the priests, thus opening and closing the day with the god's haunting clamor. In legend Quetzalcoatl Topiltzin is said to have stood on the top of the legendary Mount Tzatzitepetl—Calling Mountain—to preach his message. From

Figure 6

that eminence in central Mexico his voice resounded to the most distant coastlands, exhorting men to penitential acts and blood sacrifices. The voice deeply afflicted people. Yet what else might be expected of a god who is described as the very figuration of Ecamalacatl, the whirlwind?[9] In the *tonalpohualli* count the second of the twenty day signs was "wind" *(ehecatl)*. It was always ill-omened and competed in this with that other of the twenty signs that formed a part of the god's name, *coatl* ("snake").

But there was more in the god's nature than brutal bellowing. This other way of comprehending the wind arose from a negative feature, namely, that its voice could never be centrally located. The sky religion did not deny the square five-directional pattern of the world as taught, for instance, in the cult of the fire god, which stressed exact and formal locality and derived all directions from a center of fire, the divine hearth.[10] Ehecatl's world was round, and while the four cardinal directions were indeed of concern to him, the plasticity of day and night allowed him to pass beyond a rigid definition of direction.

Thus to the terror that the god through his stridency instilled in his worshipers was added something like a sense of cosmic illusion, or at least of indefiniteness, a loss of seat and place, and a sense of darkness. This was the very opposite of the comfort communicated to one by the hearth with its permanent location, its light, and its comforting warmth: "And when the wind increased, it was said, the dust swirled up, it roared, howled, became dark, blew in all directions; there was lightning; it grew wrathful."[11]

If for a moment we turn from a consideration of the wind as the single divine being called Ehecatl, what about the wind as multiple animistic entities? When so depicted, winds were seen to be serpents or black dragonets. These were the *ecatotontin*, the "little winds." In the Feast of the Mountains dough images were made of these helpers or pluralizations of Quetzalcoatl. The *ecatotontin* were gener-

Figure 7

ally considered to be noxious, and they played a prominent role in the underworld. As wind snakes and wind imps we see them in the *Codex Borgia* jostling together in a kind of cave of the winds, actually a huge mortuary jar where they were confined while in the underworld.[12] This passage calls to mind the cave where Aeolus, the Greek god of the winds, kept his own mercurial pack confined. The *ecatotontin* could be provoked or summoned at certain ceremonies by the waving of fans.[13] When considered in the plural, they lived in the seventh level of the heavens. Ehecatl as a single being could be found in the thirteenth, or summit, terrace of the sky, an eminence that the two high gods shared with him. In the *Tonalamatl*, however, Ehecatl is stationed in the ninth heaven.[14] Wind inhabited many levels in the sky.

We know that in the understanding of the Mesoamericans wind was a primordial force (fig. 7). We have seen that the Mexicans believed that in the initial act of creation Tonacateuctli blew his breath over chaos to divide the waters of the sky from those of earth. We have also seen that the Mixtecs taught that the two high gods (both named One Deer) performed their first acts of creation by the power of

75

wind, while we also find that the first identifiable four of their progeny were spirits of the air.[15] And it is well known from myth how Quetzalcoatl sent his hurricane breath to blow the reluctant sun out upon the first of his daily journeys, thus as wind bringing both light and time into the world. Wind is the tool by which the highest god creates, and it is thus quintessentially an instrument of power. But wind and sky to the Mesoamerican mind were indistinguishable.

The oldest avatar of Ehecatl who bears a recognizable date name is Seven Wind. He is shown in a Mixtec source as the first of the four spirits of the air, mentioned above, who were created by the two gods One Deer. He appears in the culture of Teotihuacán with his hands uplifted to the sky (fig. 8)—a corresponding scene in Xochicalco is abbreviated to the depiction of two hands upholding the sky band (fig. 24). The *nahualli* of this avatar is a raptorial bird, undoubtedly the eagle, who like the bicephalic sky dragon can be shown with two heads. Seven Wind appears in Late Classic as a young god gazing out from the open maw of the sky dragon. Seven Wind is thus a form of Quetzalcoatl so close to the original Ehecatl as to be perhaps synonymous. Further demonstrating this is the passage in myth where he created men out of ashes as the fifth sun began. Almost surely we have in him an early form of Quetzalcoatl as the sky.

One can only guess which came first, Ehecatl as a single godhead (in other words, a concept of wind as an indivisible entity) or as a pluralistic phenomenon. I prefer to believe that the two were from the beginning coexistent modes of appreciating the mystery and the power of the air, neither negating the other, but of course we have no means of finding out. It appears likely that the priesthood would have been mainly interested in developing the former, leaving the latter to the popular understanding of natural phenomena. The problem is exactly paralleled in the case of the

Figure 8

rain god Tlaloc and his many montane manifestations, the *tlaloque*.

Depictions of Ehecatl, the Anthropomorphic God

Wind of course cannot be depicted visually. It is difficult even to suggest it verbally. Wind combines impalpability with force, an unexpected twain. We are therefore not surprised to see that the god, when finally represented anthropomorphically, is arrayed in a most exotic fashion. At first glance the god is a grotesque and entirely arbitrary figure, having nothing to do with serpents or dragons, or anything else, for that matter. In his temple in Tula his image was remembered as it "lay covered, and he lay with only his face covered, and, it is said, he was monstrous [*atlacacemelle*]. His face was like a huge battered stone, a great fallen rock. It was not made like that of a man. And his beard was very long—exceedingly long."[16] This is certainly an anthropomorphic description, and the god comes through as brutish, even dangerous. This is not a commonly held opinion of the god Quetzalcoatl.

In iconography he is distinctive. To begin with, the god's body is over-all black, occasionally showing faint circles that refer to the stars in the night sky. His beard is prominently indicated, and his face paint usually consists of a stripe running down through the eyes or dividing two fields of color. Often an eye is shown extruded from its socket, a statement of blindness with the implication of autosacrifice. His mouth parts, when shown, are daubed with red.

Perhaps the most striking thing about the god's appearance is his buccal mask, which is always painted red. So strangely is the mask formed that it almost defies verbal description. On first appraisal it appears to be a bird's bill carved in wood with two sharpened mouthparts surmounted by a squared-off or broken-off nose. A curved fang or barbel protrudes from the corner of the mouth. I comment on this buccal mask more at length in the section that follows.

Also distinctive of the god is his conical Huaxtec cap, generally cut off at the top and divided into a red side and a black or blue side with a star between. This is a pictorial metaphor for the planet Venus, which always stands between night and day. At other times the cap is made of jaguar skin and rises to a peak with the star placed in the center. Or a cross may replace the star, probably an ancient glyph for the sky at its crossing from day to night. Into the cap are thrust a sharpened bone and a maguey thorn for penitential bloodletting. Extending from the front of the cap and dangling before the god's eyes is a spray of flowers with a hummingbird attached to it as if in the act of sucking nectar.[17] A headband rims the cap; this can be either an accordian-pleated undulation of material (probably raw cotton) or a fret design, which is probably a glyph for cloud-land. In addition he can wear in his hair a knotted bow of the same design as his loincloth. As an occipital decoration he wears a panache of quetzal feathers plus a fan of black feathers interspersed with stars and contrasting red quills. The fan probably represents the night sun whom Quetzalcoatl as Xolotl sacrifices in the underworld.[18] In some representations the god also wears in his hair a plaited tape, which has been thought to represent the fifty-two-year Calendar Round.[19] He is clad in a short kilt and a loincloth, the two aprons of which, in front and back, are round-ended and patterned with crossbars.

In his ears he wears distinctive hooked and tanged shell ornaments, probably mother-of-pearl. Around his neck is a collar of seashells either real or imitated in gold. As a most important talisman he wears around his neck a conch shell, sectioned to bring out the spiral structure of its interior; this is his so-called wind jewel or "whirling wind pendant."[20] While it most obviously relates to the thunderous voice of the storm, at a deeper level of symbolism it undoubtedly means also the underworld or night sky, the favored habitat of the god. He wears jaguar-skin anklets with rattles attached. He carries a priest's incense bag and a shield with a bottom fringe of aquatic bird feathers and a device showing either the wind jewel or a symbol resembling a Saint Andrew's Cross. Most important, he wields a special baton called the *xonecuilli* adorned with circular objects symbolizing stars. This too will be commented on at length.

All the above oddments we class as his divine regalia, *teotlatquitl*, and they can appear in any number of combinations. Taken together, they fully define the god as Quetzalcoatl in his human form. Each of the items had a meaning. The chronology of their attraction into his iconography would be of the utmost interest if we could recover it, for it would document the deity's development. By Aztec times in central Mexico that is the way the high priest of Quetzalcoatl was dressed. How he appeared in other places and in earlier times in Mesoamerica is not as well known. In Seibal, for instance, the regalia are different (fig. 9), while in Palenque, if the god of the Temple of the Cross is indeed Quetzalcoatl, there is no similarity to be seen. All of this again warns us of the great range of the god and of his many impersonations.

The Buccal Mask

That the Aztec Quetzalcoatl is ultimately derived from the Gulf Coast is certain, considering not only the Huaxtec headpiece that he wears but also the reference to marine shells and aquatic birds in his regalia. There is thus the possibility that some of the other items are also to be linked with the coastal areas, as for example the buccal mask.

Durán describes the mask as being that of a bird, and he not only draws attention to the warty excrescence over the

Figure 9

snout but also mentions that the image has an outstretched tongue.[21] Some late examples in art add a complete set of teeth.

Though the buccal mask so described is peculiarly this god's and is worn only by him and his avatars, there is still no consensus about its meaning or derivation. One belief is that it evolved from an original duckbill mask, to which alterations were made during the course of the centuries. In this theory the priest who wore it will therefore have been active in a cult that had to do with ducks or with a certain species of duck; in this respect we recall that the feathers of the *xomotl* duck adorned parts of Quetzalcoatl's headdress.[22] The religious officiant wearing a duckbill mask is known from Olmec, Izapan, and Mayan rupestrian art, the Tuxtla Statuette being the most famous of these. Migratory ducks occurred seasonally everywhere in the coastal lowlands of Mesoamerica and was a significant part of the diet there. We might even guess that it was the mallard (*quetzalcanauh-tli?*)[23] that with its sensational coloration first attracted the attention of the early cultists. We know that ducks possessed a clear symbolic meaning for some of the early Mesoamericans, for they carved duck heads and bills in jade to be worn as pendants.[24] As an aquatic bird the duck could suggest at once both air and water, the respective provinces of Ehecatl. The regularity of its autumnal appearance in the coastal waterways would add the idea of time and periodicity. In a relief from one of the Tajín ball courts the god Ehecatl once appears floating above a cult scene as a spirit of the air while wearing a duckbill mask (fig. 10).[25] The date of that carving is Late Classic. By Postclassic times, however, the duckbill mask that is identifiable as such has disappeared from the archaeological record.

How can we square this early duckbill mask, which is always viewed frontally, with the buccal mask shown as a pointed bill or snout with a broken nasal projection and seen in line drawings always in profile? The answer is, we

Figure 10

cannot. In our present state of uncertainty we can, however, advance a tentative suggestion that there may have
been two deities or numina symbolized in the two masks,
both coming from Olmec times. The early duckbill mask
might be the emblem of the sky as a set of temporal periods,
a kind of precalendric numen. The later buccal mask commonly worn by Ehecatl may have been a kenning for the
dragon who was a more generalized sky. This latter would
be the dragon, much as we have already described him but
with his head fantastically elaborated and enscrolled. This
mask will have been contrived of features taken from creatures as disparate as the crocodile, the tapir, the trogan, the
duck, the serpent, and possibly the jaguar. Each of the suggested animals will have had for the artist a special meaning
and a special power, and all of them will have added up to a

full definition of the sky dragon, his connections with wind and water, day and night being somehow included in the lot. Priests of the sky religion will then have carried out their ceremonial duties wearing the dragon mask, though its configuration will have varied from culture to culture. In Seibal, for instance, the mask shows a sharp, heavy stabbing bill.[26] In Tikal it is indisputably the snout of a crocodile,[27] while among the Zapotecs it is the back-rolled snout of the dragon.[28]

Behind the duckbill mask there probably stood a different cult. Let us guess that it involved a set of mantic practitioners who straddled the professions of priest and shaman along the Gulf Coast and who controlled a distinct and esoteric religion. Ultimately their specialties led them into making astronomical computations, and in doing this they must have been inexorably led to elaborate parts of the sky religion. In the process and along the way they will have discarded their very specialized mask for some variety of the dragon mask—which finally comes down to us as the orthodox mask of the Aztec god Ehecatl. Without some such mingling it is difficult to see how Quetzalcoatl can have become distinguished by a mask that means simultaneously wind and water, the planet Venus, and the calling of the priest. All of the above is pure speculation.

More will be learned about Quetzalcoatl's buccal mask when a typology becomes established. Until then we can only describe it and wonder.

The Xonecuilli

The scepter that Quetzalcoatl wielded, the *xonecuilli*, points back to a stellar background. The star lore that was once connected with the god is now irretrievably lost, but we know at least that he did have two major star connections. The first of these was his relationship with the planet

Venus; this is well known and will be mentioned in detail later. Not so well known is his connection with the Little Bear, the constellation of which the North Star is a part.

The Nahuas called the Little Bear Citlalxonecuilli, or the Club-footed Constellation.[29] It is associated with Quetzal-coatl and is symbolized by the baton that he carries. Both Quetzalcoatl and his close avatar Xolotl are seen to wield the *xonecuilli* in the Feast of the Eating of Succotash where it is a prominent feature of the dance performed at that time by their priesthood.[30] And it is at least once mentioned in direct connection with Xolotl as a cripple—as if it were specifically a symbol of his deformity.[31] From this we gather that it is the deathly aspect of Quetzalcoatl that is symbolized by the instrument.

The *xonecuilli* is a curved, short-handled crozier, roughly imitating in shape the constellation of the Little Bear (fig. 11). As a rule seven stars are shown inlaid on the curving blade or attached to its edge. Correspondingly there are seven easily visible stars in the Little Bear, joined in a sequence that has roughly the curvature shown by the *xone-cuilli*. It is easy to see why this constellation was singled out for special attention by the Mesoamerican peoples: unlike all the others it pivoted in a tight circle about its topmost star, Polaris, and never during the course of any night did it fall below the horizon. Polaris was thus the most sensational star in the sky outside the planet Venus. It was in fact the very reverse of Venus, for whereas that planet was a wanderer, much traveled and adept in disappearances and returns, Polaris was forever fixed and immobile. It was in fact a dead, a stagnant star. One may well imagine that for such a reason it could represent to the ancients the point of ingress into the land of the stellar dead, the *mimixcoa*. These ancestral spirits, whom I discuss later, had as their patronymic leader the god Mixcoatl, who is in the mythology the father of Ce Acatl Quetzalcoatl. Mixcoatl was known to be connected with the direction north, and it therefore comes

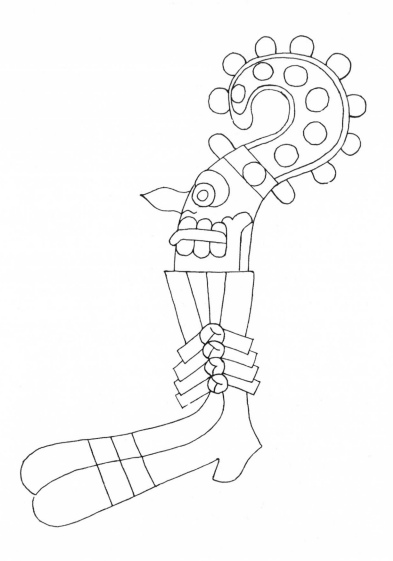

Figure 11

as no surprise to us to learn that he too wields the *xonecuilli*. There is a reference in the sources to a goddess known as Mother of the Little Bear who is mentioned in close connection with Mixcoatl; perhaps she is his consort.[32] She is surely a form of the mother of all the stars, Citlalinicue.

As the over-all spirit of the night sky and its profusion of stars, it is most appropriate for Quetzalcoatl to display the *xonecuilli* as his badge of mastery, he being the god who had assigned the guardianship of the portals of that eerie world to his scarecrow twin, Xolotl. Even more significant, in art the *xonecuilli* is attached to the sky dragon as an extension of his snout, as if to signify that, as numen of the sky, the dragon revolved through the night on the axial point of his nose, Polaris.[33] All knew that Venus was the star of risings and fallings and that it was, therefore, appropriately brought into connection with the far-roving god of warriors Ce Acatl, but it was Xolotl, the Aztec Cerberus, who was the deity guarding Polaris, that star whose feet, like those of death, were set unmovingly in the basalt blocks of night. Both of those gods were avatars of Quetzalcoatl.

The *xonecuilli* first appears in Omeyocan, the highest heaven, as an item in the regalia with which Quetzalcoatl was endowed by the two high gods when they sent him down to earth to carry out his mission to men.[34] Almost certainly it represented his power over the night sky and consequently his control of the omens that flowed from the stars. He who could hold the Little Bear in his hand was indeed an oligarch in a mighty government.

The Circular Shrine

Roundness has long been recognized as one of the diagnostic architectural forms attesting to the presence of Ehecatl. This is most evident in the ground plan of his shrines. It is of interest that, however closely apparented Quetzalcoatl was to Tlaloc, the temples of the latter were always and only square-sided. They can never be confused with the circular shrines of Quetzalcoatl. Quetzalcoatl in fact was said to have invented round temples.[35]

Round buildings, so characteristic of the Huaxteca, probably go back to pre-Teotihuacán times.[36] No doubt the circular-temple plan is an outgrowth of the indigenous round huts with conical thatching that were the common living quarters down on the Gulf Coast. We are even told that some of the villages there distinguished the chief's hut from the others by piercing the peak with an arrow, which recalls depictions in the codices of Quetzalcoatl temples with the pointed thatch pierced with the sacrificial knife or knives.[37]

The typical wind-temple platform was high and cone-shaped with the stairway correspondingly steep and treacherous. The shrine at the top was also conical and of course thatched. The peak was sharply pointed, and into it were thrust several stone knives or blades, as I have mentioned above. Or the apex might display a conch shell instead of the knife (fig. 12). These temples generally faced east, and some doorways were designed to represent the open maw of the dragon.[38] This elevated round Mesoamerican structure was unique to Ehecatl,[39] and was carried at least as far north as Casas Grandes, near the present United States border.[40]

There is a difficulty, however. Temples of Quetzalcoatl also exist with the square ground plan. The Castillo at Chichén Itzá, obviously dedicated to the Feathered Serpent, is four-sided, while nearby is the round astronomical observatory called the Caracol, which is just as certainly dedicated to Quetzalcoatl. Mayapan also had both square and circular temples to the god. In Tula there is the normal circular Temple of the Feathered Serpent, as well as the squared Temple of Tlahuizcalpanteuctli, who is an avatar of Quet-

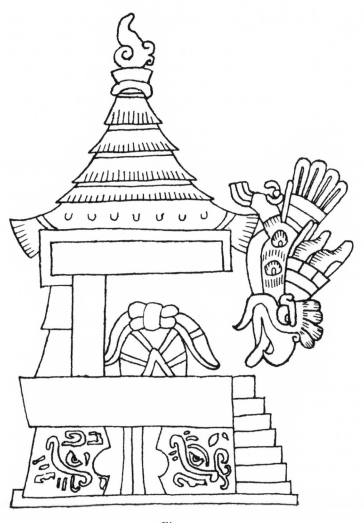

Figure 12

zalcoatl. In Teotihuacán also the god's temple is square. As far as we can see, both styles in the Postclassic period can have reference to warrior cults. One way of resolving the difficulty is to assume that the square temples point to a Quetzalcoatl who was native to the highlands (Tlahuizcal-panteuctli?) whereas the circular temples belonged to a Quetzalcoatl imported from the Gulf Coast (Ehecatl).[41] This theory at least has the virtue of agreeing with the fact that there are two outstanding appearances of Quetzalcoatl in mythology, wind and morning star. The problem has not been solved.

The God's Role in the Creation of Man

Early man ruminated endlessly on his origins. A tribe could have in its repertory of myths three or four different accounts of its first appearance, and each would be accepted as true.

The Quichés related that the creator gods set as the touchstone of man that he must possess speech and that he must acknowledge them as his lords.[42] Animals were invented first by the gods, but their languages were garbled. Men were then modeled out of mud, but they also failed to perform adequately, as did their successors, men carved out of wood. It was only after maize was discovered that proper men could be made out of the flesh of that sacred corn. These men were, however, essentially gods, for they could grasp the meanings behind things. As a consequence the creators cut back their understanding to what it is today. All of this took place in the Stygian darkness that preceded the appearance of the first sun. Men were completed only when the storm god (Tohil) took them under his protection and provided them with fire.

This is a straightforward account and can be matched in other cultures. It presupposes an evolutionary past with the human and the divine acting in the same arena but on different energy levels. Five characteristics of man are suggested here: language, religion, limited understanding, the cultivation of maize (that is, food), and the use of fire. It is difficult to see how this Quiché selection of basic traits could be improved on. Not many of the Mesoamerican peoples would have seen it differently.

There is a myth, however, that differs from the above in concentrating on Quetzalcoatl as the god most especially involved.[43] In the Quiché myth summarized above the spotlight is on man; in the second one, which is Aztec, it is on the god. It uses the old scenario of a descent into the underworld to recover a precious object—here the bones of the men of a former age that, when recovered, can bring men to life again.[44]

The myth opens with the gods designating Quetzalcoatl as the one to undertake the hazardous journey. Quetzalcoatl is accompanied by his *nahualli*, or animal double (here undoubtedly the dog god Xolotl), who acts as his guide and counselor. The reason for this choice of actors is that they represent respectively the morning and the evening star, and as such they are knowledgeable about the affairs of the underworld. The tale thus presupposes a previously existing Venus mythology. On his successful return with the bones Quetzalcoatl and the other gods assembled in Tamoanchan, where they performed autosacrifice over the relics and thus with their blood revived the race of men. The men of this last (and present) age thus owe everything to the heroism of Quetzalcoatl, his priestly skills, and his familiarity with the realm of death.

There is again a variant of this myth that has Quetzalcoatl, in his avatar as Seven Wind, creating the men of the fifth sun from ashes.[45] The god Seven Wind, at least among the Mixtecs, was depicted as Janus-faced (possibly meant to suggest twins), which may connect him with Xolotl.[46] Or again it was said that it was really the god's more common avatar Nine Wind who created men. The presence of these two alternatives does not change the picture in any essential. Quetzalcoatl is still the focal god insofar as man's beginnings are in question.

The contrast between the two myths, Quiché and Aztec, is instructive and gives us an understanding of the variety of speculation that existed in Mesoamerica. It is interesting that the creation of man could be discussed as either a historical or a religious problem. When the latter was the case, it was Quetzalcoatl or one of his avatars who was selected to move the story forward. Of all the gods Quetzalcoatl was the closest to man. The following sections will point out why this was so.

Quetzalcoatl as Culture Hero

There is a set of scenes in the Mixtec codices that displays Quetzalcoatl in his preferred role as an initiator and a culture hero.[47] It is of importance in any study of the god and is surely as interesting as the tale of his exile, death, and translation into the heavens.

Quetzalcoatl is shown to us seated in the thirteenth heaven while receiving his commission to appear on earth and bring culture to mankind. His commission is symbolized by the elements of his regalia, which are scattered about him: buccal mask, Huaxtec cap, wind jewel, priestly vest, *xonecuilli*, and so on. On the first day of the *tonalpohualli* he descends from the skies on a cobweb, landing on or near an island (Isla de los Sacrificios?). From there he begins his great work.

He first establishes shrines connected with his own cult and the associated cult of his twin, Xolotl. Annexed to these shrines are ball courts in which the dramatic events taking place in the night sky can be reenacted. He then proceeds to establish lineages and clans and to assign to them their habitats and shrines. The marriage ceremony and its sexual consummation are also depicted, as we might expect. So begins the life of the Mixtec rulers and their people under the aegis of the great establisher.

In the pertinent texts and codices the story is not told as a continuing saga. It is not an organized list like the tale of the Twelve Labors of Hercules, though it is a far more fundamental and impressive accounting than that compiled for the brawling Greek. Because of this incoherence in the Aztec myth the scholar must pick up the bits and pieces wherever he can find them.

A list of some of the items of human culture touched by Quetzalcoatl makes clear his profound implication in Mesoamerican life. He was credited with (1) the naming and therefore the organization of landmarks, (2) the discovery of maize, (3) the making of fire, (4) the culture of maguey, brewing of *octli*, and ceremonial drunkenness, (5) the institution of music and dance, (6) "curing," (7) commerce, the crafts, and the protection of travellers, (8) the laying out of the *tlachco*, (9) the creation of the *tonalpohualli*, the art of divining, and the use of the divine mushroom, (10) copulation, marriage, and the generation of children, (11) the organization of the priesthood, the institution of sacrifice, penitential exercises, and all forms of worship, and (12) oversight of the *calmecac* and the patronage of royal houses. Inasmuch as the last six items are considered at length later in this book, I shall pass over them here, considering only those that precede. Minor activities such as thieving, also a part of the god's patronage, are omitted.

On his many peregrinations Quetzalcoatl was said to have named all things, especially all unusual earth formations, bodies of water, and mountains.[48] He thus stood behind the name-giving culture of his many peoples. Such is commonly the case with culture heroes in myth, witness Adam in Genesis 2.

His relationship to the staple maize is fascinating and

complicated. In one sense Quetzalcoatl gave to man his body, for the Mesoamerican tribes generally thought of their flesh as identical with what they consumed, namely Indian corn or maize, and it was Quetzalcoatl who had discovered the whereabouts of this all-important cultigen. As we might expect, the myth relating to maize is told in several ways, but the stripped-down version of the origin of the plant relates that the god Piltzinteuctli, who was the sun in the underworld, and the earth goddess Xochiquetzal copulated in a deep cave to produce a son, Cinteotl (Maize God), also called Tlazopilli, Beloved Child.[49]

This was the rationalizing statement, but it had a rival, more popular and far more colorful. In this version maize was not created but discovered.[50] Quetzalcoatl was deputized by the gods to determine the whereabouts of the grain. Hearing that it was buried in a secret hoard by the red ants, he changed himself into a black ant and found the stored food in Tonacatepetl, the Mountain of Our Substance. He succeeded in bringing a portion of it back to Tamoanchan for the gods to sample. Their approval of this food as the secret of life caused Quetzalcoatl to return in an attempt to retrieve it all, but he was unable to lift the huge mass onto his back and carry it off. The two high gods, Oxomoco and Cipactonal, intervened at this point to decide by the casting of lots who among the gods would finish the task. Nanahuatl was the one selected, and he succeeded in the task by first shelling the corn and all the other seed plants that were hidden in the mountain. Then, aided by the four directional Tlalocs, he made off with these staples to the far corners of the earth.

This latter is a complicated myth. It concerns two divine places; two high gods; two colors of ants; the two protagonists, Quetzalcoatl and his avatar Nanahuatl; and the four Tlalocs. Its most curious feature is that Quetzalcoatl, *qua* Quetzalcoatl, does not create maize or even bring it to the world of men—he is credited only with finding it. He fails to possess it once it has been found. This failure, however, is more apparent than real, for Nanahuatl, who does bring it to the world, is a close avatar of Quetzalcoatl, acting specifically as the god in his abeyant underworld role. So in a larger sense Quetzalcoatl performs both the discovery and the retrieving. Being thrust into the tale at these two levels, Quetzalcoatl is clearly identified as a culture hero.

In the *Codex Borgia* is a scene showing the interior of the earth where various types of maize are kept to provide food for the gods of the underworld.[51] Painted as the darkened and ailing sun under the earth, Nanahuatl is shown impregnating Earth Mother (as did Piltzinteuctli in the myth) to produce maize and other fruits of the field. An avatar of Quetzalcoatl is shown escaping with ears of this corn. This is a clear visual complement to the myths already related.

In the Quiché telling of the myth we have four kinds of animals who reveal the hiding place in a distant mountain of maize, cacao, and other fruits. The creator gods, who include Gukumatz (Quetzalcoatl) and his alter ego, Tepeu, then collaborate to transform maize into the living flesh of mankind.[52] This Maya tale is really an introduction to the story of the creation of man that may explain why the act is performed by a coterie of gods, thus downplaying the role of Quetzalcoatl.

Quetzalcoatl is connected with fire only by indirection. His father, Mixcoatl, Cloud Serpent, was the first to drill fire, in commemoration of which his festival featured the making and feeding of great fires.[53] We shall have occasion later to reflect on the occasional equivalence of the two dragons who were cast as father (Mixcoatl) and son (Quetzalcoatl). Quetzalcoatl's connection with fire appears weak only if fire is equated with the flames of the hearth. If considered more abstractly as the red light of dawn and sunset, the connection is vastly strengthened.

The same conclusion that attends the authorship of fire is repeated in the myths connected with the first brewing of *octli*, the intoxicating drink, which is attributed both to Mixcoatl and to Quetzalcoatl.[54] But here the priority of the latter is undoubted. The connections of Quetzalcoatl with the maguey plant are consistently seen to be close. This is most evident in the fact that Pantecatl, the lord of *octli* and the consort of the maguey mother, was an avatar of Quetzalcoatl, wearing much of his regalia and wielding the *xonecuilli*.[55]

The myth that particularly explicates the connection of Quetzalcoatl with the maguey plant tells of a beautiful young maiden named Mayahuel who was held incommunicado in a keep in the heavens by her monstrous grandmother Tzitzimitl.[56] To bring the maiden's charms down to earth where men could enjoy her, Ehecatl, the wind god, slipped past the duenna's guard to steal the girl away. In his person as the wind he carried her off on his back, but was of course pursued by the demonic grandmother. Once on the ground he magically changed himself and the maiden into trees, hoping thus to escape detection. He himself was saved, but the demon tore apart the maiden's tree and scattered the pieces far and wide. Later Ehecatl was to gather them up and plant them, thereby producing the maguey plant so beloved of the Mexicans and their neighbors.[57]

The goddess Mayahuel was one of the more impressive forms of the Huaxtec earth mother. She is depicted with serpents on her skirt, and she carries the *chicahuaztli*, a well-known fertility baton at least once shown as formed by the rigid body of a serpent. We can assume from this that the Quetzalcoatl described in the Mayahuel myth was the one especially concerned with fertility and abundance. There is therefore the probability that the god worshiped by the Cholula merchants under the name of Meteotl, or Maguey God, was another close avatar of Quetzalcoatl.[58]

The association of the god with strong drink is simply part of a larger complex that also includes music and dance. The pertinent myth relates that originally song and dance were the possessions of the sun god in his house out in the eastern Gulf.[59] To secure them Ehecatl contrived to pass over the open waters on a living bridge made by the whale, the turtle, and the mermaid. The sun god had instructed his musicians that they would inevitably be carried off by the intruding god if they replied in any way to his blandishments. Some failed to heed the warning and so were taken back by Ehecatl along with their instruments, the most important of which were their drums.

Song and dance (together referred to as *cuicatl*) were highly sophisticated art forms among the Mesoamericans, and it does not surprise us that the god who was so noted for his sonorous voice was mythologically depicted as their discoverer. But it was more than just that which made inevitable the assigning of such a role to Quetzalcoatl. Song and dance were cult forms, their performance being designed both to entertain and to placate the gods. This meant that only that god who was the model for all priests, namely Quetzalcoatl, could by logic be credited with the introduction of such ritual necessities into the human scene.

The origins of medicine, or, better, curing, are closely connected with Quetzalcoatl, though nowhere are we given to understand that he specifically invented the art. That honor is accorded to the two gods Oxomoco and her consort, Cipactonal, who first instructed Quetzalcoatl as a culture hero.[60] Mesoamerican curing had at least three phases: the practices of the shaman, the potions of the herbalist, and the diagnostic casting of lots by the priest of Quetzalcoatl or the *curandero*. Quetzalcoatl was identified particularly with the last method. His image was brought into the presence of the sick person at nighttime, and in front of the afflicted one the priest threw twenty kernels of corn corresponding to the twenty days of the *tonalpohualli*—to discover, by the way they fell, the outcome of the illness.[61] While thus presiding over the fateful aspects of all diseases, Quetzalcoatl was the special patron of only certain ones:

blindness and eye diseases, coughs, and skin afflictions.[62] The last were considered to be venereal, and we note in this connection that the followers of the god Nacxitl, an avatar of Quetzalcoatl, are said to have introduced into Yucatán not only sin but the diseases consequent upon it.[63] In Acallan the god Kukulcan (Quetzalcoatl) was a god of fevers.[64]

Ehecatl as the Principle of Generation

Quetzalcoatl was more than just an abstractly conceived creator of children. He could be the phallus itself. In one of the well-known Mexican hymns Quetzalcoatl is hailed as the ancestral god of the Otomí Indians,[65] and we know that this ancestral god was worshiped as a huge standing pole with a possibly phallic reference. This rite was observed in the month called the Great Feast of the Ancestors, when, among other ceremonies, the merchants made sacrifices to Yacateuctli, their god of commerce and an avatar of Quetzalcoatl. This feast in turn melted into the great harvest-home celebration in which the sex goddess Tlazolteotl was honored in a dance of celebrants dressed as Huaxtecs and equipped with gigantic phalli.[66] Similarly the Etzalcualiztli festival had direct phallic references and also featured Quetzalcoatl as one of the fertility gods honored. In fact the ceremony was particularly pointed to the priests, who perforated their penises and offered small parts of the foreskin in sacrifice so that Quetzalcoatl would grant people issue.[67] To achieve the same end, the nobles in that festival danced while carrying maize stalks and pots of a porridge made of maize and beans—thus bringing together symbols of both male and female genitalia, with abundance specified as the issue.

Our knowledge of the sixteenth movable feast further confirms what the two festivals just mentioned have to say. It honored the deities of marriage, who are defined for us as a Quetzalcoatl triad, which besides the god included his father and mother, Mixcoatl and Chimalma.[68] And we know that barren women made pilgrimages to Cholula where they prayed to Quetzalcoatl to make them pregnant.[69]

Serpents of all kinds could have sexual meanings, witness the *mazacoatl* (deer snake) the eating of which endowed a man with such potency that he would die ejaculating.[70] There is one carved figure of the Feathered Serpent in the Museo Nacional that makes very explicit the ophidian nature of fertility, for ears of corn alternate on his body with quetzal feathers.

Quetzalcoatl's phallic connections are explicit though not numerous. Acting as a culture hero, Quetzalcoatl was once said to have erected a lofty stone pillar called *ueitepoltetl*, the "great phallic rock."[71] An even more vivid reference to the god's connection with sexual intercourse is the scene in one of the codices in which six couples are depicted copulating next to a gigantic Feathered Serpent,[72] while that well-known symbol of sexual activity the bicolored lizard is placed among the couples to strengthen the symbolism. Among the Mayas the frangipani tree, whose new limb ends closely resemble the penis, is always associated with Kukulcan, while the Mayan day sign for wind (*ik*), corresponding to *ehecatl* in Nahuatl, carries with it the idea of germination or of coming into being.[73]

It is no wonder that the as-yet-unborn were cast into the wombs of their mothers as *ilhuicapipiltin* ("sky children")— the generative powers of the numen of the sky thus being emphasized.[74] It appears that when petitioned for issue Quetzalcoatl was specifically called Topiltzin, the name of one of his avatars. *Topiltzin* means either "beloved child" or "our prince."

While some of the above references are indirect, the cumulative effect is persuasive. Quetzalcoatl was considered to be a phallic god. Nevertheless, we may wonder why we have no depictions of him as ithyphallic. There must be a hiatus in the archaeological record, particularly the record in the Huaxteca, where treasures still await the archaeologist's spade. I suspect, however, that most of the lack comes from the heavy overlay of symbolism in Mesoamerican art and the great antiquity of its devices. In the serpent stage of depiction the god could be read directly as a fertility symbol, but when he is portrayed as a Huaxtec priest (representing wind, air, vitality, and again fertility), we find that the items of his regalia had primary meanings other than human procreativity—however much they may have implied it. Though Quetzalcoatl was thus connected with phallicism, his iconography does not concentrate on it. The Priapean frenzy of the Huaxtecs in him had become muted.

Quetzalcoatl as the Establisher of Lineages

When Sahagún compared Quetzalcoatl with Hercules, he made an interesting if somewhat superficial connection. In mythology Hercules was never a priest familiar with penitential acts, prophecy, or learning, nor was he a culture hero in the true sense of the word. These dissimilarities aside, however, it is clear that Sahagún was still pointing to something of importance.

Both Hercules and Quetzalcoatl were demigods with mortal bodies; Hercules was the son of the sky god Zeus somewhat as we have derived Ehecatl from the sky dragon. Both were twins, though the two opposing twins, Iphicles and Xolotl, are not themselves comparable. Both Hercules and Quetzalcoatl were renowned for strength, violence, and sexual prowess, and both excelled as founders of lineages in far places. Their names as first ancestors were taken with great seriousness. Hercules' feats of strength are well known. Quetzalcoatl was regularly invoked to give a worker strength in ground breaking, tree cutting, quarrying, and so forth. He was the "manly god." Both gods were peripatetic, and once for a short time in his eleventh labor Hercules held up the sky, as Quetzalcoatl did. Both descended into the underworld, where Cerberus the dog monster can be precisely matched with Xolotl the dog monster. Finally in a climax of wonderful coincidence both heroes built funeral pyres and cast themselves into the flames, each to ascend into the heavens, Hercules as an immortal, Quetzalcoatl as the morning star.

The comparison I have made above points most particularly to the predominance of the demigod as an ancestral hero, along with a concomitant, though lesser, emphasis on sexual prowess. In fact this was probably what was in Sahagún's mind when he made the comparison. But as I have hinted, in doing this he overlooked much else of importance in the Quetzalcoatl corpus of tales. Unlike Hercules, Quetzalcoatl was a demiurge, the retriever of the bones of mankind, a priest, and a wise man. His connections with wind and water are never forgotten. And, of signal importance, he was a culture hero, whereas Hercules was not. Hercules was a mere man, and he was not modeled on or derived from any aspect of nature. Compared with Hercules, who is presented to us in Greek art and literature as crude and athletic, Quetzalcoatl was a rich and a complicated creature. So the comparison made by Sahagún, while useful, is less than complete.

We need to go more deeply into Quetzalcoatl's above-mentioned patronage of great houses. Here he is indeed the Hercules of Mesoamerica, the don of royalty, the exemplar and donor of the prerogatives of nobility. He was called "the very human lord"[75] and was the only Mesoamerican god with whom I am familiar who was reputed to have had a human body, as indeed we might expect of a first ancestor.[76] The divine model for the earthly royal marriage that would produce legitimate sons can be clearly detected in the Mixcoatl-Chimalma mating myth in which the true son, Ce Acatl Quetzalcoatl, opens the line. If a child was born on the day 9-wind (the birth date of our god as an ancestor), even though he came from plebeian stock, it was certain that he would found a great lineage.[77] Pedigree was obviously of the first importance in this Mesoamerican world. One of the sources observes:

They put great stock in family descent, and when they make offerings, they would say, "I am of such and such a lineage." They worshiped and sacrificed to their first founder, calling him "the heart of the people," and they kept him, in the form of an idol, in a secure place, offering him gold and precious stones.[78]

We can most easily understand this emphasis by first analyzing two successive festivals in the Aztec year, the Feast of the Lesser Lords and the following Feast of the Great Lords, the seventh and eighth months of the solar calendar. The rituals in these two months were mainly agricultural and celebrated the newly formed maize ears. Our interest, however, is not in these rites but rather in an extraneous set of rituals inserted into the two months that exalted the ruler and his entourage.

Two idols were used in these ceremonies.[79] The first one represented the lesser lords. The second idol was placed on a mat and wore the diadem; it celebrated the royal house. The first ceremony featured the nobles, who flaunted in public the testimonials of their male privileges, the size of their harems, and their unobstructed access to public women. Their concubines, who for most of the year were jealously hidden away behind walls, were at this time escorted out into the day, gaily dressed and garlanded with flowers. At night in a magnificent torchlight celebration the lords danced with harlots, whose long hair was unbound to symbolize the tasseling corn. Nobles were said to be "the sons and servants of Quetzalcoatl."[80]

Inasmuch as the ceremonies were held in the Temple of Tezcatlipoca, it is probable that the second idol represented that god who was the very numen of sovereignty. Nevertheless the day of the celebration was Ehecatl's day, and on that day the diadem worn by every great ruler, the *xihuitzolli*, was supposed to appear as a sign in the sky.[81] Throughout the Aztec world on that day rulers put on their crowns and sat on the *icpalli*, the mat of royalty with the backrest (described more fully below). During those two months the various wards of the city and all the dependent villages round about had to offer extravagant entertainment to the magnates at staggered intervals; in this manner the people were allowed to express their gratitude to the nobility. After this came a seven-day feast, which the *tlatoani* offered to the people as a symbol of his reciprocal care of them. Alternation of rights and duties was supposedly thus exhibited throughout the society, and the prerogative of the ruler was reiterated.

Everywhere in Mesoamerica, Quetzalcoatl was the ancestral god. In Tula he had been the legendary first ruler. Although he appears not to have been indigenous among the far-northern Chichimecs, nevertheless when they first encountered the urbanized groups on the south, they quickly adopted the god as a warranty of their more cultivated status.[82] Looking back, the Chichimecs in fact claimed Quetzalcoatl as their first ancestor, he who had been with them originally in Chicomoztoc[83] and who had led them out on his day date, 1-reed.[84] Quetzalcoatl was a form of the ancestral god among the Otomís, as well as among the Mixtecs.[85] The Aztec rulers looked back to him as their founder and the establisher of their rights, cities like Quauhtitlán, Mizquic, and of course Tenochtitlán making much of him. From the last city comes the tale that, in his flight from Tula, Quetzalcoatl sat upon a miraculous stone in the marshes to mark the spot as the future seat of Mexican royalty.[86] Aztec origination tales told of Quetzalcoatl as their divine leader anciently in Chicomoztoc, the first homeland.[87] As Kukulcan along the Tabasco and Campeche coasts he offered the same validation of royal privileges to

the Chontal rulers there. The Temple of Kukulcan in Acallan in fact belonged to the ruler personally.[88] The city
of Chichén Itzá remembered the time when the god and
his followers had first appeared and inaugurated the new
state.[89] The god's name in fact was used as a title (equivalent
to Caesar or Augustus) in Mayapan, where the ruler Hunac
Ceel became known as Ah Nacxit Kukulcan, or Lord Nacxitl Quetzalcoatl.[90] Many royal lines used the god's date
name One Reed as the date when they first rose out of the
earth to begin their migrations. Among the Mayas it was
the Quichés who believed that their rulers could actually
become Kukulcan by leaping into the deep lake where the
god lived in the form of a watery dragon.[91] To the Quichés,
Gucumatz was "the root of greatness in lordship."[92]

All rulers thus owed their dignities to Quetzalcoatl. This
perception of the divine underpinnings of rule, however,
called for confirmation procedures at stated times. That
was done by designating a primate church, as it were,
which could act as the locus for this essential rite. In central
Mexico the city of Cholula, and in Yucatán the city of Chichén Itzá (followed in time by Mayapán) filled these roles.[93]
On coming to power, the more important rulers sent formal
embassies or went in person to the prestigious cities to re-
quest the god's approval of their assumption of power.
Once this sanction had been given, no other was needed.
Full legitimacy had been promulgated.

The ceremonies in Cholula were impressive and meaningful.[94] After having their noses, lips, or ears pierced, depending on rank, these newly confirmed rulers were then
escorted home in pomp by five priests of Quetzalcoatl, who
thus acted as deponents to the home population. At the end
of every fifty-two-year Calendar Round all great rulers everywhere felt compelled to seek reconfirmation of their
lordship, in return for which they sent rich gifts to the temple in question. Nothing, not even legitimacy, was thought
to outlast a lustrum of fifty-two years.[95]

The equivalent of the throne in the Nahua parts of Meso-america was the *icpalli*, a reed mat (*petlatl*) with a cushioned back that was generally covered with a jaguar pelt. The two words used together in the phrase *in icpalli in petlatl* meant "governance" or "royal authority." A telling form of this royal seat, called the *coapetlatl*, or "serpent mat," appears in one of the Quetzalcoatl myths.[96] As the tale goes, when Quetzalcoatl arrived on the coast, fleeing before Tezcatlipoca, he created a raft of snakes and on this launched himself eastward over the waters. The *coapetlatl* was a mat woven of serpents with their heads forming the fringes; it could therefore move in any direction.[97] It possessed magical properties, and the person who succeeded in seating himself on it could be certain that he would soon become a ruler. The myth thus clearly links Quetzalcoatl with lordship.

The best known to us of all the Mesoamerican lineage associations are those of the Mexicas. It is of some interest to see how these were understood at the time. There were two views. Like all the other Aztec tribes, the Mexicas believed that they had emerged out of caves in the earth in the legendary land of Aztlan. Their first ruler there had been Quetzalcoatl, and it was he who had led them out in the year 7-reed on their historic trek into the central basin.[98] Once there, however, the god had inexplicably turned back.[99] None of the Mexicas would follow him in this reversal of course, for they had already married local women and acquired lands. Once indeed Quetzalcoatl came back and tried to persuade them to continue in his following, but they again refused. In anger at their disloyalty he announced that someday he would return and claim again his royal prerogative. Until that time the privilege of rule was to be theirs only on trust. This version connects the Mexicas with the other Aztec groups, all of whom claimed to be descended from Quetzalcoatl, but it has appended to it the prophecy of his return, a curious motif that brought into question the permanency of the office of the Mexican *tla-toani*. In a sense it even watered down the ultimacy of Huit-zilopochtli, the national god of the Mexicas, for he was their god only because he was a successor of Quetzalcoatl.

The other version is concerned with the actual facts of Mexican legitimacy and is uninterested in the possibility of the god's return. Simply put, it is a genealogy. It states that the first king of the Toltecs was Topiltzin (Quetzalcoatl).[100] It was he, therefore, who established Toltec rule. From him was descended Huemac, another ruler, and a member of the Culhua branch of the Toltecs. The Mexicas later married into the Culhua-Toltec line, which had moved to Cul-huacán and which had planted in that city the undisputed legitimacy. The second Moteuczoma was counted as the ninth Mexican ruler and the twenty-sixth Culhua ruler, though he ruled neither in Tula nor in Culhuacán but in Tenochtitlán. The Rock of Chapultepec from which Tenochtitlán received its potable water through an aque-duct was sacred to Quetzalcoatl (who had an image placed there)[101] and to Huemac, who was said to be still living in-side the rock. Chapultepec was a surrogate for the Aztlan mountain homeland, and all the great Mexica rulers had their images carved on the rock, thereby attesting their le-gitimacy. Thus were the two versions fused.

These might seem like childish vagaries not to be taken very seriously, but every Aztec royal line felt itself con-stantly under the sword and could use power only if it knew itself supported in its claims by a divine sanction. Such sanction throughout Mesoamerica was held, as I have said, only from Quetzalcoatl. When Juan de Grijalva, Fran-cisco Fernández de Córdoba and Hernán Cortés appeared off the very coasts connected in story with the god, it is small wonder that rulers throughout Mesoamerica shud-dered for the future—the god had returned! And so when Cortés finally did enter Tenochtitlán, the Mexican ruler Moteuczoma in a singular display of the power of his faith, moved out of his palace to make room for the homecome god.

It is of interest to look at another lineage founder, a personage called Xelhua.[102] He was the stem personage and the ruler god of the Nonohualco Aztecs and came from Chicomoztoc, the fabled Seven Caves, from which the various tribes had emerged. As was related of Quetzalcoatl and several of his avatars, so also Xelhua is said to have escaped from the great flood of the preceding aeon and to have become the builder of the holy city of Cholula.[103] He was said to have been the son of the White Mixcoatl and Ilancueitl (who often doubles for Chimalma). He was a holy man much in repute for his penitential practices, and he is connected in story both with the quetzal bird and with oracular religion. Not only was he the revered progenitor of that group of cities centering around Cholula and Tehuacán, but he continued to sanction the rightness of their rule.

Without any variations at all, the above was told about Quetzalcoatl, son of Mixcoatl and Chimalma. Tehuacán was famous everywhere in the Aztec world for its radical tradition of fasting and penance, all in the style of Quetzalcoatl. So it is certain that Xelhua was an avatar of the god who was worshiped by the Nonohualcas. Whatever else Xelhua may have been—even if he had been an actual historical leader—everything attributed to him had first been attributed to Quetzalcoatl. The historical person—if Xelhua had been an actual person—was put aside and replaced by the god. Xelhua was another name thereafter for Quetzalcoatl.

We can end the section on the Quetzalcoatl of legitimacy with the following summary of the *Selden Roll*, a remarkable piece of folk memory (Mixtec, probably) specifying the rule of Quetzalcoatl in the formative years of one of the tribal histories.

It begins with the well-known scene in the heavens where the two high gods have just appointed Quetzalcoatl

Figure 13

to his mission. In the year 1-reed (which was also his birth
date and which further specified him as the planet Venus)
he descends to earth, where the cave of origination (Chicomoztoc) is seen inhabited by one of his avatars called One
Jaguar. This avatar is shown as a demonic form of Mixcoatl
who has the body of a turtle.[104] His connection with Quetzalcoatl is evident when we recall that Quetzalcoatl was the
patron god of the second week of the *tonalpohualli*, which
began with the day 1-jaguar. It is this deity, standing proxy
for Quetzalcoatl, who sends a group of tribal leaders, painted
as *mimixcoa*, on a pilgrimage to the magic mountain.

The first and most important stop that this small group
makes is in front of a temple of Quetzalcoatl (fig. 13). This

shrine is most interesting. It has the usual small cella where-in is ensconced a Quetzalcoatl bundle. Immediately behind the cella and adjoining it is another edifice sharing the same frieze of *olin* signs along the cornice, as well as on the party wall. This back room has a *tlachco* (ball court) attached. In the center of the *tlachco* is the customary round marker, while over the whole preside two figures with curious buc-cal masks. Their names are Four Wind and Four Move-ment, both known avatars of Quetzalcoatl—the second one in fact is Xolotl himself, the patron deity of the ball game. Four Wind, the other figure, is therefore the deity of the ball itself. It is obvious from this scene that oracles of Quet-zalcoatl are given by the results of the games played in this sacred area.

We can guess what the oracle was in this case. The tribe will have been commanded to take up the image of Quetzal-coatl and install it as the god Ce Acatl on the peak of Mount Mixcoatl. We see this happening a few passages beyond, where a file of holy men is shown bearing the sacred bundle on a journey of many vicissitudes to the aforesaid moun-tain. The mountain is composed of the overarching bodies of two dragons, one named Itzcoatl (Knife Serpent), the other Mixcoatl (Cloud Serpent), both depicted with plumes. The face of Mixcoatl *en face* stares out of the mountain at the beholder, while he holds the quetzal bird as an emblem. Finally the image of Quetzalcoatl Ce Acatl is solemnly de-posited on the summit of the mountain, and a new fire is drilled for the requisite cult needs (fig. 14).

What follows is difficult to interpret. At the foot of the mountain a monkey figure is whirling around on a pole horizontally placed above ground level in the *tlachco*. This figure probably has some connection with Xolotl. Two prisoners of war are waiting to be inserted into the strange cultic game, while in the air overhead the figure of Nine Wind, an important avatar of Quetzalcoatl, here apparently dead, is shown falling out of the heavens. These last figures are enigmatic, and no one has as yet proposed a convincing interpretation. What interests us here is the heavy concentration of cultic and mythic references to Quetzalcoatl; he is seen in at least three of his various avatars in the same presentation.

The *Selden Roll* is a record of the legendary wandering of a people whose patron god was Quetzalcoatl. It is the god as Ehecatl who initiates the action in the sky, but it appears to be the god as the planet Venus who is involved in the tribal history depicted. The Venus cult, in which Quetzalcoatl, Mixcoatl, and Xolotl all take part, is here the center of the people's worship; this is illustrated by the intimate liaison we see between Quetzalcoatl and the *tlachco*. Obviously Quetzalcoatl in either of his two avatars, Nine Wind or One Reed, is the ancestral god of the people who recorded their past in the *Selden Roll*. Genealogy and family pedigree are the peculiar province of this god.

Quetzalcoatl in Cholula

There were several cities in Mesoamerica especially sanctified by the presence of Quetzalcoatl, cities such as Tehuacán, Xochicalco, and Chichén Itzá. None, however, was as famous as Cholula, the god's primate city.

The full name of the city was Tullan Cholullan Tlachihualtepetl.[105] Here resided the most famous merchants and artisans of Mesoamerica, known far and wide and called the Great Toltecs. A special nexus connected them with the god. Quetzalcoatl was the god of knowledge and skills; the two were equated, and both were prime attributes of the successful trader and craftsman. It is impossible to ascertain now whether the wealth acquired over the centuries by this group of enterprising men was instrumental in increasing the stature of the god there or whether—as would seem more likely—the uncommonly varied role played

Figure 14

there by Quetzalcoatl was that which originally increased the prestige of the Cholula merchants and honed their skills.

More specifically, the patron god of the Aztec merchants was an avatar called Yacateuctli.[106] The name literally means Nose Lord, and it no doubt refers to an early image of the god with a long nose or a buccal mask. In his Maya form the god in fact shows a veritable Cyrano de Bergerac nose. The name, however, should be glossed to read Lord of the

Van, that is, He Who Goes Ahead of Others. He has other names, all with related meanings, such as Lord of the Pointed Nose and Lord of the Aquiline Nose, both referring to the cunning and sagacity so often attributed to a person so endowed.

Yacateuctli certainly was a very ancient god;[107] he must come down from an aggressive culture in which the role of the merchant perforce included that of the warrior. Concerning his capacity as a trail leader we recall the role of Quetzalcoatl as the wind or tornado that preceded the coming of the rains, sweeping the ways ahead of the Tlalocs. Yacateuctli must have been a forerunner in his own right, a deity who had been early pulled into the orbit of Quetzalcoatl finally to become one of his best-known avatars. One of our sources equates him with the Greek god of merchants, Hermes,[108] while another connects him with crossroads. In the codices he is recognized by the merchant's staff and fan that he carries instead of the priest's incense bag and penitential thorns. In Cholula as in Tenochtitlán whenever that aspect of the god particularly revered by the merchants was in the ascendancy, then Quetzalcoatl was Yacateuctli, the god resident in the merchant's staff.[109]

As one of the Tulas, Cholula was a large metropolitan center impressive in its edifices and in the holiness of its traditions.[110] Although it never became as large as Teotihuacán, it was nearly as old, and it may well be considered a sister city. It had been reputedly founded by Quetzalcoatl himself when he led his retinue in from the west. It outlived Teotihuacán and boasted well over two thousand years of uninterrupted religious importance.

What distinguished it was its intense concentration on Quetzalcoatl as a giver of oracles, legitimacy, and abundance. So great was the god's reputation in Cholula that, at least in the Postclassic period, rulers from near and distant parts had their personal dynastic gods installed there in extraterritorial shrines, much like resident embassies. That is

what the Spaniards meant when they adverted to the as-
tonishing number of temples in the city—they thought that
they could count over three hundred.[111] A legend that there
had been one for every day of the year could not die, and
was later told about the admittedly great number of Christian churches that replaced the temples and which today in
various stages of disrepair still dot the surrounding fields.

Rulers from as far as six hundred miles away were reported to have sent their ambassadors to reside in Cholula
and sit for a while in the god's shadow. Every nation of
consequence possessed in that city its own inns, houses,
and shrines. The city in fact operated almost as if it were an
amphictyonic center. Because of its proximity to the coast it
attracted numbers of pilgrimages from Huaxtec and Totonac areas, lands that from the beginning had been closely
associated with the Feathered Serpent.[112]

Four elders ruled in Cholula, two of whom resided in the
temple area and particularly represented the god as the establisher and supporter of royal lineages.[113] These were the
aquiach and the *tlalchiach*, the former known by his device of
the eagle, the latter by the jaguar. It is possible that they
also may have represented the two main phases of Venus,
the morning and the evening star. Although in all cases they
were nobles from the ward in which the marketplace was to
be found, in the hierarchical system they rose through se-
niority. We can call them merchant princes, but they are
just as well thought of as high priests.

Ehecatl had other avatars besides Yacateuctli in Cholula.[114] Centrally he was of course the celestial dragon, and
his image can still be seen on the impressive Altar II on the
east side of the pyramid.[115] Construction on this pyramid
began about A.D. 100, from which time it continually expanded until it became the largest building erected in the
pre-Columbian New World.[116] The name given to it was
most appropriate, Tlachihualtepec, the Mountain Created
by Men. So breathtaking were its bulk and height that later

peoples ascribed its building to the Giants, inhabitants of the first of the five worlds, who had erected it to scale the heavens[117]—which is simply another way of saying that by building it they reached the realm of the celestial serpent and on that eminence constructed for him a house. The later ruinous condition of the pyramid was attributed to the god's wrath when he destroyed it with his hurricanes at the end of the third world.[118]

Quetzalcoatl also appears in Cholula as Quiahuiteotl,[119] or Rain God, whose date name appears to have been Nine Rain. He was one of the Tlalocs and had a shrine on top of the great mound after it had crumbled to become simply a huge grassy knoll.

Again the god could be Tonacaquahuitl, the Tree of our Substance, the life-giving tree that rises from the earth to support the heavens;[120] such a tree can be seen in a relief in the Temple of the Cross at Palenque.[121] This tree god could be worshiped also as Chicahualizteotl, God of Strength or Rigidity, who gives to toilers of the soil, fellers of trees, and quarrymen the stamina required for their work; there may also be phallic overtones in the title.[122]

The importance of Quetzalcoatl as a tree has been insufficiently stressed. In myth he twice became Green Willow Tree, once for the purpose of upholding the sky and once when he was introducing the maguey plant to mankind.[123] His arboreal cult in Cholula appears to have been of some importance. It is not certain that Quetzalcoatl was identified with the mythical Tree of Our Substance, the World Tree as a symbol of plenty, but it is probable that he was. This Tree of Our Substance is described poetically as raining down sweet songs like dew, while the quetzal bird spreads out his wings at the summit as an incarnation of the ruler.[124] That is consistent with everything we know about Quetzalcoatl.

The god is, of course, also Ce Acatl, One Reed, who was the war dragon and the morning star, though this avatar was not stressed as much here as it was in Tula and Chichén Itzá. More curiously the god could coalesce with Camaxtli,[125] another name for Mixcoatl of the nearby city of Tlascala, a fact that, however, is consonant with the filiation in myth of Quetzalcoatl to the god Mixcoatl. Finally, the god in Cholula is also Nacxitl Tepeuhqui, a variant form of Ce Acatl who historically was to penetrate the Maya areas. And we have already seen Quetzalcoatl in Cholula as Xelhua.

Thus in his most holy city Quetzalcoatl produced or displayed a wide spectrum of avatars concerned generally with rain, wealth, ancestral patronage, generation, and war. Surely this appears to be a nearly universal god.

We know little about the cult carried on in Cholula. At the time of the Spanish entry its government was typically Aztec; that is to say, it was shared by four hereditary houses, as mentioned above. These houses were traditionally derived from the original four princes of Tula (Teotihuacán?) who had accompanied Quetzalcoatl on his flight to the east and who were left behind to rule in Cholula.[126] This tradition of course contradicts the legend that Xelhua founded Cholula, but both tales at least agree that Quetzalcoatl was a first founder. Of the four houses of priest-rulers, two always held the offices designated by the titles mentioned before.

The rituals carried on there must have been singularly impressive when one considers the two millennia of religious history through which Cholula lived. We have descriptions from only the final, or Aztec, period. The city celebrated two dates with special solemnity, 7-reed and 1-reed (fig. 15). In Cholula the first date was that of the birth of Quetzalcoatl,[127] which, with the Toltec tradition that he had been born on the date 1-reed, gives a pair of twin dates appropriate to the god. The date 7-reed was a crucial one not only in Cholula but elsewhere in the Aztec world. It was a date for the inception of things, because on that day the sky was raised up, a way of saying that Quetzalcoatl was born. Every fifty-two years Cholula celebrated this holy day with exceptional splendor. The day 1-reed was celebrated in Cholula rather as the date of the god's death and his ascension as the morning star. The date 1-reed was propitiated as an especially malign avatar.[128]

One of these feasts was controlled by the merchants' guild, and for the occasion the merchants first bought a prime slave free from all blemishes and then for forty days arrayed him as Quetzalcoatl.[129] During these two Aztec months he was escorted around the city singing and dancing, constantly encouraged to give manifestations of joy. He was finally sacrificed at midnight, and his body was claimed by the merchants for a cannibal feast of potlatch proportions. From this celebration we can understand how central the merchants were in the Cholula cult. So obsessive was the religious life of the city that an estimated six thousand victims were annually sacrificed there. The two great feasts were presented with enhanced pomp every four and every fifty-two years.[130]

Inside the round Temple of Cholula that later peoples had built beside the mountainous ruins of the original temple base[131] was the wooden statue of Ehecatl painted black, red, and white and wearing the buccal mask.[132] Around him were piled riches of all kinds as befitted the darling of the merchants. Wealth and abundance were the obvious shibboleths of Cholula. Outside the temple was a raised stone platform where people disfigured with disease or racked with coughs, severe cripples, and other unfortunates came on certain festivals to act out their illnesses and miseries in the hope of persuading the god to cure them.[133] This theater was also used by others who mimed demons and animal avatars of Quetzalcoatl (mainly water creatures such as frogs, lizards, and crocodiles) and simultaneously recited myths appropriate to their appearances.

The worship of Quetzalcoatl in Cholula was surely

Figure 15

unique in Mesoamerica in being performed in such an international context. We also note the great variety of divine
roles played here by the god. Out of such complex raw
material one might have expected a god with truly universal
claims to have emerged in the last days, possibly even a god
with the first hints of exclusive godhead. We catch only the
faintest hints of these from Cholula. But then our records
are scanty.

THREE
QUETZALCOATL
AS PRIEST

In the following pages I discuss Quetzalcoatl as a sage and as a sacerdotal arche-type. I put forward the possibility that the first priesthoods were products of celes-tial religion, namely the worship of the Wind and morning star (both avatars of Quetzalcoatl). Blood sacrifice, with which the god is intimately associated, is shown to be a crucial part of that development. Sorcerers are differentiated from priests, which leads to the conclusion that the concept of the nahualli, *or animal alter ego, does not fit Quetzalcoatl. On the other hand, the pertinence to Quetzal-coatl of the* tonalpohualli *(the count of destiny days) is evident from his mythol-ogy. The connected question of the decayed gods Oxomoco and Cipactonal and their part in the making of the* tonalpohualli *is necessarily also investigated. Quetzal-coatl's expertise in the science of time is described and contrasted with that of Xiuhteuctli, the true Lord of the Year. I advance some ideas on Quetzalcoatl in Teotihuacán and his kinship with the god of rain, Tlaloc.*

The Priest

Our sources give us to understand that Quetzalcoatl was the first to invoke the gods and to institute sacrifices. He was thus the primordial priest figure. In late Aztec cult he was thought of as officiating at all cults, and in this sense he was in his person a conceptualization of religion as a whole: "Him each of the fire-priests imitated, as well as the offering priests. And the offering priests took their manner of conduct from the life of Quetzalcoatl. By it they established the law of Tula."[1]

We have a choice of two avatars whom we can plausibly connect with Quetzalcoatl's priesthood. Either we can look back to the god of the air as a mediator between earth and sky, a god whom we call Ehecatl, or we can look to the warrior Ce Acatl, whose connections are with the planet Venus but who must also be connected with celestial computation. These two are involved in any final characterization of the priest-god but with different degrees of intensity.

The usual word for priest in Nahuatl was *tlamacazqui*, "giver" or "dispenser." No doubt it had first been an epithet used to describe deity, the ultimate giver of life, sustenance, and death, and only after that was it applied to those who interpreted the gods and mediated between them and men, in other words, the priests. We note that the rain gods, the Tlalocs, were equally well designated as Tlamacazque (plural), the "Givers" of the fruits of the earth. This near-identification between deity and priest was a part of Mesoamerican religion from early times. The priest could thus be thought of as the god's "image" or "replica," *ixiptla*, though not as a "double," *nahualli*. The only difference between him and the god's statue lay in that the divine vitality

121

within the true image or statue could command action whereas the priest could only petition. In any case both the statue of the god and the *tlamacazqui* of that god were *ixiptlas*, "stand-ins" or "images."

So far so good. But the later Mesoamericans even split the concept of the *ixiptla* just described. If the *tlamacazqui* was the living image of the god, he was still a lowly subordinate and relegated to the god's daily service. He brought in the wood, tended the temple fires, swept out the divine precinct, adorned the statue, performed the vigils, and so forth. In this sense he was the god as his own servitor, however reduced. But there was another form of the living *ixiptla*, that is "the image" who literally enacted the part of the god and was, for a set length of time, the god incarnate. Generally this *ixiptla* appeared only once a year at the god's major festival. He or she was a slave or some other person chosen to mime the part of the deity as a sacrificial being. The word *ixiptla* is understood in this book to indicate this role only, and not that of the ordinary priest. The sole purpose of the *ixiptla* was to die.

At the top of the hierarchy stood the high priest, who was a fully authorized simulacrum of the god (fig. 16). For designated ceremonies he wore some or most of the regalia of his deity, whether male or female did not matter. His purpose was not to imitate the god insofar as his needs and qualities went (such as the satisfaction of his alimentary needs, eating and drinking) but rather "to be" the god only for the moment of sacrifice. At that instant it was the high priest as a "life" *ixiptla* who personally drove the knife into the body of the "death" *ixiptla*, tore out the heart as food, and collected the blood as drink for the "simulation" *ixiptla*, or statue of the god.

The priesthood was thus concerned with four levels of god affinity: (1) the icon or statue of the god, (2) the high priest as the god actively impersonating himself as an acquirer of sustenance, (3) the *tlamacazqui* as god helper per-

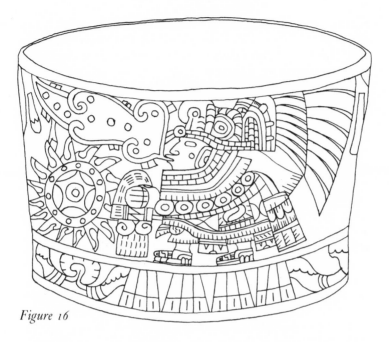

Figure 16

forming the god's daily chores, and (4) the *ixiptla* proper, the living proxy destined for sacrifice. The above analysis of the Aztec priesthood reveals the conceptual complexity of the Mesoamerican priesthood.

It may be asked, Why was it Quetzalcoatl, rather than some other god, who was chosen to be the Mesoamerican model of the priest? I believe that the answer to this question is to be found in the Ehecatl level of his godhead. Of all natural phenomena the wind alone combines power, voice, and invisibility. Other nature gods are palpable. Rain falls and then gathers into pools and channels; fire has a distinctive color and is seen only in the presence of wood; the sun can be plotted and timed and pointed out in his appearances and disappearances; earth is the ponderable bedrock of all things that have weight. One can make accurate images of all of these, and such images pile up and create further opportunities for the artist in expanding the god's iconography. But how can one locate the habitation of the wind or describe his form? The knowledge and the lack of knowledge that man possesses simultaneously about the wind leads him to project an inverted or "other" personality into any deification he makes of it. The power of the wind, greater than that of most other things in nature with which man is familiar, gives to his mythological model of it an aura of danger. Its voice, ranging from that of the zephyr to that of the cyclone, adds the elements of personality, command, and caprice. Its invisibility gives him the sense of its "otherness." These can—and I believe did—add up to the attribution to the wind of an archetypal priesthood. After all, in many cultures the priest is really "other"; he is neither a man nor a god. He has ritual access to the gods, and he knows the formulas and utterances that initiate conversation with them. And only he can at certain times countermand kings and princes in their names. But he is also in everyone's eyes plainly a man.

Wind has the least specificity and the least definition of any part of nature. It therefore allows a great deal of invention. On wind, therefore, the Mesoamericans built the priestly office.

This is a logical position for us to take, but it is not enough. There are facts concerning Quetzalcoatl as priest that involve him intimately with numeration and the observation of stellar periods and that would therefore seem to point to his Venusian character as basic also to the priestly function. I shall go into this in more detail later. Here it is sufficient to note that these possibilities deny any simple assertion that wind alone explains Quetzalcoatl as a priest.

I am in fact prepared to believe that, while wind provided the "spirit closeness" necessary to a priest in his profession, the connection with the planet Venus was at least as important in giving a content to such an intimacy. From

Ehecatl the priest perhaps first arose, but it was from Ce Acatl that he derived his power to know. It is uncertain which came first out of the bowl of the sky, wind or planet, though for the sake of argument in this book I have assumed that the former was primary.

I would briefly reconstruct it thus. The Mesoamerican sky religion early produced in the Olmec heartland a powerful and highly professional priesthood, which then spread outward. It invaded great cities like Cholula and Xochicalco and redesigned them. Although it had a necessary alliance with the cult of Tlaloc (which was an integral part of the earth religion), it never became a part of the agricultural scene. The secret of its success was in the mating of two disconnected avatars of the sky, Ehecatl and Ce Acatl, to round out the divine functions of Quetzalcoatl as a priest.

Quetzalcoatl the Sacrificer

One of the reports about the god picked up by the Spanish friars and passed on by them was the statement that he had stood out against human sacrifice, adjuring his Toltec peers to sacrifice only birds, snakes, and butterflies. This claim will be discussed later. Here it can be stated that, insofar as it concerns the Quetzalcoatl who was a divinity and not the high priest, the claim is the very opposite of the truth. In point of fact Quetzalcoatl was the only one among the gods all of whose designs were sacrificial and who alone taught the correct way in which to tear out a heart for the offering. It is indeed this very intimate association of Quetzalcoatl with blood sacrifice that puts him in the very center of the sky religion. The act of sacrifice is seen as a priestly skill and prerogative.

There were several myths concerned with the origins of heart sacrifice, it being variously attributed to the celestial Mother herself,[2] to Tezcatlipoca (Yaotl),[3] to Mixcoatl (Camaxtli),[4] to the four originating gods, and even once to Chantico,[5] a goddess of fire. The Mexicas attributed it to their national mascot and god of war, Huitzilopochtli.[6] Human sacrifice was so pervasive a part of the Mesoamerican scene that its origins were accounted for in a variety of ways, being thus assigned to any plausible god. Curiously, only one myth presents the god Quetzalcoatl as the originator, or better still the initiator, of sacrifice. That is the myth of the fifth sun, in which the first thoroughgoing sacrifices were instituted by Quetzalcoatl (in the person of his avatar as Xolotl) for the purpose of strengthening the sun preparatory to his rising.[7]

Vivid statements of Quetzalcoatl's close connection with human sacrifice come from Mixtec mythology. In one pictorial sequence Quetzalcoatl appears as his avatar Nine Wind emerging from the sacrificial knife, tied to it by the umbilical cord.[8] Pursuant then to this horrid birth he is divided into sixteen different avatars—each no doubt representing a special function—after which he is prepared in the highest heaven for his work as a demiurge and founder of dynasties. We have already described him as he descends from the empyrean clad in the full regalia of his priesthood and carrying as his badge a Venus staff with an inset sacrificial knife.[9] The statement could not have been more clearly made. Sacrifice was brought down to earth by Quetzalcoatl.

The full sacrificial cult of Nine Wind, once he is down on the Mixtec earth, is summarily displayed in another Mixtec codex.[10] In a very explicit scene Nine Wind has become his avatar, the sacrificial knife from which he was born, namely the god Itztli (fig. 17). He is shown standing in a threatening position within his shrine, which is marked with an ideogram of the sky. The shrine is doubly identified as being his because it contains his sacred bundle and has the Venus staff planted at the entrance. Itztli is generally known as an avatar of Tezcatlipoca—here Quetzalcoatl has taken him over as a logical extension of his priestly office.

Figure 17

The god is also involved with sacrifice on a cosmic scale, where the act has no application to men. In the *Codex Borgia* there is a scene in the underworld where the night sun, Yohualteuctli, is being sacrificed nine times, one for each of the infernal levels.[11] In each of the nine sacrifices a different avatar of Quetzalcoatl is doing the sacrificing, with the central heart sacrifice being performed by a Quetzalcoatl who for that occasion is wearing a hummingbird casque representing rejuvenation.

In cult the story is the same. In Tenochtitlán there were three superior priests, the title of their level of office being *quetzalcoatl*. The word *quetzalcoatl*, therefore, must be translated as "high priest," though for the same meaning one could also use *uey tlamacazqui*, a literal equivalent. One of these high priests administered the cult of the god Quetzalcoatl. One administered the state cult, that of the god Huitzilopochtli, while the third presided over the popular cult of the rain god Tlaloc.

These high priests were unique in that they were the personal appointees of the ruler. The dogma that the god Quetzalcoatl was the true founder of the royal lineage was applied by the ruler in his selection process, for it was customary for him to choose a family member, a brother or half brother, for the highest priestly position.[12] The office of *quetzalcoatl* thus belonged in the royal family and was always a firm support to the ruler himself, the *tlatoani*. From the moment of his election the high priest was considered to be the god in person with automatic access to the palace. And correspondingly, because of his quasi divinity he was forbidden to enter any other lesser domicile.[13] He was accordingly called Topiltzin after the great high priest in Tula.[14] It was he who carried to the ruler and interpreted to him the oracles of the gods, especially those that demanded additional warfare, for the purpose of replenishing the pool of captives held for sacrifice. On great occasions a high priest performed the sacrifices in person.

These political dimensions should be kept in mind when we are trying to understand the elements involved in the concept of Quetzalcoatl as the archetypal priest.[15] Blood sacrifice was the sole point of some of the Mesoamerican cults, and in all of them it was a fact that whoever controlled the sacrifices could manipulate the hunger of the gods. This not-inconsiderable power was passed down to the ruler from Quetzalcoatl, his progenitor. The ruler could use this power directly in certain cases, or he could delegate it, as seen above, to the *quetzalcoatl*.

The intimate association of Quetzalcoatl with blood sacrifice must have taken many centuries to develop. The concept of sacrifice in Mesoamerica is surely older than the nature gods as we see them finally formed. If this assumption is true, then each of the gods must have grown up, as it were, gradually abstracting from the idea of sacrifice his or her own special adaptation of it. But one of the gods, namely Quetzalcoatl, was finally designated by the late mythographers to stand for the commonalty of sacrifice everywhere. So designated, Quetzalcoatl became the chief hierophant of Mesoamerican religion, displaying to men and gods the mysteries of the heavens and of the cult of blood derived therefrom.

Autosacrifice and Penitential Practices

Lest we make too cynical a judgment on the use made by the royal houses of the god Quetzalcoatl and his doctrine of sacrifices, it should be noted here that the reverse of human sacrifice was autosacrifice, and in this the rulers played a not inconsiderable role. Here again the god Quetzalcoatl is the focal figure with a rich supporting mythology. Much of this will be taken up in chapter 6, where I describe the historic high priest Topiltzin; here I include only material that is outside that particular saga.

Figure 18

Autosacrifice was of prime importance in the religion of Quetzalcoatl (fig. 18). From the ruins of Huilocintla on the coast come two Huaxtec bas-reliefs that vividly display this form of sacrifice and relate it to the god.[16] Both show a priest deeply scarred all over his body and wearing as his badge the wind-jewel pectoral typical of Quetzalcoatl. Coiling up the legs of one of the figures is a pair of serpents. The date name One Jaguar (which is connected with the god) accompanies each figure.[17] Both wear baroque head array, on one figure a doubled casque of the head of Ehecatl with the buccal mask. The sky is depicted over both priests, as a sky dragon in one relief, as a band of stars in the other. One of the reliefs shows a figure of death and a warrior, both facing the priest. The other shows a feathered serpent (decapitated to represent the night sky) whose body forms a part of the base on which the priest stands.

Apparently the theme of both reliefs is autosacrifice, for each priest is shown passing through his tongue a long wand equipped with thorns. This was a cult act that Quetzalcoatl had taught to his devotees, and it was ranked as one of the most meritorious of all penitential gestures. Here on the Gulf Coast, which was the god's probable homeland, the rite is reported to us in all its gruesome detail. The wind god in the person of his priest here sacrifices his own blood in an essential and cosmic act.

That particular transfiguration of the god who was said to have introduced autosacrifice was known as Tlilpotonqui, He Who Is Feathered in Black. In Huexotzinco and Tlascala he was equated with Camaxtli, while in Cholula it was believed that he was a form of Nine Wind.[18] Tlilpotonqui was well known in the holy city of Tehuacán, where there was a small college of four priests who performed an ever-continuing four-year fast famous throughout the land, a regimen of almost unimaginable severity.[19] Rulers everywhere were kept informed on the state of holiness of these four, the successes of their abstinences, and the visions they experienced, for such omens could influence the tenure of their own royal offices. If one of the holy men died, it was an ill augury for all legitimate rulers and could presage the death of one of them.

The phallic side of the god also received recognition in Tehuacán. It was an accepted form of penitential service for some of the younger and more ardent of the priests of Quetzalcoatl either to split their penises or to pierce them.[20] If the latter form of autosacrifice was chosen, the neophytes would then thread themselves and hobble about, thus tied together, for the continuation of their duties. As can be imagined, this achieved a very high degree of holiness. One of the myths expatiates on penis sacrifice.[21] After Quetzalcoatl's success in collecting the bones of extinct men in the underworld, he returned with them to Tamoanchan. There the relics were ground into a powder and placed in a sacred container. Over this the god slit his penis, allowing the blood to flow down and give life to the mass. Present-day man was thus the result of an act of autosacrifice performed by this originating deity.

It was also said that the celestial gods were so pleased by the many penances performed by Quetzalcoatl's high priest in Tula that they sent down an iguana, who scratched in the earth to give promise of the abundance that would follow.[22] The iguana is connected in Mesoamerican iconography with the phallus and with abundance.

Quetzalcoatl as a Sorcerer

Our best sources refer to Quetzalcoatl as a *huey nahualli*, "chief sorcerer,"[23] or as a *nahualteuctli*, "master of sorcerers,"[24] thus adding another dimension to his already protean makeup. Mayas could describe him as a *nahualahau*, a "spirit lord," who was said to have become at will a serpent, an eagle, a jaguar, even a pool of blood, these transformations enabling him to fly up into the heavens or to descend into Xibalba, the underworld. In fact the Mayas insisted that that proclivity was his "essence."[25]

Some discussion is needed here, inasmuch as it is usually Tezcatlipoca who is credited with being the shape shifter and warlock par excellence. We would expect that a deity whose plasmic form was first serpent, then dragon, then wind and star, and finally archetypal priest would not be attracted into other animal forms—the serpent substrate in Quetzalcoatl would seem to be too solid, too basic to encourage later nonophidian appearances.

There is no agreement among scholars on exactly what the word *nahualli* means, but one of the most convincing interpretations sets it in a context of deceit, skulking, or dissimulation. The verb *nahualtia* means "to hide, covering one's self or putting on a mask," in other words to assume a disguise for the purpose of menacing or spying on a person. A *nahualli*, therefore, is a "disguise" generally in the form of a living animal. The corollary is that the mask or pelt, giving the sorcerer a shield behind which he can lurk, identifies the particular animal with which he has a supernatural rapport and whom he can use for the above ends. Because of this equivalence *nahualli* can be translated either as "sorcerer" or as "animal familiar," both of course implying shape shifting. The concept is a common one among preliterate peoples. What interests us here is that not only a man but a god can have a *nahualli*. When Quetzalcoatl descended into the underworld to retrieve the bones of men, he was accompanied and advised by his *nahualli*.[26] This *nahualli* was undoubtedly the dog, if we may extrapolate from the fact that Xolotl, who was a dog monster, was the twin or alter ego of Quetzalcoatl in the underworld (fig. 19).

There is only one animal that is brought into close relationship with Quetzalcoatl purely as an animal and not as an animal god (as in the case of Xolotl). This is the monkey, who in the lowlands of Mesoamerica was generally connected with darkness and the sky of night.[27] The monkey additionally stands for licentiousness and for the arts and crafts. He thus appears to share qualities with Quetzalcoatl or to be a kind of rebus writing for him. In fact the day sign "monkey" (*ozomatli*) can wear Quetzalcoatl's bowknot on his forehead. When, for instance, we are told that the monkey appears carved on the stone rings of the ball court, substituting for feathered serpents, we are again aware of a connection.[28] Even more revealing is that the monkey can replace Quetzalcoatl as a figure twinned with the death god in the codices. In Cholula a jade monkey was preserved as a talisman belonging to the god,[29] while in the neighbor city of Huexotzinco the thatched peak of Quetzalcoatl's round

Figure 19

temple sported the image of a monkey.[30] Today in the great hall of the Museo Nacional there are two sculptured figures of monkeys. One is a pot-bellied creature dancing on a coiled serpent while holding in his hand his own tail, which ends in a serpent's head. Most tellingly he wears the buccal mask of Ehecatl. The mouth of the other monkey is a functional water spout (in reference to Ehecatl as a rain maker), and he wears the earrings typical of the god. Finally in the *Codex Borgia* the heart of the god is designated by the day sign *ozomatli.*[31] All these examples attest to a close link between the animal and Quetzalcoatl.

In mythology, however, I know of only one tale in which both the god and the animal participate. This is the tale of the destruction of the second world (that of Ehecatl), which was accomplished by violent hurricanes blowing away all things, including men. A few men escaped the disaster but, caught in the trees, were changed into monkeys.[32] At best, however, this is a very indirect reference.

The preceding two paragraphs are the sum of our knowledge about the monkey as a possible *nahualli* of Quetzalcoatl. It does not seem to me that we are here dealing with an animal that the god used as an alter ego, as was the case, for instance, with Tezcatlipoca, when he changed himself into a coyote or a jaguar. It is likely that we are dealing rather with a kind of iconographic gloss on Quetzalcoatl, a compendium of symbolic meanings suggested by the monkey, its handiness and versatility, its sagacity, its humanoid appearance, and, in the case of the howler monkey, its booming voice in the treetops at the time of the sun's descent into the earth.

The one undoubted *nahualli* that the god should possess is, of course, the serpent. When the gods Tezcatlipoca and Quetzalcoatl determined to create the cosmos, each of them first changed himself into a serpent (certainly in this myth a boa constrictor), and between them they proceeded to catch the primordial monster in their coils and effectively squeezed her into two parts. The top part they heaved upward to become the sky; the lower part they left as earth. Omitting Tezcatlipoca for the moment from the picture, we see that this myth is merely the statement that wind, or air, separates sky from earth. As such it does not truly describe a *nahualli* situation, where the sorcerer of his own volition and for his own individual and generally deceitful ends changes himself into a familiar beast. The myth merely points to a state of nature and relates its origins. The two serpents in the myth are simply the original sky dragons.

We are thus left with an unclear picture. We know Quetzalcoatl to be the epitome of priests.[33] He is not the epitome of sorcerers as was Tezcatlipoca, and in fact he appears to escape any such definition, if we mean by this a fundamental orientation. If the buccal mask that he wears as Ehecatl had indeed once been a duck's bill, we might then conclude that such an animal was his *nahualli*. If it was so considered in the far-distant Mesoamerican past, then the buccal mask will have come down finally in vestigial form. But nothing in the sources allows us to claim the duck as the god's *nahualli*. Sorcery was never an important part of Quetzalcoatl's nature, for sorcery is particular, not cosmic, in its applications. Being derivative from the sky, Quetzalcoatl was ultimately constrained by periodicity, orderliness, and consecution. That was the very opposite of the condition of things as experienced by the sorcerer.

In brief, then, I do not know why Quetzalcoatl is referred to as a *nahualteuctli*, and I must assume, therefore, that it is merely an attempt by his priests to claim for their god a full set of supernatural skills. That would be understandable.

Quetzalcoatl and the Tonalpohualli

It was inevitable that some kind of periodic function should be acquired by the numen of the sky and objectified in an avatar. Wind, which is not reducible to intervals, is certainly not concerned here, but the sun and the planet Venus, for obvious reasons, are. When we say this, we are instantly introduced to the *tonalpohualli*.

The two great celestial antagonists, sun and planet, have a

startling coincidence in their periods. The synodical period of the planet Venus ranges from 581 to 587 days, and the average of these is 584. Five of these averaged periods equal 2,920 days, which exactly, and to us unaccountably, equal precisely the number of days in eight solar years. To the Aztecs, however, this was not unaccountable. Four was the sacred number, as was its consummator, five. By doubling four, one created a whole number enclosing a hiatus that was simultaneously both a beginning and an ending. In the heavens five and eight displayed their essential coincidence when they came together at the end of 2,920 days, at which nodal point sun and planet completed and began again their life together. The knowledge of this astronomical coincidence was one of the seminal discoveries of the Mesoamerican cultures.

When one counts things in large numbers, the counting involves reassembling the count into clusters or bundles, whether the clusters be four, five, nine, thirteen, twenty, or whatever. So is born the science of numeration. In Mesoamerica the science was put to the service not of mathematics but of divination and its handmaiden, history.

If mathematics had appeared in Mesoamerica and had been used only as a tool, then for the priests the concept of time would have diminished to the study of the relationships among the agreed-upon clusters with no relevance to man himself. Divination seized center stage, however, and caused the priests to view integers and bundles of numbers as gods in themselves. Time was thus not so much a counting as a matter of gods seen in terms of their wills and jurisdictions. The reverse of this was also true. Time had no separate meaning to the Mesoamericans—conceptually there was no such thing as time; there was only a mysterious, though still determinate, world of gods, each different but all constantly on the march, each shouldering his own baggage of integers and bunches. Time was an eerie parade, with many passing by at once but all at varying speeds. The clever man could make sense out of this, sort out the periods and read their meanings, but it was a parlous skill at best. Much indoctrination was required.

Quetzalcoatl had been the organizer of this mantic knowledge, all of it finally to be assembled in the *Tonalamatal*, the *Book of Destiny Days*. It was he, in consultation with the high gods, who had originated the *tonalpohualli*, the "count of destiny days," which was the subject matter of the aforementioned book.[34] His priests kept enlarging this learning by the addition of astronomical cycles; in some instances, as among the Mayas, the priests carried it to miracles of computation.

The word *tonalpohualli* can also be translated as "roster of days," but those days are not exactly the same days as those that add up to 365 in the solar year. On the contrary, they are 260 days in a spectral year that is forever floating across the face of the solar year and to the Mesoamerican was surely as important as the solar year. The difference is that the solar year (*xihuitl*) is defined by the successive festivals of the greater gods while the *tonalpohualli* belongs to an unnamed numen, a kind of Sibylline entity, who orchestrates the wills and personalities of the 260 gods involved. We would be wrong to call this numen Fate, but there is a resemblance. As far as I know, the Nahua peoples had no name for it. The only place where this numinous force comes out into the open is in the *Tonalamatl*, where the characteristics of the 260 days are to be found. Only trained priests could read and copy this book, for which skill they looked back to Quetzalcoatl the priest. Yet Quetzalcoatl is not the god of the *tonalpohualli*, though he is said to have organized it. Rather he is the only one among all the gods who had the wisdom to understand it. In brief, we must look upon the *tonalpohualli* as a supernatural force independent of the gods, or, better still, as a whirlpool of such forces.

The reason we are here separating the *tonalpohualli* from

the world of gods and spirits in the mythologies is just because it did posit a power that the Aztecs could not name or philosophically isolate—even though they made a place for it in their religion.[35] Indeed they profoundly felt its existence, but they seem not to have realized the essential disorder of its world as opposed to the orderly consecution of the *xihuitl*, the year with regulated cult practices and eternally repetitive seasons.

Of all his attributes Quetzalcoatl had none as distinctive as that of his connection with the *tonalpohualli*. Here he was concerned with the spirit of each one of its 260 days—in short with each day's quality as a godling. This meant that, whereas an individual might typically view a new day as merely the beginning of the visible course of the sun through the heavens, he could also view it quite differently, namely as an indivisible and motionless whole within the *tonalpohualli*, carrying a meaning distinct from that of the day that preceded or the day to follow. Each of these days was a precursory matrix, and the newborn child was related to his birth date as surely as he was related to his mother. That relationship was set, and it determined the essential role that the person would play in his lifetime. The total of all possible days was 18,980, the sum of which equals 52 years, a full round of time. There were, therefore, that many fates.

What we have said above about the *tonalpohualli* has to be matched with what was said about it in mythology. The story begins in Tamoanchan. There in a cave lives the high goddess Oxomoco. She is paired with Cipactonal, which is the first date name in the *tonalpohualli* (in the form *cipactli*) and which has been here masculinized as her consort.[36] Cipactonal in fact is seen to play the role of the red light of dawn as it floods up out of the dark earth.[37] In the myth the two are the primordial deities of the first aeon. When Cipactonal is presented as masculine, we can best understand him as an avatar of Quetzalcoatl. Literally translated, the name means Day Sign of the Cipactli. In one of our sources Cipactonal is said to have been the same as Patecatl, a god of strong drink,[38] and we know that the latter was one of the avatars of Quetzalcoatl. This would seem to confirm my statement that Cipactonal was a form of Quetzalcoatl. Whatever the meaning behind these relationships, they call attention to the fact that Quetzalcoatl as a culture hero has others standing around him.

When Oxomoco and Cipactonal consulted their grandson Quetzalcoatl about what should be the first sign of the *tonalpohualli*, the decision was made in Tamoanchan.[39] We have seen that the name Tamoanchan is Mayan and means Place of the Moan-Bird Serpent,[40] which place mythologically specifies the sky as the source of waters. The Moan bird was the screech owl, and because it was a night creature, we may suspect that it is primarily the night sky that is referred to as Tamoanchan.[41] But Tamoanchan was more than just the scenario of the sky religion, a heavenly place inhabited by Maya gods and goddesses and the seat of all good things. It was, at least in the latter part of the Classic period, identified with one of Quetzalcoatl's great centers, the city whose ruins are today called Xochicalco in the present state of Morelos. Investigations in and around Xochicalco have shown that the site ritually preserved the records of significant calendar adjustments for cities of the adjoining regions[42]—an activity quite in keeping with what we know about the god himself. The myth tells us that Oxomoco and Cipactonal devolved upon Quetzalcoatl the right to initiate the *tonalpohualli* by choosing its first sign. We have almost a visual match for that in a codex, which shows the commissioning of Quetzalcoatl in the thirteenth heaven by the two high gods, Ometeuctli and Omecihuatl. The triad of gods in the myth and the painted picture are similar. Sky, in other words, was charged by authority (the two high gods) with doing and moving the basic things, among which was the establishment of the *tonalpohualli*.

Without question Oxomoco and Cipactonal were two very ancient gods, and the intimate relationship that Quetzalcoatl has with them confirms his own antiquity. They belonged probably to that unnamed Mesoamerican culture which first produced the *tonalpohualli* and its amazing offspring, the Calendar Round. In that culture, as I have said, Quetzalcoatl was given the distinction of being its coinventor. One can guess that the canonization of an archaic *tonalpohualli* took place as early as the middle of the second millennium B.C. If so, then Quetzalcoatl as a predestinarian culture hero should be even older.

In one sense the creation of the *tonalpohualli* posits a far more sophisticated cosmogony than either the myth of the five suns or the myth of the creation of the fifth sun in Teotihuacán. Oxomoco and Cipactonal, looking out upon the unregulated nature of all life, both divine and human, chose in their wisdom to call into being an ordering device. The situation that was before them at that moment of decision was not one involving nature, for that would imply that nature existed in the shape of chaos, and chaos is not in question at that point. Rather, the situation to be remedied was specifically the lack of culture. They therefore projected the *tonalpohualli*. This turned out to be a roster of all the divinities of the universe, possibly thirteen in their original number, but certainly twenty as finally developed. To this roster of twenty, which had become a list of twenty named gods or nature spirits, was added another list of thirteen gods. The thirteen gods quickly faded away, however, and were remembered only as numbers. These two lists, twenty gods and thirteen numbers, were then set revolving upon each other, each in their immutable order—the result being a bundle of 260 days. Each one of the twenty gods was symbolized by an appropriate sign, and each one of the thirteen gods was symbolized by an appropriate number. In every case each of the symbols or numbers still carried the hazard or the good fortune of the original god. So each one

141

of the 260 days was influenced from two directions and was thus an augural composite. No 2 out of the entire set of 260 could be alike.

It would be delightful if we could recover the full rationale for the choice of the identity of the twenty gods and the reasons for putting them in a canonical order. In the myth the difficulty of settling on the name of the all-important first day was overcome when Quetzalcoatl, wisest of the wise, decided that it should be 1-*cipactli*, or 1-crocodile. This evokes "earth" and, therefore, Oxomoco herself. The rest easily followed. *Ehecatl*, "air," Quetzal-coatl's own name, followed as 2-wind. In other words, Quetzalcoatl himself followed Oxomoco. The day 2-wind was followed by 3-house, a symbol for dark interiors and one that stood for the jaguar god of the underworld, and so on, thirteen sets each of twenty signs listed always in their unchangeable order. Thus, when finally constructed, the list properly began by recalling the three cosmic levels, earth, sky and underworld. When the full 260 were painted in the *Tonalamatl*, the trained priest (*tonalpouhqui*) could read the proper fate or quality attached to each. Every child born had been sent down from the heavens by the high gods, who had assigned to it the particular day of its birth and therefore its destiny.[43] For good or evil, all was in an order known to Quetzalcoatl.

We can see that the *Tonalamatl* was in no sense a calendar as we understand it today but an instrument for the plotting of horoscopes and a plan of the structure of fate. Briefly, it was an almanac used in forecasting. As far as we can see, unlike our astrology, it did not read the fates directly from stellar positions and conjunctions in the zodiac but read them in terms of complex day-and-date revolutions.

With the passage of many centuries Oxomoco and Cipactonal eventually fell back into religious obscurity, being superseded by other gods, and thus they left Quetzalcoatl, who retained his importance, as the central character in the myth. So a tale could finally be told that Quetzalcoatl was not the grandson of Oxomoco and Cipactonal but that he and Tezcatlipoca had created them as the first human couple, from whom all men are derived.[44] Thus he finally appeared as the sole creator of the *tonalpohualli*.

The *tonalpohualli* was axial in the sky religion. This is proved by an examination of its sixteen movable feasts, which are defined as being spotted not in the calendar but in the *Tonalamatl*. Of these sixteen Quetzalcoatl and Tezcatlipoca are celebrated in four, the female sky demons (*cihuapipiltin*) in three, the sun in one, and Camaxtli, *qua* Huitzilopochtli, in one. Three others are mixed and concern the mating of sun and earth to produce abundance. Thus exactly nine of the movable feasts are concerned solely with the sky, whereas the religions of fire and earth divide among them only four.

While the above ideas were evolving among the Mesoamerican priests, the anomaly of having two contradictory concepts of "day" became apparent. On the one hand a solar day (*ilhuitl*) was one of a group of 365, and it had a seasonal and agricultural importance for the society as a whole. On the other hand, an augural day (*tonalli*) was one of a group of 260 that largely determined the fortunes of individuals. When placed side by side, these 2 "days" were seen to be disparate in quality, while in their total numbers they were incommensurable. The resolution to this dilemma, of importance for all of Mesoamerica, was advanced when, at an unknown time and in an unknown place, some priests invented an accommodation. They locked the calendar and the almanac together on their initial days, as we have said before, and then set them in motion revolving on each other, each day changing its partner 18,980 times, a period equal to fifty-two years—this bringing the two groups back to where they began again simultaneously on their initial days. Scholars refer to this as the Calendar Round, and it is thought to have come into existence at least by 1200 B.C.

The fifty-two year period, or lustrum, that was thus discovered became immediately something far more than either a calendrical entity or a horoscope. It became the final definition of the nature of time itself, for the expiration of a lustrum meant that time at a precise point either would begin again or would not. The infinitesimal hiatus between two lustrums was therefore no longer centered on the individual (through the *tonalpohualli*) or even on his society (through the solar calendar) but on the entire universe of gods and men. This meant that, when the collapse of the fifth sun and the extinction of time should occur, it would have to come at one of the junctures uniting two lustrums. Over such great wisdom as this Quetzalcoatl presided.

The *tonalpohualli* is one of man's most arbitrary inventions. It was an attempt to measure and thus to control the fluctuations of fate. Many peoples in the past have given fate a name—Tyche, Fortuna, or whatever—and have let it go at that, knowing it to be unlimited, uninterested and alien. Mesoamerican fate, as made evident in the *tonalpohualli*, was a trifle different. It was neat, knowable, and therefore to some extent pliable. However complicated it might be, it still showed a well-engineered form. With care one could become more and more expert in its interpretation and manipulation. Quetzalcoatl was the god who could read and teach to others the signs, and, therefore, while he could not be said to have invented fate, it was he who discovered the secrets of its curious consecutions of signs and numbers and codified them.[45] In the performance of this task he was a culture hero of notable stature.

Quetzalcoatl and Time

The sky dragon must originally have had one broadly imagined definition, as well as several more partial and concrete ones. All of these were able, of course, to intermingle in a kaleidoscopic effect like a dance of avatars around an altar. Many meanings could be drawn from this celestial quadrille, the most obvious being that concerned with the sky's periodicity, namely the oscillation between light and gloom. Sky provides early man with practically his only challenge to intellectual speculation and measurement. Once speculation has started, however, it creates in societies the need for what we might call "speculation maintainers," or priests. A hierarchy is then called for, which in turn imposes on the priests a need to expand the cult. The latter, however, is unrelated to the substance of my theme, and so I only mention it here.

In discussing Quetzalcoatl's implications in time, we are almost wholly limited to Aztec sources, which themselves look back to earlier cultures. To the Aztec man, time moved in a staccato rhythm—five aeons in all, each separated from the others by a chasm of nontime. The quality of this Aztec time was progressive, sacred, and finite. As is well known, the five aeons were defined as gigantic days, or suns, and each of these suns was a different solar avatar, the first four standing in the order of elements, earth, air, fire, and water, which when translated into gods usually come out as Tezcatlipoca, Quetzalcoatl, Tlaloc, and Chalchiuhtlicue. The fifth sun, which is the present age and the last, has been something of a puzzle. As an element of nature it represents "movement," *olin*, or "earthquake," and the god into which this sun translates is Nanahuatl, who is a form of Xolotl, who in turn is Quetzalcoatl's twin and avatar. No more than five suns are possible; thus Nanahuatl is the last of the solar avatars. From this we can see that Quetzalcoatl is the most prominent god in this unfolding of time, for he is the only one who is twice represented, once as himself and once as an avatar. As the second sun he is air, one of the four natural elements; as the fifth sun he is a force for final destruction and a way to seal up forever the divagations of time. Note how differently the Maya thought about time. They saw time as infinite and stressed its basic indivisibility.[46] For the Mayas time itself was a divinity, though, like fate, it had no name. For the Aztecs time was the name for the organization of the universe, in brief its underlying pattern. Both peoples took time seriously and were acutely aware of the shared nature of past and future time.

The Aztec myth of the five suns is not so much a creation myth as a tale of ordering. It begins with the four divine children of the original pair. It is these four who decide upon the act of cosmic arrangement, but they then depute the matter to two of their number, Tezcatlipoca and Quetzalcoatl. Most interestingly, the arranging of this universe is not precedent to the appearance of the first sun but follows the collapse of the sky at the end of the fourth sun. To repair the cosmic damage, as I have pointed out before, Tezcatlipoca and Quetzalcoatl transform themselves into two dragons who coil themselves around the earth monster and divide her into two parts. It is the installation of the sky that is the main point of this cosmogony. Elsewhere we learn that the two demiurges first traced out the Milky Way across the heavens, and that this marvel took place on the first day of the year. The focus of interest is on the sky, not on the earth.

In the Maya area we find the primordial claims of sky also clearly displayed. "All by itself sky existed," says the *Popol Vuh*; "the face of the earth was not yet visible."[47] Only then are mentioned the formless waters in which lie abeyant the two divine beings, Tepeu (Majesty) and Gukumatz (Feathered Serpent). A higher numinous being, who is really four gods and who is called the Heart of Heaven, presides over the wide world.[48] It is he who enjoins the two to create all things, which they then proceed to do, beginning with the earth.

Although widely separated in time and space, the two cosmogonies, Aztec and Mayan, described above are almost identical. Their celestial orientation is clear. Both posit an authority in the sky that is glossed as four consulting gods and that authorizes the action. Companion demiurges then appear, in both myths conceived as serpentine and celestial. Quetzalcoatl is specifically named in both myths as one of the two dragons, and in the Maya version it is almost certain that the companion god Tepeu is the equivalent of Tezcatlipoca. Thus in both myths the two demiurges are identical pairs. Such a close affinity is impressive. It assures us that we can see Quetzalcoatl as essentially the same divine being wherever he is found in Mesoamerica.

Acting in concert with a companion god, Quetzalcoatl is thus found at the very sources of Mesoamerican time. Before these two there did exist a high level of supernatural beings, but this level is there simply to confirm the supernatural context in which action can take place. Tezcatlipoca and Quetzalcoatl are the protagonists who translate into actuality a preexistent potential toward cosmos.

But Quetzalcoatl also wets his feet in other oceans. He not only stands at the springs of Mesoamerican time but, along with the same companion, stands at its end. In the person of his son Nanahuatl he is the fifth and final sun, which will come to an end when Tezcatlipoca steals it out of the sky. The world's end is prophesied to take place on a day 4-movement, a date name for the fifth sun. Four Movement is another name for Quetzalcoatl's dark and deformed avatar, Xolotl, to be described later.

It is difficult to make a judgment on the quality of Quetzalcoatl as he encases time from its beginning to its end. The acknowledged god of time as we know it was Xiuhteuctli, who is both the Old God and the Lord of the Year. If any deity fully symbolized time (*cauitl*), it was surely he. Yet I can find no connection between him and Quetzalcoatl. It may be that what the Mesoamerican peoples revered in Xiuhteuctli, the god of fire who sat deep in the center of the earth, was the passage of historic time, while in Quetzalcoatl, a sky god, they revered time as future-oriented.

And yet, unaccountably, while many tales were told about Quetzalcoatl, it seems that no myths of any consequence whatsoever were told about Xiuhteuctli.

It is Quetzalcoatl's derivation from the sky dragon (out of whose periodicity came the original impulsion to chart time) that is in question here. Quetzalcoatl is not himself a symbol of time, but the nature matrix out of which he came could and did eventuate in solar and stellar observations and computations, whence the connection between the god and time per se. The amazing intellectual products arising out of such a connection encouraged the priests to accept Quetzalcoatl as the patron of their wisdom. Xiuhteuctli, who was warmth and the preparation of food, remained tied to the hearth fire and its daily service during the solar year. There is nothing surprising in this. Xiuhteuctli thus became the god of the calendar with its rigid recurrence of seasons and festivals, while Quetzalcoatl became the god of the priests, who understood the periods of time and used them prophetically.

Chichén Itzá, in Yucatán, was one of the cities sacred to Quetzalcoatl. His temple there, the Castillo, is a remarkable and superbly designed building. It is really an architectural glyph proclaiming the god's prescience. Ninety-one steps lead to the top on each of the four sides, plus an additional step on the north side.[49] They total 365 and refer to the number of solar ascents and descents in the sky. The bulk of the pyramid, therefore, represents not a mountain, as one might think, but the celestial vault itself. In addition to this the Castillo is made up of nine superimposed terraces symbolizing the nine levels of the night sky. Each of the four sides of the pyramid base has fifty-two projecting panels, the number of years in the Calendar Round. The two columns between which one passes into the sanctuary are designed as twin feathered serpents sustaining the sky. Finally, the west stairway was oriented to the summer solstice. In brief, the temple was a complicated symphony of themes from both the calendar and the *tonalpohualli*. The god who was in the shrine was thus identified not only with the sky but with the complex calculations of fate as well. Here, translated into stone, Quetzalcoatl's special connection with time was made manifest.

Quetzalcoatl and Tlaloc in Teotihuacán

The often-quoted statement of Sahagún that Quetzalcoatl as the wind was the herald and road sweeper of Tlaloc presents him to us as a mere subordinate of that great god of rain. Yet another source defines him as a "friend and relative" of Tlaloc, while a relief from Tajín shows the two closely associated in cult.[50] The Aztecs variously identified both Quetzalcoatl and Tlaloc as gods honored in the first festival of their year, as though they were not sure which god it really was.[51] The fact that the little winds (*ecatotontin*) have a relationship to Quetzalcoatl which is a duplication of the relationship of the *tlaloque* to Tlaloc also points to a connection. We see from the codices that in Four Wind, an avatar of Quetzalcoatl, we are faced with a god who is an obvious fusion of the two.[52] Up to now we have been assuming the uniqueness of Quetzalcoatl. Could it be that this assumption is questionable? Quetzalcoatl's nature will not be adequately probed until he is set beside Tlaloc, and the two are compared.

Both Tlaloc and the sky dragon had existed in Olmec times. The Olmec god who is depicted full face at Chalcatzinco has the goggle eyes and the pointed cap of Tlaloc; thus we may assume him to have been Tlaloc's prototype, if not the fully formed god himself. While this particular representation cannot be dated accurately, it must be placed somewhere between the middle and the end of the second millennium B.C. The sky dragon of that early period is also depicted in the same complex of rock carvings; thus it would appear that the dragon is differentiated from the Tlaloc god. From this we can argue that it is permissible to refer to the Olmec sky dragon as Quetzalcoatl. In our late Aztec sources Tlaloc is the storm king, a mountain god who is custodian of the clouds that appear around the peaks; therefore, he is of the earth, whereas Quetzalcoatl was always celestial, being wind and the planet Venus, and further back, the sky itself. The two gods are quite differently constructed.

Artistic and archaeological evidence for both gods is plentiful in Teotihuacán. We can for the first time be certain of a developed religion of Quetzalcoatl supported by a powerful sacerdotalism in that city. The positioning of his temple in the exact center of the city bears this out, as does the great number of subsidiary shrines surrounding it. Quetzalcoatl's shrine was erected early, sometime between A.D. 200 and 300. Yet two greater temples, those of the Sun and the Moon, preceded it. A possible interpretation for this priority of the other two deities is that the religious constitution of the state as understood by the populace had already been set by the time the more elite priesthood of Quetzalcoatl became powerful. This could imply a change in rulers, where a hypothetical dynasty from the coast moved in with its own national god, that is, Quetzalcoatl.

About A.D. 650, after centuries of grandeur, the city Teotihuacán began giving evidence of population contraction, and around 700 the city was destroyed in a catastrophic conflagration. By 750 the city was to all intents and purposes deserted. It was during these last centuries that artistic representations of armed and bellicose deities became more common. Quetzalcoatl, however, remained prominent in the art throughout all the centuries and survived to the end.

From the archaeological evidence we can be sure that Teotihuacán was a theocratic state, and it is reasonable to expect that its decline will have been accompanied by—

perhaps even precipitated by—drastic cult confrontations. This antagonism must have involved all the gods but particularly those whose priesthoods were the most entrenched. In the archaeological record Cholula does not participate in the dire events that overwhelmed Teotihuacán and would logically then have been the site to which the remaining Quetzalcoatl cultus was transferred. Furthermore Cholula was a center of Quetzalcoatl ritual perhaps as ancient as that of Teotihuacán; certainly it was a venerable pilgrimage center. Admittedly, this is a reconstruction of the events that may have taken place, but at least the archaeological evidence does not contradict it.

Besides the archaeological record, however, I believe that there is historical evidence as well, though it is carefully disguised. A short but useful summary about the city of Tula is found in Sahagún.[53] It is presented as though it referred to the Toltec capital, that is the city in the present state of Hidalgo. Sahagún points to that city as the place where both the year count (*cexiuhtlapohualli*) and the count of augural days (*tonalpohualli*) were first used. The priests there were learned in star lore, they knew about the various levels of the heavens, and they worshiped the high gods, Ometeuctli and Omecihuatl, who ruled over the twelve levels below them, they by implication being in the topmost, or thirteenth, level.

The name of the city—Tullan in Nahuatl—was a generic term referring to any commanding metropolis, however, not just to the city in Hidalgo. Teotihuacán was also known as Tula. Now all the details adduced by Sahagún almost certainly fit Teotihuacán better than they do the capital of the Toltecs. The latter was immersed in its military-sacrificial cult and seems to have been on a perpetual war footing. Teotihuacán on the other hand was dedicated to commerce and the priestly arts in the days of its apogee, all of which is consistent with Sahagún's information.

I believe that the above identification of Tula as Teotihuacán also applies to the famous tale of Quetzalcoatl as Topiltzin, his priesthood, his temptation at the hands of an evil god, and his subsequent exile. This great corpus of stories will be analyzed *in extenso* toward the end of this book. Here I must state my belief that those tales originally referred to Teotihuacán and were only later applied to the Toltec capital. My reasons for transposing the events of those stories to an age four hundred years earlier than usually thought will be given later. Now the Aztecs who passed the stories on to the Spaniards were unable in their historical thinking to separate the Teotihuacanos from the Toltecs. To them the entire millennium past, which included the two successive cultures in the area just north of Lake Tezcoco, Teotihuacano and Toltec, was indivisible. There was undoubtedly the knowledge among the Aztecs that historically the ruins of Teotihuacán preceded the ruins of the Hidalgo Tula, but mythical and legendary material from the two cultures would not have been rigorously allocated.

All that we know archaeologically about Quetzalcoatl in Teotihuacán shows that he was important and that he was involved in the sciences of computation and augury. After the fall of that great city this would not have been easily forgotten, and his mythology and legend there might easily have been attributed to the successor city, Tula in Hidalgo, which was in any case less than twenty-five miles away. We thus have two channels of knowledge leading to an understanding of Quetzalcoatl in Teotihuacán, the archaeological evidence and the written material purporting to refer to the Toltec Tula.

The archaeological material from Teotihuacán shows a developed cult, for Quetzalcoatl appears there both as a dragon and as a priest. So far as I know, he and Tezcatlipoca are the only Mesoamerican gods depicted duomorphically. Other deities can have other forms—generally animal—as their *nahualli*, but the *nahualli* forms cannot

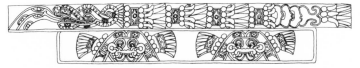

Figure 20

stand alone as the designated god and as him only. The Feathered Serpent, however, is always to be interpreted as Quetzalcoatl.

In Teotihuacán the dragon is plainly portrayed as an overarching sky motif, a path for stellar objects. He is a plumed rattlesnake, and he is often paired or twinned. He can also be identified, from the quincunx (the five points that together form the emblem of the morning star) that adorns him, as the planet Venus (fig. 20). As a dragon his head is that of either a serpent or a quetzal bird with floods of water occasionally pouring out of his mouth. When he appears as the priest-god, he wears the dragon helmet with a huge quetzal-feathered crest. He dispenses signs of fertility and seems to be speaking of the virtues of human sacrifice. Sometimes he casts out over the earth the visible signs of holiness and sacrifice, heads, hands, hearts, dogs, buccal masks, and so forth. In his priestly guise he is also associated with the quincunx.

In the design of his temple in Teotihuacán, where the dragon head alternates with the masked Tlaloc head, Quetzalcoatl reveals his close association with Tlaloc.[54] We are aware that the latter, being clearly seasonal, could stand for the solar year, or *xihuitl*, and accordingly in Teotihuacán he wears as a headdress the glyph that, at least in later times, stood for the solar year of 365 days. The temple in question has six tiers, these being the ascent, which when doubled for the descent give twelve, with the shrine on top making up the sacred number thirteen.[55] Four staircases led up to the summit, one on each of the four sides. Each staircase had thirteen steps, the whole equaling fifty-two, the number of years in the Mesoamerican lustrum. Running around all six tiers of the pyramid base were (probably) 366 dragon heads and the same number of Tlaloc heads—this was as close in terms of architectural symmetry as one could come to 365. Thus both the *xihuitl* and the *tonalpohualli* were recognized in the temple's plan. The corollary is that the respective patron gods whose heads are there displayed, Quetzalcoatl and Tlaloc, had a close identity. All of this implies a sophisticated priesthood adept in accommodation.

Images of Tlaloc in Teotihuacán are not easily categorized.[56] The basic Tlaloc appears to be crocodilian in nature and to represent water, therefore as being terrestrially derived. This is the Tlaloc who later becomes the Mesoamerican mountain king, an earth deity who emits rain clouds and hurls the lightning from the crags. Although both Quetzalcoatl and Tlaloc are sources of water and consequently are fertility-oriented, the terrene source (Tlaloc) is strictly limited to that conceptual role, whereas the celestial source (Quetzalcoatl) plays many other roles as well: wind, lineage patron, morning star, and others. Depictions of Quetzalcoatl in Teotihuacán show that, while he necessarily and importantly overlaps Tlaloc in the water sphere, they are nevertheless separate gods and are not avatars of each other but companions.

The sophistication of Quetzalcoatl's cult in Teotihuacán can be seen in the presence there of his two most important avatars, the evening star (Xolotl)[57] and the morning star (Ce Acatl). I shall discuss both of these at length later; here I merely note how early such major elements of the god's mythology appeared. A particularly fine representation from the period shows Quetzalcoatl as a human face held in the jaws of the dragon, while the ornate crest of quetzal feathers features the wind jewel.[58] The head itself is shown emerging out of a mounded form, undoubtedly to symbolize the earth at dawn, which is glossed with skulls and wind jewels, a perfect symbolization of the Ce Acatl we know from later Aztec times (fig. 23).

The affinity of Quetzalcoatl for Tlaloc lasts down through Aztec times. The connection of both with serpents continues without interruption. Tlaloc occasionally appears in an avatar called Epcoatl, the Mother-of-Pearl Dragon, and the goggles and mask that he always wears are often made of coiling snakes.

Both Quetzalcoatl and Tlaloc were of first-rate importance in the pantheon, and their alliance is always obvious. In one listing of thirteen gods they together stand at the head of the list.[59] In myth each of them becomes one of the five suns. "Wind" and "rain" are both day signs in the *tonalpohualli*. Both gods stand for the withholding or the presence of abundance. In Cholula, Quetzalcoatl would seem to be almost a double of Tlaloc in his avatar Nine Rain. As the god Five Wind, Quetzalcoatl is definitely one of the Tlalocs who bring rain. Both gods are connected with trees. In the feast of the first month Tlaloc is represented by one of the great fir trees brought down from the mountains and called Tota, Father. In myth we have already seen that Quetzalcoatl became one of the trees supporting the heavens, and in Cholula he could additionally be worshiped as the Tree of Our Substance. These are just a few random examples of the nexus that binds the two gods together.

All of the above can be explained. Water and snakes were thought to be coincidental by the preliterate mind. It is therefore no wonder that the storm king of the mountains and the god of hurricanes should resemble each other. Tlaloc's guardianship of the waters stored in the mountains was universal, and so he controlled all mountains and the clouds that formed around them. With Quetzalcoatl the case was different. Only when his name was given to a mountain did he become a Tlaloc.[60] In Cholula the great pyramid was thought to be a mountain, which is why it was understood to contain waters within it. Finally, epiphanies in the forms of trees are not unusual for gods who control aspects of fertility.

The hypothesis of the existence of a single god who was then split to become two is essentially a weak one. What basically aligns Quetzalcoatl and Tlaloc is their mutual implication in fertilizing clouds and water—that and that only. What differentiates them is the disparity in the source of those waters. Tlaloc controls tellurian waters, arcane pools within the earth that are seen to issue as springs from the mountainside and as clouds from the peaks. In his avatar as Ehecatl, Quetzalcoatl does move among the *ahuaque*, the clouds, scattering them about—but his waters are clearly celestial. They fall, often catastrophically, from the ocean in the sky. Tlaloc's rain comes in answer to prayers and offerings. Except in Cholula, Quetzalcoatl's rain was not sought, at least not in Aztec times. After all, one might well distrust any rain that was flung about at second hand by the violence of the wind. This removal of Quetzalcoatl by one step from rain bringing meant that his control of abundance was thought of in very general terms; it could be not only the seasonal harvests but commercial wealth as well.

The two gods differ greatly in appearance. Both wear buccal masks, but they are otherwise dissimilar.[61] Tlaloc's mouth mask is serpentine, whereas Quetzalcoatl's, whatever it may be, is definitely not associated with snakes. Yet this all seems backward, for of the two we would expect the latter, who is the Feathered Serpent, to wear a serpent's mask.

The rest of the regalia of the two gods is also unlike. Tlaloc wields the thunderbolt (shown as an ax) and the lightning (shown as a snake). Only very occasionally does Quetzalcoatl carry these symbols. Quetzalcoatl carries the priest's incense bag, the penitential thorns, and the *xone-*

cuilli. Tlaloc carries instead a thick flowering rush and a shield with the design of a water plant. Here the distinction between them is pronounced.

When converted into multiple smaller gods, the two are also distinct. The Tlalocs were thought of as dwarves or small gods, and because of that they were believed to prefer children as sacrificial offerings. Only in Cholula, where his temple was thought of as a mountain, are child sacrifices recorded for Quetzalcoatl. The images of the mountains were called *tepicme* and were squat, legless mounds of dough with inserted corn kernels as eyes. The images of the winds, the *ecatotontin*, on the other hand, were made of dough plastered over gnarled tree roots and branches, being thus depicted as snakes.[62]

Again the parts that the two play in the calendar are different. Tlaloc can wear the year sign, as we have seen; Quetzalcoatl cannot. This may reflect the dominant role played by Tlaloc in the calendar, where he appears in seven of eighteen monthly festivals, whereas Quetzalcoatl appears briefly in only four of them. Tlaloc's cult reflected mankind's immemorial anxiety about food. Quetzalcoatl's role was more diluted. Tlaloc was a testy god who was served by a vast state priesthood. Quetzalcoatl represented the interests of more select groups—merchants, priests, and great lineages. Quetzalcoatl's weak hold on solar time is a reflection of the fact that the calendar had been elaborated as an aid to the toiler in field, and to a great extent it always retained that orientation. The calendar was in fact pro-Tlaloc.

There is a poem reputedly composed by the ruler Nezahualcoyotl wherein the poet identifies himself with a god called Ilhuicaateotl, Divine Sky Water, a deity situated in the region of the dawning. The poem appears to designate the east as the land where this god was endowed with his green feathers, his curved scepter (*chicuacolli*), and his fan, all of which recalls Quetzalcoatl. Sky Water is the common Nahuatl term for ocean, and it points to the firmament considered as the floor of a celestial ocean, the great hyaline plate supported by Quetzalcoatl on his shoulders. Divine Sky Waters appears to be the essential Quetzalcoatl, a god far removed from the Tlaloc who lived below him in the hollow places of the mountain.

FOUR
QUETZALCOATL
AS A GOD
OF WARRIORS

In these pages I examine Quetzalcoatl's war-dragon avatar Ce Acatl or One Reed, a far remove from the priestly avatar treated in the preceding chapter. When considering Ce Acatl, one necessarily also discovers two other related gods, the morning star considered as a warrior, Tlahuizcalpanteuctli, and the god Mixcoatl, both connected with the dawn. The entire corpus of Mixcoatl myths is taken under review in some detail because of the paternal relationship of that god with Quetzalcoatl. These two forms of the morning star are seen to be connected with Quetzalcoatl in different ways. The role of the morning star in mythology is found to be so central that the scenario in the myth of the fifth sun is summarized to elucidate the interpenetrability of the sun and the two forms of the planet Venus. A fuller elaboration of the sun's role and his avatars follows, this analysis being necessary to the chapter that follows.

The Warrior Hypothesis

Black Elk, one of the last of the medicine men of the Oglala Sioux, said in reference to the power of the morning star, "Here you see the Morning Star. Who sees the Morning Star shall see more, for he shall be wise." In the great Amerindian complex, of which Mesoamerica is a part, the planet of the dawn had many meanings. It was looked upon as the key to the day. The sun story could not be told without reference to it; the underworld could not be thought of except as its house; the blowing up of the last night's ashes into a red glow for the new morning was like the celestial fire that enfolded that star and finally destroyed it. The wondering Mesoamerican mind could deal in many ways with the restless planet, but two visions of it were common: it was seen as the fount either of wisdom or of valor.

For our purposes this suggests Quetzalcoatl's two avatars, Ehecatl, the wind, and Ce Acatl, the hunter and warrior. We have already considered the first. Here we turn to the second, to him who, according to the Tlascalans, was the most "valiant" of all the gods.[1] At first it seems contradictory to find in one god both heroism and a knowledge of esoterica. We tend to believe that hunting skills and heroism differ radically from the qualities associated with priesthood. This antithesis is one of the many problems connected with Quetzalcoatl.

In the long list of Quetzalcoatl's avatars are three who stand apart from all the others. They form an obvious triad: Tlahuizcalpanteuctli, Mixcoatl, and Ce Acatl. The first is the morning star, the second is the hunter and tribal warrior, and the third is the war dragon. We note that the latter is a date name and therefore presupposes another deity whom it designates or from whom it shoots off. It would seem obvious that one of the other two was this presumed god, and as I develop my theme, I shall give reasons for believing that Ce Acatl was a date name for Mixcoatl.

While all three avatars are tied together by a devotion to war, there is another common denominator that unites them, namely fire. This connection is tenuous but important. We note, for instance, that both Ce Acatl and Tlahuiz-calpanteuctli ruled weeks of the *tonalpohualli* jointly with deities of fire (the eighteenth and twentieth weeks, respectively), and we also know that it was the god Mixcoatl who first drilled fire.[2] Indeed his name was given to one of the three supporting stones of the Aztec hearth.[3] Similarly, among the Tarascans the morning star was known as the High Priest of Fire.[4]

This connection of the three avatars with fire has to do, however, not so much with the hearth as with the fires of dawn and the sparkling star they cast up. In other words, because dawning is an early fire in the sky, therefore fire must be connected with the three gods, all of whom are forms of the morning star. Yet these three are not true gods of fire at all, as was Xiuhteuctli. Xiuhteuctli was an animation of actual flames to be seen in any conflagration. These three were rather gods who were encased in a red glow in the sky. Fire may be said to be their matutinal habitat, whereas Xiuhteuctli, dwelling in the earth's center, was the father of wood fires and volcanic flares—not of fires in the sky.

We begin then with a set of three avatars who can be seen equally as warriors, as spirits in the dawn, and as companions of fire. One of the Maya groups defines this deity as He Who Awakens the Earth—and who is in his appearance a plumed serpent.

The Mixcoatl Corpus of Myths

The most vivid body of speculation about the sky religion that the Aztecs inherited and then made their own is contained in the Mixcoatl cycle of myths. We can isolate five of these myths[5] and arrange them in a roughly logical order as they shift their focus from the Cloud Serpent (Mixcoatl) to the Feathered Serpent (Quetzalcoatl) seen in his avatar as Ce Acatl. It is an interesting, self-contained collection, and it speaks particularly to the problem of this chapter, which is the nature of Ce Acatl. The five myths are paraphrased below. Some have been mentioned before.

The First Myth.[6] The great earth and water goddess whose name was White Jade Skirt produced four hundred sons, who were the first *mimixcoa* ("cloud serpents"). It was Grandmother Maguey, however, who suckled them as they were being reared in the Seven Caves, down in the darkness. Their father was the sun, and he had enjoined them to provide him with food and drink. But this first brood of *mimixcoa* failed dismally in their filial duties, rioting about in drunken fashion and neglecting their parents. In fact, at one point, as they reeled and staggered, they all tumbled down into the ocean. At this point the goddess produced five more *mimixcoa*, who were specifically instructed to subdue the unruly ones. These five were Mixcoatl (Cloud Serpent), Eagle Dragon, Hawk Mountain, Master of Waterways, and Wolf Woman. When finally grown, these filial five ambushed their brothers, killed them, and then with their hearts and blood feasted the hungry parents. Those of the four hundred remaining surrendered the Seven Caves to the heroic five. And thus began the ritual slaying of victims to feed the gods.

A version of this myth is told about Camaxtli, an avatar of Mixcoatl.[7] The numbers of the *mimixcoa* are reversed in this version. The five appeared initially in the eighth heaven and were enjoined to create war as an energizing institution. They fail in this and, wandering aimlessly about, fall into the ocean. They then return to the eighth heaven, while Camaxtli creates an additional four hundred (who are identified as the ancestors of the Chichimecs). Hostilities erupt between the two groups, and out of the resultant sacrifices the gods are finally fed. Camaxtli thus brings war into the world.

The Second Myth.[8] In this myth the four hundred *mimixcoa* are defined as early wandering Chichimecs, that is, the ancestors. Itzpapalotl, a goddess of fire, captured and ate them. Only White Mixcoatl escaped. He hid in a great cactus that defied all the goddess's attempts to rip it apart. Finally he reappeared, summoned up the four hundred, and with them turned the tide of battle. They shot the goddess to death with arrows, afterward burning her body. From her ashes they ground the black paint for the eye masks that thereafter distinguished the *mimixcoa* and all mortals when they dressed for war.

The Third Myth.[9] Two of the *mimixcoa*, Xiuhnel and a younger brother, Mimich, one sunset went tracking a pair of two-headed deer who had descended from the sky and then turned into women.[10] One of them gave Xiuhnel blood to drink, whereupon he raped her and then sacrificed and ate her. The other brother then drilled fire, into which the remaining woman disappeared. Mimich leaped after her into the fire. In this incendiary world he followed her all night and until the following midday, when he finally caught up with her and shot her. The first woman, now a celestial demon, or *tzitzimitl*, reappeared as the goddess Itzpapalotl. Thereupon the fire gods and the two *mimixcoa* threw her into the fire. In the fierce heat she exploded into five different-colored stone knives. From the five Mixcoatl selected the white knife, wrapped it in a sacred bundle, and thenceforth carried it about on his back. The white knife became his god as he set forth on a career of conquest.

The Fourth Myth.[11] On one of his hunts in the land of Huitznahuac, Mixcoatl once met the gigantic, naked mistress of the land. Her name was Shield Hand. So powerful was she that she scorned to defend herself, easily avoiding the four arrows that he shot at her. He then for a time left the scene, while she retired into a deep cave. But Mixcoatl began molesting the women of the land, who appealed to Shield Hand for redress. She returned and allowed Mixcoatl to copulate with her. In the end she suffered a four-day parturition and died at the birth of the child. This child was Ce Acatl. He was nourished by the goddess Quilaztli.

The Fifth Myth.[12] The sons of Mixcoatl (here the *mimixcoa*) burned with envy of their brother Ce Acatl because he was their father's favorite. In a plot to kill him they found a pretext to send him up onto Burning Rock and then treacherously set fire to the hillside below. Cleverly he escaped death there, after which he hunted down a deer (emblem of the sun), returning with it as a gift to his father. The brothers next lured him up into a high tree and then shot at him with arrows, but he feigned death and again escaped. Afterward he shot a rabbit (emblem of the moon) and brought it as a gift to his father. Mixcoatl discovered the crimes of his sons and rebuked them, whereupon they turned on him, killed him, and secreted his bones in a distant land. On setting out to recover his father's remains, the pious Ce Acatl was told by his brothers that Mixcoatl had been changed into a mountain. He found the mountain and ascended it but was instantly beleaguered by his brothers seeking to dispatch him once and for all. He killed all of them with arrows and then held a great victory celebration.

Another ending to the tale was current.[13] When the bereaved Ce Acatl asked the whereabouts of his missing father, a vulture revealed that he had been murdered by the *mimixcoa* led by Apanecatl and then buried on the Mountain of Mixcoatl. Ce Acatl journeyed there, recovered the bones, and erected a temple on that spot in which to enshrine them. The wicked brothers tried to forestall him but failed, for Ce Acatl had called up the moles to burrow into the mountain. Through the central cavern that they opened up within the mountain he was able to ascend, emerging finally on the peak. The *mimixcoa* attempted to light the sacred fire on the mountaintop, but Ce Acatl forestalled them and was the sole one to perform that important ceremony. He then captured Apanecatl and the other brothers, tortured them, and finally dispatched them by tearing out their hearts.

There are really only two themes in this body of five myths. The first is the introduction of ritual sacrifice as a crucial act in the imposition of a cosmic pattern; the second is an elucidation of the recurrence of the day, using as actors earth, dawn and dusk, the stars, the two phases of the planet Venus, and the nocturnal sun. The myths use the ancient symbol, found in almost all preliterate cultures, of the stars as the issue of sun and earth, but they expand this to also equate the long-dead ancestors, thought of as warriors, with those stars. The *mimixcoa* thus fluctuate ambiguously back and forth between the poles of ancestral and stellar being. Such an ambiguity allows war and sacrifice, which are human activities, to be projected back upon the sky religion and to cast the stars as the sanctifiers of war, its perpetrators as well as its victims.

All the actors in the drama are nature gods, and their identities are easy to arrive at. The *mimixcoa*, as we have seen, are the stars, who are simultaneously celestial demons and the souls of the ancestors. Specifically, the four hundred are the stars in their legions, whereas the five, each named, are early Chichimec deities. Mixcoatl (or Camaxtli) is the central character and is a kind of genius of the night sky, having something to do with the sun descending into the underworld. Ce Acatl is the dawn or the aborning sunlight, seen concretely in the person of the morning star. Itzpapalotl is fire experienced as both the hearth fire and the fires of dawn and dusk. Xiuhnel and Mimich are the traditional hero-twins morning star and sun. Chimalma, or Shield Hand, is the earth.

With the exception of the last, every one of the actors is some aspect of the light, either the setting or the rising sun, the extinguished light of the sun in the total darkness, the evening or the morning star, or the dawn as partial light. With our logic-oriented minds some effort is required to accept the fact that such a rich drama reduces itself to the simple tale of heavenly light and dark sky. A more extended analysis can perhaps be useful.

Taking Itzpapalotl first, we note that in one of the myths she consumes the *mimixcoa*. We can interpret this event as the light, or the fires of dawn, blotting out the stars. Yet the *mimixcoa* revive and with the aid of Mixcoatl shoot her to death. In this event we can recognize night or the starry hosts, led by the declining sun, putting out the fires of sunset. In another myth she appears as sisters, dawn and dusk. She attempts to seduce the descendant sun in the underworld, but is herself consumed as her fires also go out. The other of the two *mimixcoa*, Mimich, who must here be the revived light that is about to appear, also overpowers her, that is, outshines her to become the new day.

Besides being fire—a hearth fire, as it were, in the sky—Itzpapalotl is the knife used for sacrifice in the cult of Mixcoatl. The whiteness associated with the knife is a color symbol sometimes associated with the north, the direction to which Mixcoatl was assigned. From other myths we know that the sacrificial knife descended from the sky, as did Itzpapalotl in myth; in fact, among the Mesoamerican artists a common way to depict the starry sky was to show a band of stars alternating with bloody knives (fig. 21). However incongruous it may seem to us, the Aztecs considered knives to be celestial in origin.

Itzpapalotl is one of the most graphically described of the Mesoamerican goddesses. She is also centrally located in

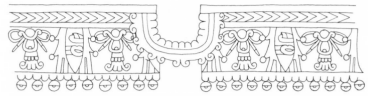

Figure 21

the Mixcoatl mythology. Without her the celestial color of
those tales would not be as striking. Out of her crepuscular
fires glowing under the horizon were born both night and
day. And out of the burning of her body warriors gathered
the charred bits of wood with which they painted black
circles around their eyes. Their eyes were then thought to
be stars glittering through the night. The underworld sun
and the two phases of Venus are given male roles, but
"rosy-fingered dawn" can be female.

Mixcoatl is more difficult to grasp than are his many
brethren. He was thought of as a warrior, a hunter, a merchant, and a star. His warpaint, mentioned above, is shown
in the codices as a black area over the bridge of the nose and
around the eyes, surrounded by white circles that denote
the stars. He carries as his badge of authority the *xonecuilli*
baton, which represents power over his siblings, the stars.
His imagery thus shows him as a genius of the night sky,
which is exactly our understanding of the nature of Quetzalcoatl. But this imagery must be further interpreted. As
the spirit of the night sky, which includes dawn and dusk as
its terminal points, he necessarily also connotes the twin
appearances of the planet Venus, that of the morning and
that of the evening. This further association is made evident
not only by the association of a fire deity with him in his
mythology but additionally by the fact that he was the first
god to drill fire (that is, the dawn), thus bringing it into the
world for gods and men. Dusk and dawn circumscribe his
bailiwick, and night is necessarily an integral part of it.

We can go further still. The night sky we know to be a picture, or a replica, of the underworld. Two contrasting definitions of the underworld were put forth by the Meso-americans: on the one hand, Mictlan, the abode of the dead, and on the other that chill obscurity into which the sun and the evening star dipped together. The latter is the one that concerns us here, for Mixcoatl as the genius of the night sky is also the sun who, as a dying or sacrificed hero, gives meaning to that underworld. Mixcoatl is thus the dead—but ultimately the redeemable—light. We can see that he is in no sense the *sol invictus* that generally informs the myth-ologies of mankind. That role belongs to Tonatiuh, the sun of the daytime, who does not appear in any of these myths.

The fourth and fifth myths describe the great victory, the return of light to the heavens after its burial in the earth. Mixcoatl the sun enters the dark earth (Chimalma) and there produces his successor, who will have two forms, the morning star and a new sun. The fifth myth gives us a great deal of folkloristic detail. It begins with the dusk. The earth at this perilous time bears the name Burning Rock. The sun or the evening star—it is a matter of little moment which—sinks into the underworld as Mixcoatl. In that stifling and deathly place Mixcoatl dies and then reproduces himself as Ce Acatl. The demons of the night, namely the stars, had attacked both father and son down there and had succeeded in killing the former. Mixcoatl is buried in the obscurity of night. The perilous hiatus in legitimacy is bridged when his pious son becomes his successor by penetrating the caverns of earth and retrieving his bones. His appearance on the summit of Mount Mixcoatl is the equivalent of the appear-ance of the morning star over the ridges of the east. His vic-tory in this final myth is seen in that it is he, not the other stars, who can light the ceremonial fire (the dawn). A true son of his mighty father, Ce Acatl (now to be taken as the rising sun) blinds the stars with his light and destroys them. In conclusion he gains their vitality by sacrificing them.

In one sense this is all very confusing; it seems to be a palimpsest of smudged meanings. In another sense it is absurdly simple, if one realizes that all the actors are aspects of the light that disappears in the dusk, is totally extinguished, and then returns in the morning. Each one of the celestial actors can be, as the needs of the tale demand, the sun, the stars, or the planet Venus. Only Itzpapalotl is confined to the role of the crepuscular light and the redness of blood. In one curious sense a cast of actors does not exist at all in these dramas. There is only one actor, Mixcoatl, alone on the stage. He dons and doffs various masks as he moves about, miming the vicissitudes of the embattled light.

Ce Acatl

Ce Acatl is a calendar name and means "1-reed." Date names such as this presuppose a person or god allegedly born on that day who otherwise carries a descriptive personal name. Inasmuch as *ce acatl* is the day on which sky came into being,[14] we may begin by believing that Ce Acatl was once upon a time the sky god given an epithetical name. By the time of the Spanish entry, however, we see Ce Acatl more loosely interpreted as an alter ego of Mixcoatl.

In this more restricted form Ce Acatl ws probably the date name adjudged to Mixcoatl at least as far back as the Toltec period. This near-identity of Mixcoatl and Ce Acatl was broken up by the priests when they cast Mixcoatl and Ce Acatl as father and son. The earlier identity of the two, however, was never forgotten. Ce Acatl is generally coupled with Mixcoatl in both iconography and mythology. And as Mixcoatl is found in close alliance with Itzpapalotl, a fire goddess, so his son Ce Acatl is paired with Chantico, another fire goddess (see fig. 18). There can be little doubt that Ce Acatl is Mixcoatl.

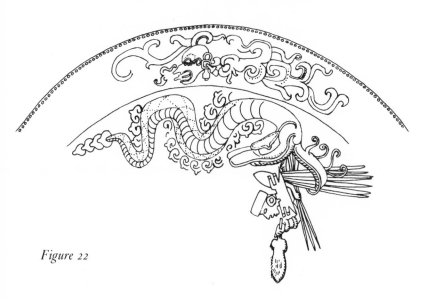

Figure 22

Ce Acatl is Mixcoatl in the form of a dragon or feathered serpent. In other words Ce Acatl is an avatar of the Cloud Serpent *qua* dragon. Inasmuch as the god Mixcoatl is the warrior par excellence, so also is the dragon Ce Acatl a new formation, in the world of chimerical beasts, of the profession of arms, and the cult of sacrifice.

There is an interesting extension of all this into the realm of warfare, so crucial to many of the Mesoamericans. In the reliefs at Chichén Itzá where the dragon rampant appears above the battlefield, we have to see him as the *nahualli*, or élan, of the warrior (fig. 22). This carries the further meaning that the warriors depicted as engaged in combat are "cloud serpents" exactly as are the Chichimecs of Cuauhtitlan, who are specifically said to be *mimixcoa*, or, as we may loosely translate it, "followers of Mixcoatl."[15] The warriors in Tula and Chichén Itzá were *mimixcoa* in the same sense, if we may judge by the rebus writing on their sandals. Inasmuch as the stars were thought of as hosts of regenerated warriors aloft, so warfare on earth must have been interpreted as celestial in all its implications. The warrior served in a surrogate role in the millennial struggle in the heavens. Again it was the sky, not the earth, that provided mankind with a model for his life.

To understand the relationship between Mixcoatl and Ce Acatl more adequately, we can think of the former as the patron god of hunters and warriors, whereas the latter was more simply the quintessence of savagery in war. Ce Acatl was both the warrior who sacrifices and the captive who was sacrificed.

This symbolism is made even more specific in representations of the Feathered Serpent that show it with a knife either in its tail feathers or in its mouth. The most common form of Ce Acatl, however, was the writhing, upended serpent thrashing about in the sky over the battlefield. Oftentimes a warrior is shown outlined against the dragon as if one were a gloss for the other. This dragon is certainly the god of the Toltec squadrons. In a vivid depiction from Chichén Itzá he is rearing up behind a priest who is tearing out a prisoner's heart, while a coil of the dragon's body, arched upward, serves as the *techcatl*, the block over which the victim is pinned awaiting the final blow.[16] In the sky religion these are fundamental icons.

Ce Acatl's closest identification is with the planet Venus rather than with air or windy violence. In Chichén Itzá one can see Venus glyphs encased in each coil of the dragon's body.[17] Also from that site comes the magnificent wooden lintel depicting the cosmic challenge that the morning star offers to the new sun.[18] In this portrayal the radiant sun is seated on his jaguar throne shouting imprecations at Ce Acatl, who is armed and wearing in his hair the two eagle feathers that denote the warrior. Behind him coils his glyphic representation, the dragon. The whole scene takes place *within* the body of the two-headed dragon of the sky. We thus have Quetzalcoatl depicted in three stages or ava-

tars of his existence: the ancient sky dragon, an anthropomorphic Mixcoatl, and the Feathered Serpent, who is Ce
Acatl, the morning star. This scene is the most dramatic
confrontation in all of Mesoamerican mythology, a passage
at arms where the morning star, who is the older brother,
fails to prevent the rising of his younger brother, the sun.
Daybreak is the consequence of that duel.

What the Aztecs are telling us when they declare that the
heavens were created on the day 1-reed is that the role of
Venus is crucial to any understanding of the cosmos. We
shall see later the reverse of the medal, where Venus as the
evening star defeats and sacrifices the sun. The obverse,
which we have described above, shows Venus as the morning star defeated by the sun. The tale can be told with either of two sets of actors, father and son or older and
younger brother. But what we are really being told, however indirectly, is that the sun and the planet Venus, though
separated for the purpose of storytelling, are essentially one
fluctuating unity, each being adequately resolved only
when considered as a gloss on the other.

The true role of the planet Venus in the development of
the Mesoamerican cultures is still not understood. It might
not be far wrong to look upon the Mesoamericans' great
skill in numeration as a child of that planet and to state that
their intellectual life pulsed to its periods. Certainly a significant portion of their mythology involved the planet, and
their concepts of family legitimacy and challenge were colored by the bonds that united the planet to the sun, the
fount of all authority. It is also possible that over the long
centuries the commensurabilities and divergences that obtained between the two helped appreciably to build the
Mesoamericans' view of the cosmos. Particularly impressive to them must have been the fact that five synodic periods of Venus exactly equaled eight solar years and that the
rise-set position of Venus on the horizon swung north to
south and back again, making one such journey to the sun's

eight. The ability to apprehend such gigantic periodicities must have given the Mesoamerican elite a social position that could turn away almost any challenge from below.

Among the Aztecs the magic of such endings and beginnings was celebrated in several festivals, and one in particular should be mentioned here. A most solemn ritual was held every eighth year on the day 1-flower. This festival, the Atamalcualiztli, was not a Venusian cult, and so we need not describe it in detail, but it did, like the eight-year synodic cycle of Venus, advert to and ritually complete that section of time, defining it as the lifetime of the maize. There can be no doubt that the number eight was ascribed to this all-important staple because of the Venusian definition of time.

Tlahuizcalpanteuctli and the Dragon Pillars

When we think of Ce Acatl not as a dragon but as the essential warrior, he is to all intents and purposes indistinguishable from Mixcoatl. But Ce Acatl is also a configuration of Tlahuizcalpanteuctli, who is both the planet Venus and the crepuscular fires of dawn and dusk. Tlahuizcalpanteuctli is the first and last light, and, to comport with his high significance, he inhabits that level of heaven just under the meridian Omeyocan.

The name of this deity is important. It means Lord in the Dawning. The verbal stem is *tlahuia*, signifying a lighting of the way as with a torch held aloft. There is specified about the dawn a host of related concepts, such as redness, heraldry, presagement, and early fire. From the verb is built the noun *tlahuiztli*, "emblem," "insignia," or "coat of arms." *Tlahuizcalli*, the common word for "dawn," might seem to mean therefore "the house of devices or arms," or simply "the armory," but more likely it is to be dissected as "the place of reddening." Possibly both lend their flavor to the word: (1) the appearance of a flambeau held on high in advance of a greater one and (2) a reference to the red east as the scene of recurrent battle and bloodshed. Tlahuizcalpanteuctli is thus a bearer of the light precedent to the sunrise as well as the sun's challenger.

When depicted in the codices, the appearance of the god is completely consistent with this characterization.[19] He is generally painted with red and white body stripes (common also to Mixcoatl and Camaxtli), which indicate the warrior who chances capture and sacrifice. His face is a skull denoting his affinity with the underworld. He is always equipped with the atlatl and darts.

The first appearance of the morning star is described in the mythology of Quetzalcoatl. According to one account it took place at the moment when Quetzalcoatl down on the coast cast himself into the fire.[20] His ashes drifted up into the skies to become a bevy of caroling birds, while his spirit descended into the land of the dead, remaining there for four days moribund and inert. Then for another four days he underwent a transformation into the person of another god, providing himself with darts and preparing for a life of war. Thus at the end of eight days he rose above the horizon as the god Tlahuizcalpanteuctli (fig. 23).

It is clear that Quetzalcoatl's cremation and death relate to the last day on which the evening star was visible in the west, thus beginning the eight-day period of inferior conjunction. After this hiatus the first sighting of Venus again is in the east as the morning star, and equally obviously this appearance is referred to in the rising out of the ashes of Quetzalcoatl's heart, which becomes the god Ce Acatl. In another vein the Aztecs said that Ce Acatl made three attempts to escape from the caverns of the underworld, at each attempt emitting a burst of light. On the fourth attempt the god broke loose and, shining with a baleful and supernal light, frightened all who beheld him.[21] These four bursts of light possibly betoken the four phases of the planet

Figure 23

Venus. For thirty-six days preceding (and for thirty-six days following) inferior conjunction, the planet shines most brilliantly—these appearances were undoubtedly considered to be marvelously baleful.

The intent of the myth in any case is clear. It means—or was intended to achieve—reincarnation. We need not be too concerned with the astronomical calculations. What is crucial is that we have here a statement of the most famous transfiguration of deity in Mesoamerican mythology: Quetzalcoatl, who can normally be thought of as Ehecatl, becomes in this myth a totally distinct god. And the instrument of transposition has been sacrifice by fire; in other words, a celestial deity (sky or wind) has become another but unrelated celestial deity (dawn or the morning star) through burning. The names and the iconography of the two have nothing in common. Ce Acatl can perhaps best be seen as that avatar who spans the gap between the two deities Quetzalcoatl and Tlahuizcalpanteuctli.

It is curious that the Mesoamerican peoples thought of the morning star so consistently as malign. He was to them, whether they were Aztecs or Mayans, the very father of calamity. The dates of his heliacal rising were forecast so that the dooms ahead could be adequately read and prepared for. His sparkling rays became swift darts with which he could strike down various categories of people, or even such crucial gods as Cinteotl and Chalchiuhtlicue.[22] There were five such categories. If the heliacal rising occurred in the *trecena* (a "bundle" of thirteen days) that began with 1-*cipactli*, then the aged were imperiled; if 1-*olin*, then children; and so on. Significantly his malice could also be directed at rulers, for if he arose in the *trecena* opened by 1-reed, then great lords sickened and died. The origin of his malevolence can be guessed. The planet Venus spends a significant part of its career of 485 days under the horizon, where it is of course invisible. During those days therefore the planetary god was contaminated by death and darkness. Wisps of mortal contagion thus came trailing after him when he appeared again, an alien, in the land of light. No other heavenly body had such an intimate acquaintance with oblivion. The Great Star, as he was commonly named, was an evil eye. The Mayas gave to the planet Venus the date name Hun Ahau, a day connected with death and darkness.[23]

There was a widespread pillar cult in Mesoamerica connected with the risings of Venus that has hitherto gone almost unnoticed. Stone pillars have been found in several places in Mesoamerica, in the highlands from Xochicalco to Kaminaljuyú, and along the Gulf Coast, notably in the Veracruz area. They were variously sculptured. One is spiraled upward like a waterspout and surmounted by a head of Ehecatl wearing the buccal mask and the Huaxtec cap.[24]

The magnificent one now in the Museo Nacional is a slender nine-foot Quetzalcoatl with a young man's face but lacking the buccal mask. From Teayo came specimens with dates connected with Mixcoatl or with dragons standing on their tails.[25] From Xochicalco comes the famous set of two squared pillars showing sky bands and Quetzalcoatl's face in the dragon's maw together with the dates 4-movement and 7-wind, avatars of Quetzalcoatl (figs. 24, 29). From Veracruz comes a plain stone column surmounted by a large head of Quetzalcoatl, a true herm.[26] From Teotihuacán and Kaminaljuyú come plain stone columns carved with only the rattles of the rattlesnake, a shorthand for the dragon.[27] Finally, in Tenochtitlán at the time of the Spanish entry we hear of an imposing stone column that the Mexicans called Ilhuicatitlan, In the Midst of the Heavens.[28] It had a peaked thatch cap, as did Quetzalcoatl's temples, and at its foot great numbers of sacrifices took place, particularly at the heliacal rising of Venus; associated with it inevitably was a skull rack.

The above do not comprise an exhaustive list. They and others are vestigial pieces left over from an ancient celestial cult possibly indigenous to Tabasco and adjoining coastal regions. As a matter of fact, undecorated stone pillars are found in the Guatemalan highlands dating back to Preclassic times.[29] Probably they were once painted with designs taken from the sky religion. The thought naturally arises that such pillars might also indicate a phallic cult, but I find no evidence for that.

The antiquity of this cult can be seen in the commemoration on the pillars of several of Quetzalcoatl's important avatars: Ehecatl, Tlahuizcalpanteuctli, Mixcoatl, and the youth in the dragon's maw, who is probably Quetzalcoatl himself. Nothing else so clearly points to the close relationship that unites these gods within the network of a great sky religion. I suspect that the Maya stelae from the Classic period, which are now known to be connected with chro-

Figure 24

nology, lineage, and rule, may ultimately be derived from these dragon pillars.

The First Dawn

The myth of the fifth sun is one of the central tales of Aztec mythology. One section of that myth particularly relates to the thesis of this chapter—that is, the duel between Tonatiuh, the sun, and Tlahuizcalpanteuctli, the morning star. I have already adverted to it as it is found in art. Here we need a more extended analysis.

After the diseased god Nanahuatl had thrown himself into the fire in order to become the sun, the gods present at the occasion were appalled to see the first glimmerings of dawn in each of the four directions. Of all the gods only Ehecatl (the wind), the *mimixcoa* (the stars), and Tlazolteotl (the moon) divined that the correct direction was to be the east.[30] Just as the splendid appearance was about to take place, however, an obstacle arose. The sun wavered on the horizon, refusing to begin his climb to the zenith unless the sixteen hundred gods assigned absolute sovereignty to him and in token of it offered him their hearts and blood. The champion of the gods, Tlahuizcalpanteuctli, reacted and in a rage shot three arrows at the sun but missed. The sun retaliated, shooting his challenger full in the face and thus destroying him. The morning star was cast down to become Cetl, the god of frost, who thenceforth lived in the underworld. In an alternative telling, the sun killed all the gods, that is, the stars.[31]

There are other versions, but the most interesting to us is the one in which the gods, under their leader, Xolotl, offer themselves as sacrifices to achieve the rising and the coursing of the sun. In this version Xolotl sacrifices all the gods and finally himself. A variant has Ehecatl selected by the concourse of gods to perform this first of all sacrificial acts.

He does so, but Xolotl demurs and, weeping, flees away. Yet finally even he has to submit. There is an important addendum to the myth. It says that with all this the sun still refused to move, in response to which crisis Ehecatl raised a wind of such cyclonic violence that the sun was blown out on his course, which he has been following ever since.

The scenario of this myth of the origins of celestial movement has not yet been fully grasped. To grasp it, we must identify the various actors, all of whom act as antagonists to the sun. Who are they? As it turns out, all of them except the goddess are transfigurations of Quetzalcoatl: Nanahuatl is his son, Xolotl is his twin, Tlahuizcalpanteuctli is the morning star (who is Ce Acatl), Cetl is the god Ixquimilli known from the *Codex Dresden* to be a form of the planet Venus.[32] Finally there is Ehecatl, who is one of the archetypal forms of Quetzalcoatl. The first four are forms of Quetzalcoatl as the planet Venus; the last is Quetzalcoatl as the wind. In other words a remarkable gathering of gods, all of whom can be considered as emanations of one overriding numen, here play the role of antagonists to the sun god. And all, including the sun himself, are celestial (Tlazolteotl, who is primarily the Earth Mother, here is found in the role of the moon). But there is something even more remarkable than that in this history of the first dawn: Nanahuatl, who approximates the evening star, is that very god who by his sacrifice emerges as the sun.

In short there is now only one actor in the entire myth, a point I have made previously. When analyzed, the protagonist melt together as a numinous whole.

Thus it would be better to move to a higher level of interpretation and to understand it not as the myth of the appearance of the fifth sun and the vindication of his sovereignty but rather as the myth of an ambivalent period, namely the dawn, in which both sun (day) and stars (night) participate and in which an underlying homogeneity of godhead is present. Some of this myth was translated into cult by the Aztecs at the beginning of their year in the Feast of the Flaying of Men (Tlacaxipehualiztli). Much has been written about this gruesome paschal event, but the fact that it is a rendition in cult of the myth of the first sunrise has been noticed only infrequently, if at all.

In this myth the sun is Xipe, the god of valor and of renewals. During the festival the duel between the sun and his enemies in the underworld was acted out by living actors on the famous gladiatorial stone. Fastened to this round stone, the captive, a warrior of proven ferocity, fought singly against a series of well-armed braves. The victim, therefore, was the *ixiptla* of the sun who had to die and make way for his successor, who would appear as a hero emerging from the shadows. Among the ritual warriors were four (each colored differently to indicate one of the four directions), called the "four dawns."[33] They represented the experimental light of the first dawn spread around the whole circumference of the horizon and not yet assigned to the east. The death of the captive is the foreordained death of the sun at midnight, which death was lamented by a priest dressed in a shaggy skin and called Old Wolf, a personage who surely takes the place of Xolotl.[34] The exact coincidence is difficult to determine, but we note that, just as Xolotl in the myth flees from the sacrificial butchery weeping copiously, so Old Wolf in his performance in the cult howls and moans lugubriously at the death of the victim. He is furthermore the "uncle" of all the stellar gods, a not-unexpected title for the evening star in the underworld. But if that passage is somewhat unclear, an exact coincidence does exist in that part of the ceremony in which all the gods, in the persons of their *ixiptla*, are sacrificed.[35] This corresponds to that episode in the myth in which the sun demands the blood of the sixteen hundred gods, who are thus forced to accept death on the sacrificial block. The *ixiptla* of the god Quetzalcoatl was prominently a part of this rite, and we can assume a connection between this figure and the Ehecatl of the myth whose blasts forced the reluctant sun to rise.

Thus the essentials of the myth were reproduced: the death of the sun in the underworld, the uncertainty about the direction of the first dawn, the anger of the gods at the sun, the presence of Xolotl and Ehecatl as sacrificers, and the immolation of the gods to support the new sun. The scenario depicts the situation that leads directly to the matutinal rising. Nevertheless the ceremony is presented in the calendar as a specific annual event, and so the meaning switches easily from the daily sunrise to the seasonal coming of the springtime. The cult ends on a note of flower offerings, which probably has an equinoctial meaning. Xipe thus not only is patterned on the sun at his daily rising but for cult purposes is the sun standing at the spring equinox.

From other sources we know of Xipe's close association with Quetzalcoatl.[36] The former, while still identified in his solar role, can also wear all the regalia of the latter.[37] In the *Tonalamatl* they are treated as companion gods, both of whom performed penitential acts on a legendary Thorn Mountain. Both Xipe and Quetzalcoatl's twin, Xolotl, share the name Four Movement. Both could bear the title Topiltzin.[38] I think we are to gather from such disconnected items that the connection between Quetzalcoatl and Xipe is ancient. At first sight, however, there would seem to be little connection between the two. Whereas Quetzalcoatl's body paint is black, Xipe's is red as befits a god of the ardent sun. They carry different staves: Quetzalcoatl has the *xonecuilli*, while Xipe has the *chicahuaztli*, a badge of office that is carried by deities of fertility but seldom by Quetzalcoatl.

We are in the presence of an eerie set of reciprocating concepts: the sun tracked into the underworld by a demonic evening star, a double or joint death in the darkness, and then the renewal of exactly the same confrontation in the gigantic persons of the sun and the morning star. There is more than rebirth suggested here. Identity is also stated.

We know for instance that in cult the *ixiptlas* of both Nanahuatl and Xipe were flayed and their skins worn by others
to express the principle of recurrence.[39] And Nanahuatl, as
we shall see below, is a form of Quetzalcoatl.

The priests expressed this impressive conflation of ideas
in the title they gave to Xipe's special priest. This priest was
known as Yohuallahuan, He Who Becomes Drunk in the
Night, the reference being to rebirth. Drunkenness was
thought of as a taking away of life and a falling down in the
stupor of death, followed by resurrection. Both Quetzalcoatl and Xipe possessed attributes of fertility, and that was
probably sufficient for the priests to see them as related.
Nevertheless the Xipe in the ritual of the Tlacaxipehualiztli
is not to be confused with the Tonatiuh who arises splen-
didly every day, destroys the stars, and easily assumes the
celestial sovereignty. Both were sun gods but with different
emphases.

The Sun's Place in the Sky Religion

Our investigation of the role of the morning star has led
us to a point where we can see that planet drawing closer
to the sun, seeming at times to merge with it or somehow to
be absorbed in it, even perhaps to *become* it. This very
real ambiguity needs more analysis if we are to make it
believable.

If one were to designate a priori the pivotal character in a
hypothetical sky religion, one would naturally opt for the
sun. One would assume that the major myths would re-
count first the deeds of that luminary, his amours, and his
peregrinations. Day would be defined as what it was simply
because of the sun's presence. Night would be defined as
his absence. The moon would be his wife, and the stars his
issue. It would necessarily be a paternalistic and a heroic
picture.

In the Mesoamerican sky religion the role of the sun is not as straightforward as the above. In fact the sun is *not* a totally dominant figure in that religion. A word of caution, however: There did exist in the late period a sun cult, contrived solely for the knightly orders, which featured the sun (Tonatiuh) centrally. This, however, was a subculture in the sky religion and was designed solely to reinforce the social standing of the knights. It did not basically affect the more labyrinthine picture of the sun put forward by the priests.

In Aztec mythology the simplest statement of the multiple meanings attached to the sun's performance is to be found in a variant of the central myth.[40] This variant says that an eagle snatched Nanahuatl from the pyre and carried him up to the high gods, Tonacateuctli and his consort, who thereupon enthroned him in the sign 4-movement. But inasmuch as that sign points generally to the underworld, we have to believe in a sun the complexion of whose being was nocturnal and whose springing into full life in the daytime sky cannot eradicate this propensity toward darkness. Thus he cannot be thought of as dominant.

The real role of the sun in the late period of Mesoamerican history was to underline an important dogma in the sky religion, namely that blood sacrifice had a celestial origin. In the actualization of that dogma the sun is indeed central, yet he can act only in the presence of Quetzalcoatl or one of his avatars. The dogma requires a sacrificer as well as a victim, and, as we have seen, the act of cosmic sacrifice finally produces a full cast of identical—or closely related—actors, so large a cast that the anticipation of the action, the central act, its devolution, and the final astounding climax become the focus of our interest. The plot becomes more compelling than the mere contemplation of the hero. Because of this, the sun in Mesoamerican mythology has become a very complex and irresolute being.

From the impersonal *tona* ("to be a sunny day" or "to be

hot") the sun derives his name Tonatiuh, He Comes Forth Shining. The allusion is obviously a heroic one, referring as it does to the dayspring. Certain parts of his mythology describe this eminence. His palace is situated far over the eastern waters. He appears with the dawn at the jeweled gates serenaded with music and the clash of arms. His retinue is composed exclusively of brave warriors who have fallen on the field or who have been sacrificed on the stone of sacrifice.

We have called the sun Tonatiuh. The word describes him, but it should not be thought to have been his real name—that is to say, his calendrical name. He had several avatars, each of whom possessed a particular date name, but the Aztecs worshiped him first as Four Movement. It is not at all strange that he shares this name with the god Xolotl, whom we shall consider in chapter 5. Here for the sake of clarity we shall consider the name Four Movement to be uniquely his.

Yet now we must pile Ossa on Pelion and inform the reader that 4-movement was not the date of the present sun's birth, which it should be if indeed it was his real name.[41] This sun, the fifth, was born on the date 13-reed, and that was therefore his canonical name. The reasons for this perplexing situation follow.

When the priestly mind in Mesoamerica began developing ideas about the universe as an entity, it utilized the sacred numbers four and five as the measurements with which to standardize it. Cosmic history was divided into four past chapters and the present one, making five. We note, however, that each of these packets of time was placed under the aegis of a god who, to exercise his (or her) rule, became for that period the sun. In brief the sun has been five times the *nahualli* of a different god. Because of certain imperfections each of the first four suns came to a catastrophic end, and in each of the cataclysms the gods died. Thus each aeon was a self-contained slice of time, finite and unconnected with the others. The fifth god who took the sun as his *nahualli* was Nanahuatl. The previous suns had been given divine date names beginning with the coefficient four and followed by the sign that signified their dooms, fire, flood, and so on. In accordance with this orthodoxy, this last sun became Four Movement. The "movement" element in the name can, and here specifically does, mean a movement of the earth, or an "earthquake." The whole name thus signifies that the present age will be destroyed in a final earthquake.

The doubling of date names was explained by the Aztecs in another way. They concluded that both date names were authentic, being dual because in actuality two gods were being talked about: Nanahuatl, who threw himself into the fire to become the sun on the day 13-reed; and Tonatiuh, the god he became who first appeared above the horizon (that is, was born) four days later, namely on 4-movement. The sacrificial death and the new life that it produced were one and the same, while still pointing to distinct and reciprocating avatars—wherefore the distinction in name.

The sun's date name 4-movement is thus not a reference to heroism at all, as is the case with the name Tonatiuh. On the contrary, it looks ahead to defeat and the final cloture of time. This finding supports my statement that in the sky religion the sun played a role far removed from that of a *sol invictus*. It is furthered by the fact that Tonatiuh, as we have said, is not a fully formed deity like the others but is rather a *nahualli* figure. This weakening of solar centrality was conceived by Mesoamericans who were adept in celestial computation, and it accords with a priestly, not a natural, logic.

Thus the sun was not a clear-cut deity in Mesoamerican mythology. Some of the ambiguity is undoubtedly due to the fortuitous accretion over a long period of time of several sun gods, each with slight differences, all of whom were committed into a solar corporation. That he is blurred, however, is largely owing to a powerful and very real religious apprehension by the Mesoamerican peoples. On the one hand the sun is a young and virile conqueror; on the other hand he is a tragically doomed puppet. He oscillates between the pole of pure nature, where he is the shining disk of the sun above us, and the pole of nocturnal absences and anxieties that are so often alluded to in the mythology. No other god in the sky religion plays such a curious role. In contrast to Tonatiuh there is of course Xipe, whom we have seen to be a sun god who is an integrated and whole deity. Xipe dies, it is true, but his rejuvenation comes easily and without the uncertainties that are built into the concept of Tonatiuh. Tonatiuh is thus unique.

In accord with the above we can separate the several avatars and epithets applied to Tonatiuh into two lots, those referring to him positively and those referring to him negatively. I list the former ones first.

The sun was referred to as the Manly One, the Brave, Our Conqueror, the One who Falls Gloriously in War, and the Turquoise Shield. He could even be called the Unique God. Such epithetical names are to be expected, and they comport with the characteristics displayed by four of his avatars: Xiuhpilli, Piltzinteuctli, Xochipilli, and Macuilxochitl, all of whom were variants of the rising sun. Precious Son (Xiuhpilli) was, like Xipe, the principle of springtime, of green fields and new life; he is definitely the sun who springs up in the morning. A more important god of the newly appearing sun was the Lord of Children (Piltzinteuctli), whose mythology shows him to have been of some antiquity. On the one hand he arose from the underworld after defeating the demons of darkness in the ball game; on the other hand he was the sun who coupled with the Earth Mother (Xochiquetzal) and had by her a son who was the spirit of maize. Another ancient sun god was Flower Prince (Xochipilli), whose date name was One Flower and whose images show him to have been a god of the rising season and of flowers. Both he and the equally prominent Five Flower (Macuilxochitl) were especially worshiped by the nobles and the people of the palace. Five Flower in fact was widely revered for his patronage of luxury, song, dance, and the excitement of gaming—he was certainly connected with the early light. The two latter gods are so closely identified that it is almost impossible to separate them. His name appears to have been also Lord of the Dawn (Tlapcoyohuale).[42]

We mentioned in an earlier chapter that the sky dragon takes on a special form when he is brought into relationship with the sun. At such times he is Xiuhcoatl, which, literally translated, means Turquoise Dragon but which commonly is referred to as Fire Serpent. As the latter name implies, the Xiuhcoatl who lives on the fifth level of the heavens spews forth flames, comets, and other portents of the sky.[43] He is probably an animation of the daytime course of the sun across the sky, for he is shown carrying the sun on his back. In mythology he becomes the fiery weapon hurled by the victorious sun at his enemies, the stars.[44] And as Quetzalcoatl represents the waters to be found in the sky, so Xiuhcoatl represents the fires to be found there. His connection with the blazing sun of day needs no further comment.

Behind all these forms of the sun god looms that antique one who comes down to us as the Lord of Abundance (Tonacateuctli), whose date name was Seven Flower.[45] He is without a doubt the sun god of ancient Teotihuacán. By Aztec times Tonatiuh had taken his place, but he was still remembered as a venerable figure enthroned in the highest heaven and sending down to earth the heat of summertime and the young of all the races of man.

All the above deities are modeled on the heroic conceptualization of the sun, the *sol invictus*. The somber side of the sun is apprehended in other epithets of his, such as

Falling Eagle (Cuauhtemoc) and Earthbound Sun (Tlal-chitonatiuh), but even more so in the calendar name Four Movement.

There is a god of most difficult definition, an alter ego of Tonatiuh, who is undoubtedly one of these more somber avatars. This is the Lord of the Night (Yohualteuctli). Whereas Tonatiuh, the daytime sun, carries the date name Thirteen Reed. Yohualteuctli, the sun in the night, is that god who properly owns the name Four Movement.[46] The logic of this latter fact is that the fifth sun, which is also the last sun, is the present *nahualli* of an essentially nocturnal deity, namely Nanahuatl.

Yohualteuctli, who in one of the codices is seen being sacrificed nine times,[47] once for each of the levels of the underworld (fig. 25), is also that god who brings children into the world, much as was said about the high gods.[48] The creation of a child is at least once interpreted in the sky religion as a result of a game of *tlachtli* played in the night sky between the Red Tezcatlipoca, who stands for the power of rejuvenation, and the terrible Earth Mother, Tlazolteotl, here presented as the moon.[49] In the center of the court, which is the color of blood, death as a demon is shown giving birth to a child. This is given as the end of the game—death in the center of the court as an act of renewal. Yohual-teuctli's death is thus given to us in two visual equivalents, heart extraction and a losing game of *tlachtli* (fig. 25).

With all this we are not surprised to find that Yohualteuc-tli, this daimon of the night sky, is more than an emanation of the sun; he is also a transfiguration of Quetzalcoatl as the planet Venus, who is named One Crocodile after the initial day of the long series that makes up the *tonalpohualli*. If Ce Acatl is the emblem of the morning star and Xolotl that of the evening star, then One Crocodile will probably be an intermediate and permanently nocturnal form of the planet Venus. He is closely connected with the jaguar and is de-

Figure 25

picted in the form of that animal floating in the night sky. His name tells us that he is equivalent to the old high god Cipactonal (the consort of Oxomoco), whom we thus discover to have been the light of the first dawn, before ever the rising of either the planet or the sun. In other words we are talking about a deity who performs as does Yohualteuctli, Lord of the Night, but is the planet Venus instead of the sun.

A summary of this complicated god can now be presented. One can say that there are two suns, the hero of the daylight and the nocturnal captive who suffers a sacrificial death. The former follows the latter as a son follows his father. In the sun's coursing there is a hiatus at noontime, when the retinue of braves leaves its champion as the zenith is attained. At that point, where the changeover occurs, the male warriors hand him over to an escort of equally heroic but deathly amazons, who take him down into the earth. Thus, from noon on, the divine one falters until he is finally seized by the earth dragon. Night thus begins at noon and comes to an end at midnight at the very moment when the sun, who has become Yohualteuctli, falls under the knife of his nemesis, Xolotl. This cosmic sacrifice ends the period of tragedy; out of it there appears a youthful and a vigorous hero, son and successor to the former celestial king. Or, as we have seen, the scenario can take the form of a game played in the *tlachco* between the sun and his opponents. With victory attained in any case, Tonatiuh then rises through the fires of dawn or issues forth from his eastern palace, depending on which version one prefers, and the sequence begins again. The father-son relationship permeates the Mesoamerican understanding of the day, but for birth from the womb it prefers to substitute a miraculous rejuvenation through the act of sacrifice.

There were many interpretations suggested by the above myth. The Totonacs even extrapolated from it the concept of a future savior, the child and legitimate successor of the sun, who will come someday to rid the world of evils.

I have kept this analysis of the sun purposely brief so that we can continue our concentration on Quetzalcoatl. What follows is a further development of this riddle of the skies, but in terms now of the evening star.

FIVE
QUETZALCOATL
AND THE
UNDERWORLD

The deathly meanings attached to the god of the evening star, Xolotl (himself an avatar of Quetzalcoatl), are set forth here, while his animal background and close connections with the underworld are scrutinized. As a twin of Quetzalcoatl, Xolotl was a god of the malformed and the diseased. He is identified as one of the heavenly gods who fall into the underworld, and as such he merges imperceptibly into the sun, to become a conjoined avatar called Four Movement. Xolotl's place in the sky of the underworld is shown to be symbolized by tlachtli, *the ball game of which he is the patron god. The game as a pan–Middle American nocturnal cult of the heavenly bodies is commented on, as well as its connections with fertility— the latter seen in the person of Nanahuatl, who is the seed corn in the ground before sprouting. Finally Quetzalcoatl's identification with death is considered and rejected.*

Xolotl Introduced

We have seen that Quetzalcoatl was the sky, and we have considered some of the deities known to be his avatars. The most curious of these, and in many ways the most focal, is Xolotl, whom we examine in this chapter (fig. 26). We find him first in the myth of the recovery of the bones of man, discussed earlier. He is always an ominous and repellant deity but a necessary one.

When the gods decided that a race of menials should be produced, they sent Quetzalcoatl down into the underworld to locate the bones of a former race of men, which they would then revivify. Three versions of the myth exist, all of them, however, telling a consistent story. In one Quetzalcoatl descends alone into that dark world. In another he is accompanied by his *nahualli*, who is not named. In the third it is the god Xolotl who descends. Xolotl we know is generally depicted as a dog.[1] We know also that the *nahualli* was usually an animal, and thus the three versions come together to inform us that Quetzalcoatl's *nahualli* was a Xolotl animal. Xolotl is in brief that alter ego that Quetzalcoatl assumes whenever he must operate as a denizen of the underworld. That does not, however, remove Xolotl from a basically celestial orientation. The reasons for this seeming contradiction will be given later.

In some early stage of the Nahuatl tongue the word *xolotl* undoubtedly designated a species of dog or some doglike animal. By late Aztec times the common words for dog were *itzcuintli* and *chichi*. *Xolotl* is not found as a pure synonym of those words. A primary meaning of the word when used in compounds appears to have been that of something or someone kneeling, wrinkled, possibly twisted.[2] An im-

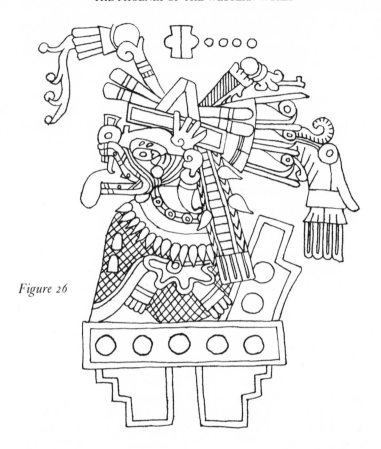

Figure 26

portant line of meanings comes out of this. The word *xolotl* can secondarily mean "beast," "servant," or "page," and from this (perhaps because of the common use of midgets and hunchbacks in the royal courts) the meaning "freak," "prodigy," or "monster." It can also mean "penis."[3] When the name Xolotl appears as an Aztec glyph, it is simply the head of a crop-eared animal, most probably a dog. Dogs were killed at funerals to guide the disoriented soul down the paths of the underworld.

Xolotl appears in Mesoamerican iconography either as an animal or as a being with a human shape but an animal's head. The species of animal is not always clear. It can be a composite; in other words, while mainly canine, it can show the talons of a monster, as well as mixed traits that recall the tapir (*tlacaxolotl*); the opposum, an animal thought by the Quiche's to belong to the predawn darkness;[4] or even the badger, which was said to have been born in the underworld. More precision than this is not attainable, and we have to realize that the god Xolotl, being very ancient, wears for us an elusive mask. He was probably not biologically intelligible even to the Mesoamericans who depicted him. It is therefore probably best to think of him as anatomically a canine-based chimera, a creature whose animal parts were put together so far back in the past as to have been forgotten (fig. 26). Briefly he was monstrous, and, being a monster, he was greatly to be dreaded.

I have mentioned his antiquity.[5] Only seven gods were reported to have survived the deluge,[6] and he, along with Ehecatl, was one of them. In one of the codices he is shown as twins in the highest heaven at a time long before the birth of Ehecatl.[7] These Xolotl twins are shown acting as retainers of the two high gods in Omeyocan. In one of the myths he doubles for Quetzalcoatl as the leader of the sixteen hundred gods,[8] a datum that certainly points to his great antiquity. In fact the question may arise, Which of the two, Quetzalcoatl or Xolotl, was the model god, and which the avatar? In the *Selden Roll* the latter, in the form of a stone in a bundle, is clearly connected with the rise of lineages, exactly as if he were Ehecatl, and that takes us sufficiently far back in time.

There is no doubt that the earliest form of Xolotl was distinct from that of Quetzalcoatl the sky dragon, though they were early brought together by the priests. At the beginning Xolotl was undoubtedly chthonian, and he can even be understood as a fetish in the form of a rock.[9] As against this, Quetzalcoatl was celestial from the beginning and always remained so.

It was early man's need to interpret intellectually the loss of all daylight objects in the recurrent obscurity of night that must have brought the two gods together. What allowed the joining was the crepuscular light, that indeterminate mingling of the day and night skies precisely at the nodes of dawn and dusk. Dawn belonged to the day, dusk to the night. The mythical creatures who summed up these two forms of half-illumination were the morning and evening stars, respectively, hypostases of a sinister planet.

We believe that Xolotl was originally a stifling presence, a numen of the underworld, if not indeed another name for it, and thus could be logically cast as the evening star. This in turn necessarily paired him with Quetzalcoatl who already was Ce Acatl, the morning star. It is impossible to state when this joining was first made. Out of it came the casting of the two deities as twins.

Xolotl's chthonian characteristics are very evident in his mythology. We have seen that he was leader of the sixteen hundred gods as they dropped into the underworld, all of them dispatched by sacrifice. In stellar terms this was the evening star preceding the starry host as they fell under the earth in the west. Xolotl can thus be thought of as the psychopomp of the gods, a Mesoamerican Hermes as it were. He was certainly not death itself as a self-supporting, abstract power; he was only one aspect of it, namely its eerieness in association with darkening skies, with the idea of descent, and with the horrors of blood sacrifice.

Xolotl appears in two myths laid in the underworld. The first shows him slipping down into Mictlan to secure the bones of men. We have already noted this. In the other myth—a priapic tale—he forces the goddess Xochiquetzal into the underworld and there rapes her.[10] Violence is part of his nature.

Xolotl has a female counterpart, a goddess called Chantico who was changed into a dog by the high god.[11] She too was an underworld deity and bore the descriptive name Xolotl Head, though she is not to my knowledge so depicted. Inasmuch as her date name was Nine Dog, we can interpret the name Xolotl Head to be the equivalent of Dog Head (Torquemada translates it as Wolf Head).[12] She was the patroness of the eighteenth *trecena* of the *tonalpohualli*, which began with the day 1-wind, a well-known festival of Quetzalcoatl. The few representations of Chantico show a completely anthropomorphic being with no bestial traits whatever (see fig. 18). Scholars continue to repeat that she was a goddess of the hearth, but I am not aware of hard evidence for this. She is mentioned here solely to add to our picture of Xolotl as a god important enough in his own right to produce divine duplications and to influence other gods.

In the great *Codex Borgia* there are two adjoining plates that introduce us to the important relationship that Xolotl has with Quetzalcoatl.[13] An interpretation of these scenes is difficult, but it is worth attempting if only to demonstrate that neither god can be understood without the other (figs. 27 and 28).

The plates show two temples whose roof areas are interpreted by the artists as the sky. The temples themselves suggest different things. The first temple (fig. 27) is the usual conical, thatched shrine of Quetzalcoatl. The god, painted black to represent night, is seated inside confronting Tlahuizcalpanteuctli, that is, himself as the morning star. The other temple (fig. 28) is a grotto in the underworld, and in it, also seated, is Xolotl. On the front porch of the first temple a figure of the god Xipe lies in state, which is as much as to say that the spring sun has not yet returned. On the porch of the underworld temple a goddess lies supine, her heart having been torn out in sacrifice. In the cavity of her body thus opened up, new fire is being drilled. New fire represents here a renewed period of sun. Out of this fire a small figure, symbolizing a spark and

Figure 27

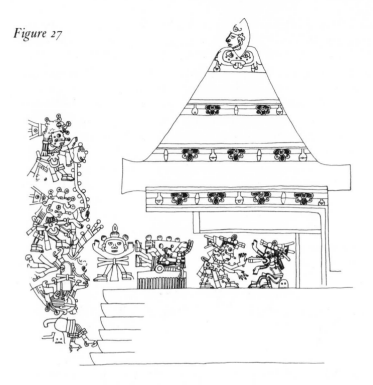

wearing the wind jewel, escapes and races toward Xolotl, who is shown here in his common monster form, though he is additionally defined as a being who is playing the part of the sun in the underworld.

Facing each temple a sacrifice is taking place. The victim is identical in both scenes, being a curious and almost formless demonic being. The god performing the sacrifice in the first scene is Quetzalcoatl himself with all his nocturnal characteristics exaggerated. The sacrificer in the second scene is a form of Xolotl, also with nocturnal characteristics augmented.

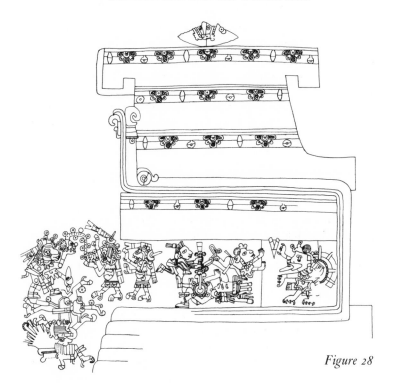

Figure 28

All of this gives us a fairly clear picture of the role played by Xolotl. He inhabits the underworld, where we know him not only to be a form of the planet Venus (that is, the evening star) but also to be mythically premonitory of the new sun who will be resurrected in the underworld. In other words the blackened sun in the underworld, before he can be renewed, passes through a transformation that is effected by Xolotl and in a sense *is* Xolotl.

Our reading of these two scenes brings out a vaguely seasonal meaning. Yet there is no reason why a diurnal reading is not also possible. In such a case the first temple would symbolize the dawn (night giving way to day), while the second would recall the failing daylight ending in the nadir of deep night. The subject matter of both scenes is the same, namely the resurrection of the sun as a result of the actions of the planet Venus seen in its two main phases. The actors in the drama are avatars of Quetzalcoatl, while the recipients of the action are different versions of the sun god.

Freaks and Twins

Mesoamerican man responded to monsters and others deformed by disease or congenital defects in a way that may seem startling to us: he deified them. These unfortunate ones not only served as the usual buffoons and objects of ridicule in the courts but also acted as templates for the clearer visualization of certain gods, Xolotl among them.

A number of finds from the Preclassic and Early Classic periods illustrate what was in all probability an important cult of freaks. These are the two-headed and two-faced figurines, the ceramic faces from which the flesh on one side is stripped away, the famous hobbledehoys of the Olmecs, and others. Even the great god of fire was not immune to influences from this cult, and he is early shown telescoped and cruelly doubled over. Grotesquerie, inversion, the disquieting, and the repellent were felt to be great powers. One aspect of this was the patronage of certain families of diseases by selected gods. Quetzalcoatl for example specialized in the infliction of disorders of the skin and eyes and of course in the curing of them.[14] An interesting aspect of his cult in Cholula, in fact, was the appearance of persons thus afflicted coming to display and act out their disorders. In contrast, badly crippled and deformed people were under the patronage of Xolotl and his avatars.

In the cult of Quetzalcoatl twinning was an almost necessary concept. It stemmed from four causes: (1) the linguistic feature in Nahuatl that the word "snake" also meant
"twin," (2) the concept of the birth of twins that was adjudged to Xolotl,[15] (3) the early doubling of the sky dragon
in iconography, and (4) the recognition that the planet Venus possessed two faces, morning and evening star, separate
yet conjoined.

I find no clear indication in the sources which of these
four options may have been the overriding motive causing
the early priests to mate the two gods Quetzalcoatl and Xolotl, otherwise so unlike. If we see Xolotl as having been in
origin a Venus god, particularly the evening star, and if we
correspondingly see Quetzalcoatl as having been, in some
other culture, also a Venus god, though unrelated, then we
may be able to understand how the fitting may have taken
place. Yet in the course of time neither assimilated the
other; they moved in parallel courses into the mythic consciousness of later Mesoamerica. In other words, though
they were fellows, they were not polar to each other. For
example, Xolotl never appears as a serpent or a dragon,
though he was Quetzalcoatl's twin. As a matter of fact he
may have been the more ancient of the two. All of this is
permissible speculation, but is of course unproved.

Because doubling, and therefore twinning, was so basic
in the draconian origins of the sky religion, it appeared
prominently in myth and art. Quetzalcoatl and Xolotl were
definitely said to be twins. Again Xolotl himself appears as
a pair of identical though differently colored twins in one of
the codices.[16] In the world of nature the Mesoamericans understood all twinning per se to be an expression of the god
Xolotl. Indeed he was said to have changed himself once
into a doubled ear of maize and again into a doubled maguey stalk, prodigies in the world of nature.[17] In iconography, however, and in spite of the insistence in myth that

Quetzalcoatl and Xolotl were twins, they bear no resemblance to each other.

In Teotihuacán, Quetzalcoatl is shown at least twice as twins.[18] In the *Popol Vuh* there are two sets of celestial twins. The first set certainly, and the second set probably, contains Quetzalcoatl as one of its members. Mixtec myth tells of a pair of gods, born to the two high gods, who are plainly Quetzalcoatl and Xolotl under thinly disguised names.[19]

We must not think of this twinning of deities as in any sense a religious dualism. Scholarly works sometimes cast Quetzalcoatl and Xolotl as, respectively, life and death, but there are no indications of that understanding in the sky religion. Quetzalcoatl himself, particularly when he is acting as Ce Acatl, has so many violent and death-dealing aspects that he could not possibly stand for the principle of life. It is true that he brought life to the bones of men, but he did not bring them maize—that was left for the deformed Nanahuatl, one of Xolotl's avatars. Thus there exists no distinction between the two gods sufficiently extreme to be thought of as polar.

We have mentioned that the twinned sky dragons on the Gulf Coast appeared in Huaxtec art as early as the Protoclassic period. In one instance the counterpoised dragons enclose the face of a personage who from his earplugs can be identified as Quetzalcoatl.[20] Almost twelve hundred years later the Spaniards entered the land and found that in that regard little had changed, for an Aztec glyph emblematic of the god Quetzalcoatl could be a double-headed serpent superimposed on the face of the Venus monster.[21] Cognate or twin dragons were thus an enduring element in the iconography of the god.

From Cholula, the center of the Quetzalcoatl religion, comes indisputable proof of the contrapuntal nature of the god. There was recently discovered on the south side of the great Cholula pyramid a patio with altars on three sides. These altars featured great rectangular slabs of stone horizontally placed at ground level and in one case carved with twin dragons.[22] The three altars were incised with sophisticated volutes derived from Huaxtec art. This vast open area was given over to the cult of the sky religion, which doubtless had been brought in earlier from the Gulf Coast. The rolling volutes are abstractly conceived and indicate clouds; only the twinned dragons are representationally presented. At some time in the past this sacred area was intentionally attacked and the altars thrown down, reminding one of the deliberate destruction in the Temple of the Morning Star in Tula or the defacement and toppling of the figures at the Olmec sites. Such revolutions can always be expected where social and religious elements have become frozen under the rules and dogmas of ancient and encrusted religions. But who were the destroyers of the Cholula altar to Quetzalcoatl we do not know. The destruction in Tula, legend tells us, was the work of adherents of Tezcatlipoca who reversed the Quetzalcoatl reforms instituted by Topiltzin.

Hero-twins were common in American Indian mythology. In the Hohokam culture as early as A.D. 500 to 600, Xolotl-type twins appeared on ceramics, as well as double-headed serpents spanning the sky.[23] Among the Pueblos farther north the Little War Twins (who are really older and younger brothers) were sons of the sun, Herculean culture heroes and hunters.[24] In fact, they, like Ce Acatl, set forth on travels to seek out their father. At the southern limits of Mesoamerica we see the twins appearing as the sun and the planet Venus playing the deathly ball game in the underworld. These few illustrations are meant not to establish the most distant outliers of the Quetzalcoatl-Xolotl cult but to demonstrate that there was a basic scenario behind the sky religion and that twinning or pairing was one of its salient features.

The Descenders

The descent of the sun and the putting out of the fires in the sky had a hold over the Mesoamericans' imagination easily surpassing the interest they showed in the sun's victorious ascent to the zenith. They imagined the descent in terms of a lurid chain of mythical beings and actions. As the sun begins his fall, a set of avatars unlike any others walks onto the stage of this Gargantuan play. The sun's part as a doomed light-bearer is played by Tlalchitonatiuh (Earth-directed Sun), the evening star is enacted by the Venus Monster, while Yohualteuctli, the Lord of the Night, appears as a vaguely conjugated version of both the sun in the underworld and the evening star. We therefore cannot possibly discuss Xolotl as the evening star without also discussing his peculiar relationship to the sun as it traveled through the world of night.

There is a well-known scene in the codices depicting the cosmic event of dusk as the confrontation of the sun god and the evening star.[25] No longer is the sun a paladin; now, defeated and pierced by a dart, he is bound in the cerements of the grave. Under him the open jaws of the earth dragon are waiting to engulf him, while Xolotl, who is shown wearing Quetzalcoatl's regalia, confronts him. Xolotl is menacing the sun with a knife as an earnest of the sacrifice that portends. Yet both gods, so far apart in many ways, wear identical headgear. Encircling the scene are the waters of the ocean, this determining for the viewer that the event concerns the cosmos and therefore has universal application.

We have mentioned previously the two names in Aztec mythology that designated the stages of the sun's fall from the empyrean. First he was Cuauhtemoc, Swooping Eagle, and then Tlalchitonatiuh, Groundward, or Setting, Sun. This is the sun who has been wounded by a dart, and we cannot be far wrong in identifying the author of that assault as Xolotl in his avatar the Venus Monster.

The Venus Monster is highly specialized. This chimera is an emblem of the demonry felt in the dusk and in deepening night. As the evening star rushes down in pursuit of the sinking sun to destroy him under the earth, he represents the quintessence of all that is menacing. That menace was presented in a most singular icon. The creature is depicted front face; he has the jaws of a jaguar, the wings of a bird, the tongue of a serpent, and the spraddle-legged stance of a toad or a crocodile. Beautiful fans of quetzal feathers wave from the back of his head. What with elements of jaguar (earth's interior), bird (sky), and toad (water), this variant of the dragon proclaims himself to be a numen of primordial night, black-browed and brutish. As the spirit of the evening star, he is the most sinister of the descenders.

The Venus Monster is almost a homologue of the earth dragon, and he thus represents the being furthest removed from the celestial dragon—yet he still has connections with sky, in this case the night sky. One source spells this out when it gives us One Cipactli (the earth monster) as one of Xolotl's names and shows him in that form as an infernal jaguar.[26] Here sky and earth religions mingle to produce a monster congenial to both.

We first see this chimera in Teotihuacán, wearing a headband on which the glyph of the morning star alternates with the *olin* glyph, which is generally connected with Xolotl.[27] Toward the end of Teotihuacán times in Xochicalco the monster appears with a human face in its open jaws (fig. 29). This face, seen on the Xochicalco stelae, has up to now been identified with Quetzalcoatl, which forces one to interpret the monster as a *nahualli* symbol or casque worn by the god. I believe it to be the other way around, namely that the dragon is primary and that the god depicted in the monster's jaws is Xochipilli, the new sun who will emerge

Figure 29

as the hero of the next day. The monster from whose jaws he emerges must then be Xolotl or more specifically the Venus Monster. My reason for this interpretation is that Stela 3 in Xochicalco specifically identifies the deity as Four Movement (fig. 29), and Four Movement in my opinion is neither the sun alone nor the evening star alone but a compendious numen that encompasses the entire complex of meanings in the sun's descent, his death in the underworld, and his resurgence, all in interaction with forms of Quetzalcoatl. In brief, Four Movement is the totalization of the chthonic chapter in the sun's story, which we now turn to.

Four Movement

I have pointed out that the sun played an inconstant role in Aztec religion and possibly in the earlier stages of Mesoamerican religion as well. He was indeed the flamboyant and incomparable hero aloft in the sky—his common stance in most of the mythologies of the world. The myth of his appearance as the fifth sun is evidence of that. Yet a competing dogma described him equally as prey to disaster, horribly threatened, and finally extinguished.

The sky religion so concentrated on developing all angles of this situation of the light's peril that we can almost see it as a religion of anxiety wherein the sun's beleaguerment rather than his victories was pivotal. That is why the storehouse of cult practices and myth that the Mesoamericans created makes so much of Quetzalcoatl and his various avatars, who were all in some manner or other connected with the night sky. Only by understanding them and arranging them in a proper relationship do we arrive at an appreciation of this peculiarity of the solar situation as seen by the Mesoamericans. Two gods are of special interest here: Four Movement and Yohualteuctli. We have already discussed the latter.

Four Movement was not so much a god as a vast numen that subsumed a total situation including night, sacrifice, and the *tlachco*.[28] In one codex he is called Earthquake Dragon;[29] he can be shown as a stone fetish probably acting as a warden at the portals of the underworld,[30] and he may have been originally an underground god who shook the earth.[31] He very definitely was also an avatar of Xolotl.

The sign "movement" (*olin*) can be translated as "earthquake," or "a running, rolling, or coursing."[32] In the *tonalpohualli* the patron god of this sign was Nanahuatl, the crippled form of Xolotl who became the fifth sun.[33] The signification of the *olin* sign is uncertain, but some of the earlier forms make it appear to be two short lengths of cord crossing each other as in a netting, almost in the form of an ×. Later there was added to the point of juncture an eye, standing for a star, almost as if the glyph for "crossing" had now been made to read "crossing of an astral body." If this was the case, our interpretation could point either to the sun or to the evening star. On the other hand, it is possible that the sign may have the meaning "twin," but here I am obviously guessing. In Tajín the *olin* sign is closely connected with the ball court.[34]

Whatever its origin, the sign is of great importance in the sky religion. The dates 1-movement and 4-movement are both names of Xolotl, while the latter is additionally a way of designating the numen (solar? stellar?) to which we have drawn attention above. Xolotl as the evening star, in concert with the Xolotl who presides over the sixteenth *trecena*, is identified as Four Movement.[35] The date is said to be Quetzalcoatl's special feast day.[36]

If Four Movement is indeed Xolotl's true date name, then Tonatiuh, the sun god, who carries the same date name (though it is not his birth date), must in some sense be the same divine personage as Xolotl.[37] What a curious thing this is! To confuse the evening star with the westering sun seems to be an extraordinarily irresponsible thing to do, until we consider, as I pointed out above, that the date sign 4-*olin* is first and foremost the name of a numinous passage at arms. It is not so much a deity discrepant within himself as an entire situation which acts as a supernatural. Only secondarily is the divinity Four Movement attached to either of the two antagonists in the myth.

The famous Sun Stone bears this out, for it is a full statement of the cosmic event referred to. When seen in this light, the stone is easy to interpret. The cosmos is here defined solely in terms of the two faces of Venus and the sun in declension. The center of the stone is the abode of Four Movement, who by his attached talons is shown to be demonic. Inside Four Movement is a face with a knife of sacrifice issuing from its mouth.[38] This is the face of the sun in the underworld, and we can without any doubt identify it as Yohualteuctli, Lord of the Night, a god whose feast day took place on 4-movement.[39] Around the periphery of the stone, which includes spatial as well as temporal coordinates (that is, the four directions, the twenty day signs, and the four elapsed aeons), circle the twin sky dragons, the fires of dusk and dawn. The stone is thus an epitome of the central dogma of the sky religion, the premise that the Great Death occurs within the enclosure created by the twin stars of the morning and evening and that that death is defined as sacrifice after capture. When thought of in this way, Yohualteuctli becomes Xolotl. Yohualteuctli is in fact a recomposed illusion of Xolotl, of the night sun, and of the whole process of engulfment.

Four Movement came to be an avatar of Xolotl through the fact that he was the divinization of the prophecy that the world was to end on that day and on no other day. The current aeon was the age of the fifth sun, whose name most ominously is Four Movement—and Four Movement is Xolotl. This ultimate catastrophe, about which the priests were well informed, would come about by earthquake, an event comporting with Xolotl's early subterranean stone nature.[40] So we are now looking at an evening star who is at the same time an earth shaker! The god of the evening star finds identity with the earthquake god even as the morning star found identity with the god of war. In such a fashion has the sky religion reached down into the bowels of the earth.

The dogma elucidated above cannot be older than the first appearance of a style of life oriented around war and sacrifice. We are ill-informed about such beginnings. Teotihuacán would seem to be a logical center where such a development could first have occurred, but then there is still too little known about the cultures along the Gulf to eliminate even earlier appearances of such an elite style of life there. My own feeling would be that warlike cultures did indeed appear first on the Gulf Coast. I would further guess that by that time the sky religion had become basically Venusian rather than aeolian. This level of the religion had been preceded by the more popular understanding of the early food producers, namely that the dragon was the circumambience within which the sun moved and that violent winds characterized him. Such a dragon would later function as a spirit of war and the morning star.

The Underworld as a Tlachco

It must be apparent by now that an understanding of the underworld is essential to a full understanding of the Mesoamerican sky religion and particularly of Quetzalcoatl's connection with it. There were at least six models or evocations of the Mesoamerican underworld about which we are informed: (1) the night sky itself, (2) the Teotlachco, or Divine Ball Court, (3) Mictlan, the land of the dead, (4) Chiucnauhcan, the Land of the Nine Levels, (5) the cavernous hollows of Mother Earth, and (6) Tlalxicco, the source of fire and the home of Xiuhteuctli. Of these only the first two have relevance to our discussion.

We need first to describe the typical *tlachco* and the game played there in Late Postclassic Mesoamerica.[41] Because it was thought to be an entrance to the underworld, as well as being the night sky in that underworld, where possible the ball court was excavated below ground level, or else the same effect was achieved by encasing the court within high walls. The newly constructed court could be dedicated only at midnight, this taboo being consistent with the fact that all activity within the court was considered to be nocturnal. The rubber ball flying and bounding about in the *tlachco* was the sunken sun itself, reeling about, attacking, feinting, and defending itself.

The orientation of the court was generally on a north-south axis so as to bring out the seasonal implications of the play.[42] As shown in the codices, the floor of the court was quartered to display the four directions, and just as the upper world had a midday point or zenith at the apex of the heavens, so this inverted world had a midline drawn across the center of the court between the side walls to represent the nadir, the players being spaced on either side of the demarcation. This line, drawn on the surface of the court, was crucial, not only because it represented the frontier between death and life but also because in its center was embedded a round stone marker through which one descended into the abyssal waters contained in the earth.[43] In the codices it is sometimes shown as a skull placed in the center of the court. On that spot was decapitated the leader of the vanquished team in those games that were played as a part of ritual. The sacrificial blood flowing over the stone plate at the game's end brought forth the life of a new sun in the morning, or, if seasonally interpreted, it brought forth the spring season. It may be that there could also be read into the act of decapitation a lunar meaning, namely that the sun had dueled with a hostile moon, vanquished her, and finally dismembered her—such a reading is preserved for us in the myth of the gigantomachy, where Huitzilopochtli decapitates his evil sister, Coyolxauhqui, in the center of the *tlachco*. This latter meaning, however, is not fundamental to an understanding of the *tlachco*. When so considered, the moon's death appears to be intrusive into a mythical situation not originally designed for it. Variant interpretations were thus possible, providing only that they explicated celestial phenomena.

On both sides of the court at midpoint two stone rings protruded from the vertical walls, one on each side. If by some great stroke of luck or skill the ball was driven through either of those two holes, it was an automatic win for the achieving side. The two rings represented the portals through which the astral bodies entered or left the underworld.

Consonant with the celestial concept of the ball court, the two competing teams could be appropriately attired. In Chichén Itzá, for the final sacrificial act in the court members of one of the teams appeared clothed as dragons.

This unique sports area thus conceptually related the underworld and the sky of the underworld, which sky was a mirror image of the night sky appearing above earth after sunset. The confluence of ideas made possible by this ambivalence and its actualization in architectural form is unique in the history of building in stone.

We have seen that for the Mesoamericans the night sky was a kind of model, an icon if you wish, of that great reservoir of demons that was the underworld (fig. 30). This sinister connection was proved to their satisfaction by the visual fact that the concourse of stars arose from the earth after dusk. We have seen that those stars were thought to be the unblinking eyes of demons and hell hags staring down from above out of a holy blackness, while other demons, named and unnamed, lurked in the underworld ready to do

Figure 30

mischief to the crippled sun. For its combination of ur-
gency, sport, horror, and mythical grandeur, this representation of the underearth is unparalleled among the religions
of the world. One of the central tales from Tarascan mythology can be summarized here to illustrate the point.[44]

Sun once played a ball game with Night and, because he
lost, was sacrificed in Xacona, the House of Night. He left
behind a posthumous son, whom Night raised as his own.

One day the son went hunting and, coming upon an iguana, learned from him where his real father was buried. With this knowledge he exhumed the body of his father and carried it off on his back. The dead father thereupon revived as a maned deer and dashed off into the north.

At the heart of this myth is the statement of the filial relationship of the dawn sun to the preceding sun of the dusk. The implication is that there has been a not-unexpected death of the sun in the underworld followed by its disappearance—that is, burial. The fact that the adoptive father of the unfledged sun was the night itself is of great interest in revealing the Mesoamerican linkage of even seemingly disparate things. However closely he may have been related to the old sun, the morning sun was nevertheless a new and different personage. That is a mystery acknowledged by the myth but not stressed. Our Tarascan scenario describes sunrise and sunset, but a gloss was added to account also for the seasonal swaying of the sun between north and south. In most Mesoamerican mythologies the deer was accounted a solar animal; this tale presents the sun as a deer with the sun's rays streaming from him as he moves northward into the summer season. The locus of the myth is the *tlachco*, which serves as the area of confrontation between the sun and the furies of night. Night's victory over the sun is specified as an act of sacrifice in the night sky. It is a complete death; the sun can never rise again. Only a pious son in a miraculous transfiguration can become the next luminary. Thus did the Tarascans present the brutal and creative events that swirled around the sun in the underworld.

Another version of this game comes to us from an Aztec source. We can see it depicted in one of the codices,[45] and we can find hints of it in the difficult Atamalcualiztli hymn of Sahagún.[46] The former identifies the four gods who are involved in the game (which is played in the Sorcerer's Ball Court) as Quetzalcoatl and the Earth Mother

(Cihuacoatl) opposing Ixtlilton and Xochipilli-Cinteotl. The textual source mentions essentially the same deities, Quetzalcoatl and the Earth Mother (here Tlazolteotl) with Xolotl substituting for Ixtlilton, and Xochipilli appearing instead of his close avatar Piltzinteuctli. The only substitution needing comment is the god Ixtlilton, whose name means Little Black Face and who is a form of the night sun (or possibly a demonic stellar being) vaguely connected with newness and youth. My guess is that he is here a reading for Xolotl, just as Piltzinteuctli is surely a reading for Xochipilli. Our players are thus the morning star (dawn), the moon, the evening star (dusk or the sacrificed sun), and finally the sun renewed after death and about to rise into the new day.

Three possible levels of meaning in the *tlachtli* are to be extracted from the above: (1) the death of the sun in the underworld followed by blood sacrifice that enables his successor to arise, (2) the renaissance of the growing season as the sun moves out of the south, and (3) the consequent return of all vegetable and animal life. The fertility aspects in fact appear to be almost as compelling as are the astronomical ones. New growth eventuates from the vigor with which the contestants play the game; flowers, corn, and young lords, all of them coequal symbols in cult, reiterate this emphasis on fecundity. The Aztec festival wherein the impersonators of the above gods ceremonially paraded in the *tlachco*, as if playing a game, was the Tecuilhuitontli, or Lesser Feast of the Lords, a festival of flowers and sex.

The fertility implications of the *tlachco* are abundantly clear in the festival of the Atamalcualiztli, which was held every eighth year, a significant interval. Eight solar years exactly equal five Venusian years. In other words, on a known day every eighth year the beginnings of the solar calendar and the synodic calendar of the planet Venus coincided. The Mesoamericans used this point of significant conjunction to celebrate the renewal of maize. The reason is obvious. When the seed corn was buried in the earth and lost from sight, it was thought to die in the underworld. But the corn god died in another way as well. In the daily preparation of food corn was incessantly being dismembered by Indian women, crushed under their grinding stones to make cornmeal, and then scarred with roasting. There comes a time when corn can no longer accommodate himself to this sustained and callous ill treatment, and he (the god Cinteotl) dies. A period of eight years was chosen as the length of his life as a friend to man and his subsequent renewal because at the end of that period a genius of the underworld (the planet Venus) and a genius of the upper world (the sun) renewed themselves together. We have no trouble deriving this situation from the lineup of contestants in the ball game we have described above; in it we see Quetzalcoatl and Xolotl participating as the two aspects of Venus, we see the sun in his avatar of the young corn, and finally we see the earth, which provides the locus of renewal.

All of this is for background. What specifically of the role of Xolotl? It is known that he was the patron deity of the ball court, which is tantamount to saying that the demon of the "down"—in this case the evening star—was in a sense the central actor.[47] We have already discussed the difficulties of trying to disengage the sun, in his fall and in his stay in the underworld, from the evening star who follows him down, the two together forming one entwined concept of capture and renewal through sacrificial death. That Xolotl was a twin simplifies our understanding of this, for it is possible to view Quetzalcoatl and the sun as brothers, older and younger, respectively, or as twins, this concept being at the heart of the sky religion.

For amplification of this point we turn to the Quiché Mayas. From them comes a splendid account, given in great detail, of the functions and meaning of the ball court.[48] It will help the reader in understanding the following myth to be told beforehand that he will meet in it two sets of hero-twins, the second set affiliated to the first. The twins of the first set are named One Hunter and Seven Hunter. Those of the second set are Hunter and Jaguar Deer. The name of the underworld, as well as of its ruler, is Xibalba.

The myth begins with an invitation issued by the lords of Xibalba to the first set of brothers, who lived in the upper world, to play a game of *tlachtli* with them. The twins made the initial mistake of not taking their own ball to the game. Their descent to Xibalba took them through treacherous country whose dangers are spelled out in fascinating detail. Because they did not know that the lords had plotted to sacrifice them, they did not win. In the end One Hunter was decapitated and his head stuck in a tree, which at the moment of impalement burst into fruit. The fruits already hanging on the tree were gourds that looked like skulls. The lords placed an immediate taboo on the tree.

An underworld maiden named Blood Girl defied the taboo and approached the tree. Inadvertently she allowed the skull of One Hunter to spit into the palm of her hand, whereupon she became pregnant. To escape the enraged lords, she fled up to the surface of the earth, where in due course she gave birth to the second set of heroes, Hunter and Jaguar Deer.

These two grew up to become famous ballplayers—so famous that the lords became irritated and demanded their presence in Xibalba to play a game with them. The two did not, however, fall into the several traps set for them and indeed ended up by totally disconcerting the lords. They played against Xibalba himself in a court where the center marker was a skull. The prize for the winners was to be flowers from the forbidden gardens of the underworld. Hunter, who was apparently defeated in this game, was duly decapitated, and his head was substituted for the ball. But now a higher god came down, and, as the dawn reddened in the east, he revived Hunter. In the end Xibalba was defeated by Jaguar Deer. After performing prodigious feats of sorcery, the two brothers then by deception turned the tables and sacrificed the lords. They thus avenged the death of their father. After all this they entered the sky as the sun and the moon. Throughout the texture of this account of the second game of *tlachtli* is woven a story of the dawn and its five attempts to produce a true sun.

Almost everything previously mentioned about the ball game is to be found in this myth, either patently displayed or hinted at. Let us briefly mention them.

The most obvious thing is the contrast between the two sets of brothers, for they represent on the one hand the doomed sun and on the other hand the sun about to rise. The two sets are tied together by an act of magical impregnation whereby the dead sun is enabled to produce his successor.

We note that, insofar as the above actors are concerned, the game of *tlachtli* is the equivalent of death and appropriately takes place in the underworld. The kind of death is specified as sacrifice by decapitation, and this is amply confirmed in Mesoamerican art. The contestants are astral heroes pitted against death demons (who can also be thought of as stars). There can be no doubt that one of the first set of brothers, One Hunter, is the sun in declension while one of the other set, Hunter, is the rising sun of the next morning. The ball, as it metamorphoses into the hero's skull, is a simulacrum of one or both of these suns.[49] The tree of the underworld was doubtless suggested by the poles normally erected in or near the *tlachco* on which to display the heads of the losers. The fruiting of the tree was the symbol of the abundance that comes out of the dark earth. In this respect we note that next to the great *tlachco* in Tenochtitlán was the *tzompantli*, or skull rack, which so impressed Cortés and his followers with its estimated 136,000 skulls. This gruesome trellis was not only a display rack but also an espaliered tree of abundance.

222

The renewal of the sun in the underworld follows a magically conceived sexual act, though not a coitus, and describes the renewal as the birth of a posthumous son. This is glossed as a prize of spring flowers for the victor. But where is Xolotl in all this? And Ce Acatl, the morning star? The Quiché myth says that the second set of brothers became the sun and moon. But it is known that the moon in Mesoamerica is always female and is always an aspect of Earth Mother. Among the Mayas she is Ix Chel. Among the Huaxtecs and the Aztecs she is Tlazolteotl. She is thus a poor choice to posit as one of the brothers. On the other hand, we know that there are two well-known celestial brothers in the mythology of many North American Indians, the older one the morning star, the younger one the sun. In any such equation Xolotl would acquire the status of an older brother. There is no reason therefore to doubt that each of the two sets of brothers represents the planet Venus and the sun, though Venus in the first set is the evening star, while it is the morning star in the second.

This is theoretically a sound interpretation and makes Seven Hunter an avatar of Xolotl. But we have already noted that Xolotl as Four Movement is the numinous concretion of both the *tlachco* and the events that take place in it, which is also a way of describing Yohualteuctli.

The *tlachco* is further described for us as the field upon which sorcerers demonstrate their skills. The Aztecs told of legendary ball games between sorcerers in the tribal homelands of Teoculhuacan and Chicomoztoc.[50] These legends are probably to be connected with the Aztec vision of the northern sector of the night sky, wherein the North Star and its circumpolar neighbors are referred to as Citlallachtli, the Ball Court of the Stars.[51] The stars in the far north were thought of as the ancestors, and we have already discussed the night sky as conceptually a field of conflict. In other words, the gods playing ball in the festival of the Atamalcualiztli are at the same time playing in the Nahuallachco, the Sorcerer's Ball Court in the sky. And finally we are told, in the Quiché myth just paraphrased, that the second set of brothers won because of their powerful sorcery. Thus the Mesoamerican game, which required such amazing physical dexterity of its human devotees, among gods and demons was played with sleights and magic deceptions.

Nanahuatl

One of the more enigmatic figures in Mesoamerican mythology is the diseased god Nanahuatl. The name itself is curious. *Nanahuatl* is the word for afflictions of the skin, generally running or pustulous sores. The god's name is thus simply the name of a disease, and he may be considered to be the god who sent the disease and who can also cure it. Human sacrifices made to him in fact were chosen from among those who suffered from his diseases. He is thus the "disease" Quetzalcoatl. He must have been a very old god, for he appears to have had a limited cult at the time of the Spanish entry, yet he is the central figure in the myth of the five suns that originated in the days of Teotihuacán.

His name also appears as Nanahuatzin or Nanahuaton, both translated as Little Nanahuatl, the implication being that he was a dwarf or was thought to be strikingly small in stature. He appears among the Quichés as Nanahuac and is one of their early creator gods, along with Gukumatz (Quetzalcoatl), and he is called by them "dwarf," or "green," that is, young.[52] I believe that he was the seed corn, which, put away underground, is later brought out for sowing in the earth and renewal; that is why the myth stresses his youth. And again, like dried-corn kernels, he is wrinkled and misshapen. In this connection we may recall that the young maize god Cinteotl is often referred to as "the fatherless or wretched child."[53] This identification as the underground or stored corn in no way invalidates our believing

Nanahuatl to be also the "disease" Quetzalcoatl. The one easily flows into the other.

The clearest indication that he is indeed in origin a corn god comes from the myth of the finding of maize described earlier. While it was Quetzalcoatl who had discovered the hiding place and the uses of corn, it was Nanahuatl who alone was able to thresh the stocks of grain in the Mountain of Our Substance.[54]

Let us list the facts that support this view. Two versions of Nanahuatl's parentage are given. In the first his father was Piltzinteuctli.[55] His mother was Xochiquetzal, who conceived him in a sacred mating deep in a cave in the earth. The young god's permanent abode was Tamoanchan. Exactly these same details appear in a description of Cinteotl, the god of maize, who is also a form of Xochipilli, the youthful sun god under the earth.[56] In the second version we have his father given incorrectly as Itzpapalotl (who was female) while his mother is given as Cornflower Necklace.[57] In still another source Quetzalcoatl, no doubt in his figuration as a fertility deity, is said to be the father of Nanahuatl, there being no mother mentioned.[58]

Let us now return to the myth of the fifth sun and look at it from the point of view of Nanahuatl alone, disregarding all other elements. The fourth sun had died, and the cosmos weltered about in a sullen gloom. The gods then decided that they must create another sun, which they would initiate through a sacrificial act—in other words, one of their number would have to die so that a new sun could come into being. A great fire was accordingly kindled on an eminence in Teotihuacán, this being the only beacon in the darkness. The myth thus opens with a presolar fire, which must be seen as a statement of the creative and purificatory half-light—whether dusk or dawn. In contrasting versions the myth allows us to see that Nanahuatl either volunteered himself or was chosen. All the sources, however, agree that he was repulsive to look at and indeed was the last being whom one might think worthy of becoming the sun.[59] We have already discussed his disfigurement, and so we are not surprised to learn that the gods threw him into the fire because of it. Variants exist here as well. It is Cinteotl who persuades him to leap into the fire. Or the two most venerable of the gods, Tonacateuctli and Xiuhteuctli, ancient deities of the sun and of fire, call upon him to fill the part. Or again Quetzalcoatl, his father, hurls him into the fire. In all of these he is homologue for Quetzalcoatl performing autosacrifice.[60]

Generally, however, the wretched god volunteers. He does so either as a genuinely humble and selfless person or because, being a great sorcerer, he can perform the act with impunity. The latter version is revealing. A situation is presented to us in which all the gods are eager for the honor of becoming the sun and all contend for the distinction. But Nanahuatl through his magic powers either descends into the underworld or enters a world of flames whence he returns laden with jewels. With these he purchases the coveted honor.

On a page in the *Codex Borgia* Nanahuatl's sacrificial journey into the infraworld is given in fascinating detail.[61] At the top of the page he is shown being sacrificed as an *ixiptla* by Quetzalcoatl[62]—this undoubtedly referring to a common cult act and therefore not to the myth where he is the victim of fire sacrifice. There follows below a set of five scenes, each of which is a gloss on the events that ensue. In the first he is ingurgitated by a dog monster standing for the horrors of Mictlan, while in the second he is destroyed in the *tlachco* by the balls and playing sticks hurled at him by four of his own avatars. In these two scenes he is covered with sores. These statements of death are climaxed by a third, where he is, as a deathly avatar in the underworld, being sacrificed at the crossing of the four infernal roads. Out of his dead parts five differently colored and crippled counterparts appear. He was thus not only destroyed in life—he was destroyed in death as well. The special Nanahuatl who emerged from the heart of the dead god was then cooked in a great pot, a reference to the cannibal meal that always followed sacrifice and, therefore, a statement of final annihilation. The final scene has the crippled god emerging from a conch shell floating in the ocean of the underworld. He carries a weapon usually thought of as the lightning. Though he is still in the underworld, a resurrection is hinted at.

It is the motivation of this astounding sacrifice that is in question. It is possible to see in the multiplicity of versions a number of different cultures or chronological levels, each adding its own special understanding of the core narrative. Two elements in the tale, however, are always present: fire and corn. Some of the versions hint strongly that Nanahuatl was the numen of the corn, which seasonally springs up out of the earth responsive to the heat of the sun. Other versions stressed Nanahuatl's association with fire alone (that is, the dawn), his sacrifice therein (the evening star), and his renewal (the new sun). These two elements, fire and corn, may seem to us at first unconnected, but both were understood as essential items in the myth. Might it be that the fire motif was that one favored by the earlier hunter groups, while the corn motif came into the myth a bit later with the rise of the urban-peasant cultures?

We see Nanahuatl doing duty for one or both. He is thus a swirling configuration of Xolotl, Ce Acatl, and Xochipilli-Cinteotl all at the same time. And it is precisely this association that gives him his affiliation with Quetzalcoatl. This ambivalence is exactly the same as that we find in the other god connected with the *tlachco*, Xochipilli-Cinteotl, the sun god rising in the red east who is also and at the same time the sprouting corn. We therefore have two gods who represent seasonal revivification and who are essentially the same being, the only real difference being that one was modeled on the planet Venus and the other on the sun. This explains

Quetzalcoatl's sometimes enigmatic connection with the sun, a seeming anomaly in a god of hurricanes and of the planet Venus.

Xolotl can claim Nanahuatl as an avatar of his by virtue of common deformity as well as by an intimate connection with cosmic sacrifice in the underworld. Indeed Nanahuatl is explicitly called Four Movement in Tlaxcala.[63] His further qualities as a patron deity of the underground maize, however, find no echo at all in the makeup of Xolotl, who represents the purely demonic. To all this can be added two revealing statements found in our sources: one that Nanahuatl was none other than Quetzalcoatl Topiltzin of Tula,[64] the other that he was the son of Quetzalcoatl.

Nanahuatl has one other kinship tie that must be mentioned—his connection with Xipe. By his sacrifice Nanahuatl becomes Tonatiuh the sun, whereas Xipe is also the form the sun takes as the renewer. The tie is vague, yet it certainly exists. In cult the *ixiptla* of Nanahuatl was flayed, which was the sacrificial death prescribed also in the Xipe rites. Both gods patronize the same skin diseases.[65] Nanahuatl was worshiped in the shrine called Netlatiloyan, the subterranean room into which the used and rotted skins of victims flayed in Xipe's worship were finally cast.[66] If Nanahuatl is indeed a form of Xochipilli-Cinteotl, then we should not be surprised to find a further fertility connection with Xipe.

Quetzalcoatl and Death

All of Quetzalcoatl's avatars are closely tied in to the night sky, to blackness, or to the underworld. If we leap from this, however, to the conclusion that Quetzalcoatl was a god of death, we shall be in error. The line separating them, however, is narrow and difficult to grasp.

Let us present the evidence for the god's identity with death. The codices call him either the "son" or the "brother" of Mictlanteuctli, god of death.[67] Also, in the codices he is depicted twinned with Mictlanteuctli, the two figures being joined back to back to form a creature with two disparate legs and four arms (fig. 30).[68] In one of these representations each god holds a *chicahuaztli*, a scepter symbolizing increase or rejuvenation; yet Quetzalcoatl holds the one marked with the death sign, while Mictlanteuctli carries the one marked with the abundance and fertility sign, the reverse in both cases of what we should expect. Furthermore, Quetzalcoatl is depicted there as a nocturnal monster, his body painted with soot, while his joints, as was customary with demons, have become horrified eyes and clashing jaws. A Huaxtec sculpture shows him with a kilt of skulls or wearing a skeleton as a dorsal cape (fig. 31).[69] Two references in myth repeat this deathly motif. In the myth of the creation of flowers we find a bat, always a symbol of death, springing from Quetzalcoatl's semen,[70] while we are elsewhere told that the god once erected a palace complex in Mictlan (if indeed this is not a reference to the building of a temple to Quetzalcoatl in the city of Mitla).[71] Finally, we have the statement that Xolotl was another name for the god of death.[72]

From the above there can be no doubt that Quetzalcoatl operates in the underworld with something of the power of death. But the power of death, which is fully exemplified in Mictlanteuctli and his spouse, the Lady of the Dead, is a numinous and final power. Quetzalcoatl's death references are not of this absolute type. A scene in the *Codex Borgia* to which I have already alluded can perhaps explain this.[73] There are shown nine avatars of Quetzalcoatl, all sacrificing the mutilated and wrinkled figure of Yohualteuctli (Four Movement), who is the sun in the world below. The ninth and central avatar is unique in being clad as a humming-

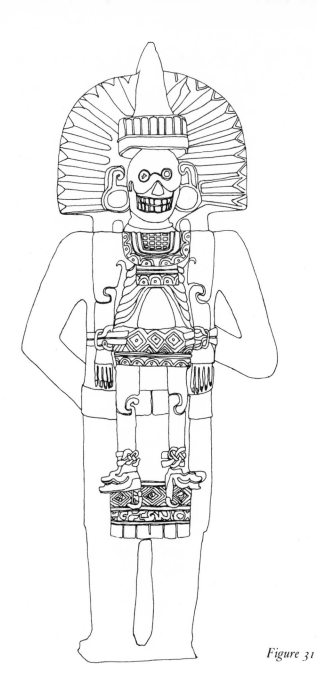

Figure 31

bird, which was the sign for the revivification of the land after the winter's drought (see fig. 25). In other words, Quetzalcoatl does not stand for *life* as against *death*, nor does he stand for the reverse. He stands rather for the mysterious mechanism by which the two are related to each other in religious thought and which could be activated in the blood of sacrifice. This is a radical redefining of the usual conception of Quetzalcoatl.

From this it follows that one must develop also a quite different understanding of the sky religion itself in which Quetzalcoatl was so central a figure. To undertake this task, let us now turn our attention to the god Tezcatlipoca—whom for obvious reasons we have hitherto avoided.

SIX
THE PLACE
OF TEZCATLIPOCA
IN THE
SKY RELIGION

Because Quetzalcoatl cannot be understood apart from Tezcatlipoca, the latter is here singled out for analysis. Both gods were geniuses of the night, and from them developed the joint god Yohualli Ehecatl, a conceptual avatar of both gods. Next I take up the legends clustering around the great priest of Quetzalcoatl called Topiltzin. Each of the main events is studied: the confrontation between the gods Quetzalcoatl and Tezcatlipoca and the former's fall from purity, his exile, and his flight to the coast. At this point the two contradictory resolutions of the story are considered: Quetzalcoatl's transformation into the morning star and alternatively his sailing over the water to Yucatán, where he appears as Kukulcan. The enigmatic figure Hueymac is also considered, and it is concluded that he is manufactured of both Quetzalcoatl and Tezcatlipoca. The religions of the two gods are then summarized and contrasted.

Introducing Tezcatlipoca

In this book I have isolated a Mesoamerican sky religion and have defined it as derived from a concept of the sky as a dragon (or, better, as two dragons). From that archetype were extracted all the celestial and atmospheric gods, as categories and forms are extracted from an essential whole. Basic terrene concepts were not included in the scope of this religion, but formed a separate religion entirely, which I have alluded to in this book but not investigated. The earth religion enshrined different attitudes toward supernatural power.

I have stated that the sky numen had two facets, the diurnal and the nocturnal, the latter of which, by being imaginatively moved into the underworld, correspondingly extended the writ of the sky religion into the world under the surface of the earth. Such augmentation never gave to the sky religion control over the forms and meanings of Earth Mother, but it did provide Mesoamerican man with a higher and more plastic set of divine terms and ritual theatrics. The sacrificial cult itself belonged essentially to the sky religion, even though Cihuacoatl, Earth Mother, and Xiuhteuctli, the genius of fire, demanded their share of hearts and blood. I certainly cannot claim that the sky religion was primary or that it demanded greater allegiance from men than did the worship of the Mother, but I do claim that it alone elaborated a sophisticated mythology of blood sacrifice. The sky religion may well have been too speculative and too complex to compete with the intuitive simplicities of the Great Mother. In fact, it became so distinctive that we today can produce this model of it, a model in which

Quetzalcoatl, not the sun, becomes the principle of the whole.

We now approach a difficult problem. One might think that the Mesoamerican priests would have seen a dichotomy of earth and sky, that they would have had an awareness of two alien structures, perhaps even a hostility between the two that should have appeared in the mythology. That was not the case. Instead, the elements of estrangement, malevolence, and opposition that are or seem to be embedded in the ways of nature were pointed up in the persons of two deities, Tezcatlipoca and Quetzalcoatl. Yet these two did not represent day versus night, as one could logically expect.

To devote a whole chapter to Tezcatlipoca in a book that revolves around Quetzalcoatl might seem superfluous. The ties between the two, however, are so strange and so close that Quetzalcoatl can come into focus only if he is finally understood in the presence of this other god (fig. 32). One of the early friars likened Tezcatlipoca to Jupiter and Quetzalcoatl to Hercules,[1] which would make them father and son, respectively, the one a god, the other a demigod and hero. However interesting this theory may be, it is still not enough. Like two drops of quicksilver in a dish these two jostle each other, suddenly join into one globule, and then shatter just as suddenly, becoming separate and distinct again. To add to this confusion, Tezcatlipoca is not by his nature within the sky religion, as I have noted above. He forms the single member of a way of religious thought wholly his own, and he enters the other religions only when their own mythologies have a need to present reality as at bottom unstable.

Tezcatlipoca had many faces. He was the surreptitious all-knower, the pansophist, with all the frightening power that this aptitude confers. He was the shaman, the deceiver, and the shape shifter. He was the berserk warrior and the Apollonian young man. He was the cajoler and the mocker.

Figure 32

He was sudden wealth and the equally sudden fall into squalor and wretchedness. He was the forgiver and the forgetter—when it so pleased him. He was both implacable and whimsical. He alone of the later Mesoamerican gods exercised a plenary power. Thus he could stand for untrammeled authority. In this book we are not particularly interested in these many facets of Tezcatlipoca. We are interested in him only as he appears in the sky religion and in the Quetzalcoatl story, where he is needed to help unravel the tangled cross-webbing of that god's nature.

We begin by noting the curious fact that, while all the gods with whom we are familiar are basically discrete deities, these two, Tezcatlipoca and Quetzalcoatl, are in a sense inseparable. This anomaly in the Mesoamerican pantheon must have a meaning. The anomaly is most readily apparent when we consider that curious attribute displayed by Tezcatlipoca, namely his amputated foot and its replacement by what has traditionally been called a "smoking mirror" but which is probably meant to gloss as "speaking mirror." Quetzalcoatl never shows this peculiar form of crippling; for Tezcatlipoca it is diagnostic.

To clarify this disabling of Tezcatlipoca, we can point to three representations in the codices, each showing a young god standing in oceanic waters.[2] One of his legs has just been torn off below the knee by an aquatic monster (fig. 33). In one codex the god is identified as Tlahuizcalpanteuctli; in the two others he appears to be an avatar of the sun that has just dropped into the underworld. In either case the missing limb is a visual symbol of an injured astral body. We thus have concrete evidence of a lost myth, or myths, that must have had originally at least three elements: a cosmic confrontation involving a sky god and a *cipactli* monster, the loss of a foot by the former, and finally its replacement by a mirror from which scrolls arise.

The god in the myth must be one of the two forms of the planet Venus or a form of the sun in the underworld—or possibly even a concurrence of all three. What interests us here is that the lost myth must have told of the replacement of the severed foot by an oracular mirror, which arrangement thenceforth identified the god as Tezcatlipoca. Yet the god depicted in one of the codices, as I have stated, is already identified as Tlahuizcalpanteuctli, the planet Venus, which we know to be a form of Quetzalcoatl. Ergo Tezcatlipoca could be there identical with Quetzalcoatl—in other words, Tezcatlipoca might have been in origin the planet Venus.

This is an extreme position to take. Perhaps I had better simply say, as above, that the two gods in mythology are

Figure 33

inseparable. Nevertheless, the above thesis is not without some validity, as we shall see in what follows.

Quetzalcoatl and Tezcatlipoca as Sky Gods and Creators

In the folk tales of the North American tribes there often appear two spirits responsible for the establishment of the world and the present constitution of its parts. They are variously referred to. They can be older brother and younger brother, the Little War Twins (of the Pueblos), and so forth. They are hunters, or they are animal spirits, or they are even grotesque were-animals. And very often one of the brothers or cocreators is a trickster, notoriously childish, inventive, perverse, and disorderly. Against this Paleolithic model of the personae of creation let us place Tezcatlipoca and Quetzalcoatl. Two Aztec myths speak to the facts of this juxtaposition: the myth of the five suns and the myth of the creation of the cosmos.

The former makes clear that the structure of the cosmos is fundamentally a function of time itself, which is fivefold and finite. Time proceeds in sunbursts or aeons, five and no more, each one being unique. The common denominator is the physical sun, who is the god Tonatiuh. This sun was five times possessed or invaded by different gods, this possession eventuating in the naming of each sun after its appropriate deity. The order of the five suns was generally as follows: Tezcatlipoca, Quetzalcoatl, Tlaloc, Chalchiuhtlicue, and Nanahuatl. In part 5 we considered the manner in which the last of the five succeeded in becoming the sun. The significant factor here is the appearance of the two gods at the beginning of the list of names. This indicates their primacy.

The first sun was experimental and produced only a tenebrous light.[3] It was in keeping with the character of Tezcatlipoca that he transformed himself into this first of the completed suns. At the end of thirteen 52-year cycles Quetzalcoatl Ehecatl attacked Tezcatlipoca, knocking him from his solar station into the sea. Ehecatl then became the second sun, which endured an equal length of time. At the expiration of that period Tezcatlipoca turned upon Ehecatl and knocked him out of the sky, thereby letting loose upon the world destructive hurricanes.[4]

No hostilities or struggles are mentioned in connection with the next two suns. The fifth and present sun, however, which is the *nahualli* of Nanahuatl, son and avatar of Quetzalcoatl, will finally be snatched out of the sky in a final act of knavery by Tezcatlipoca, thus forever ending cosmic history.[5] In this tale of five gods only our two are referred to as antagonists.

The nature of their cosmic confrontation is decidedly not that of opposites, however. It is not, in other words, an incipient dualism but is something much more complex. Before turning to this subject, however, let us briefly consider the second myth mentioned above, that of the creation. Two major versions are extant, the highland Mexica version, which we have in Aztec sources, and a Maya version found in the *Popol Vuh*.[6]

The Maya version is the more folkloristic of the two, but one can still see behind its details the outline of an old creation tale involving the two primeval brothers. The tale opens on the mention of a great ogre, Seven Parrot, who lived in a world tree before there was any sun at all. He was married to Chimalmat, the Earth Mother (who is Chimalma, the mother of Quetzalcoatl, in Aztec mythology). The presumption and vainglory of this monster were evident in his constant boasting. That brought about his downfall, for he was finally killed by the twins One Hunter and Jaguar Deer. In the affray one of the twins lost his arm.

This simple scenario is duplicated and expanded in the episode immediately following, which involves the two sons of Seven Parrot. The first, the orogenic monster Cipacna, lived in the waters, created the mountains, and carried them about on his back; his name recalls the Nahuatl *cipactli*, the caiman, who was the primordial earth monster floating in the ponds and slime of early chaos with its ridged back protruding. The second son, Two Leg, a personification of the earthquake, had the power to shake down not only the mountains but the sky as well.

Now the twins who had killed Seven Parrot proceeded to plot the death of his two sons. At this time Cipacna had just succeeded in killing a coterie of brothers who upon their death had become the stars in the sky. One Hunter and Jaguar Deer attacked Cipacna and disposed of him by thrusting him under a mountain. They then turned upon his brother, Two Leg, who had been trying to outdo the sun, killing him also. As a finale to the tale the heroic twins were transformed into the sun and the moon.

The old motif of the two creating brothers, one of them quixotic and perverse, is here split into two sets of brothers, the first set purely heroic, the second set (clearly connected with the earth) just as clearly perverse. Seven Parrot is a numinous foreshadowing of his two refractory sons.

A more rarefied set of twins is given us under the names Gukumatz and Tepeu, two dragon beings who live in the deeps and who are always mentioned jointly.[7] It was they who began the creation by calling up the mountains out of the waters. The names of the two mean, respectively, Feathered Serpent and Conqueror. I need hardly point out that the first is Quetzalcoatl, while Tepeu was a common name for Tezcatlipoca among the Nahuas.

The Maya myths tell us that in the time precedent to the creation of the sun the main actors were brothers. Earth in this prototime rises out of its encompassing waters and claims the stars, which thenceforth must always rise out of the terrestrial darkness. Our interest, however, is rather in the brothers or twins who cooperate as demiurges but who are somehow still hostile. We further note that their creation includes the whole of the cosmos, heavens and earth.

Contrast this somewhat disjointed account with the standard Aztec myth of creation. The two gods Tezcatlipoca and Quetzalcoatl either decided themselves or were deputed to perform the creation. Identified respectively by their date names One Wind and Nine Wind, they were sent down by the mighty Mother Starskirt, who was the Milky Way.[8] First they brought fire, or light, into existence and followed this with the entire inventory of things and living beings. They paid particular attention to the creation of the earth. Floating like a log in the ocean, which they had previously called into being, was the torpid monster Cipactli. For the final act the two demiurges changed themselves into two dragons, as we have seen, and by twining around the monster crushed it into two parts. The upper half they

242

lifted up, and it became the sky; the half that remained below became the earth. From the parts of this baser half they then created all earthly things: vegetation, rivers and springs, mountains and caves. A slightly different version concentrates on the making of the sky.[9] The fourth sun ended when the sky fell from its great height and covered the earth with its ruins, thus allowing the celestial waters to gush out. Gods and men perished in this catastrophic flood. Tezcatlipoca and Quetzalcoatl thereupon entered the body of the earth monster (that is, they went underground), driving four roads into the interior to join and make a crossroads in the center. Together they heaved up the sky again and fixed it in place with the aid of four gods, each of whom thenceforth supported one of the four corners of the sky. Tezcatlipoca and Quetzalcoatl then changed themselves into two world trees, giving further support to the sky. In accomplishing this splendid reconstruction, the two gods wore a path through the wilderness of the stars, that was to become known to men as the Milky Way.

The Two Gods as Darkness and Night

In an earlier chapter we came to the conclusion that Quetzalcoatl had been originally the sky and that out of this numinous essence Ehecatl was refined as the god of air or wind. We also discovered, somewhat unexpectedly, that Ehecatl found darkness more congenial than the blaze of day, though this aspect of him was perhaps no more than an emphasis at first. Consequently, we had no difficulty in accepting him as an appropriate deity in the creation myths that concentrate on the *tlachco* and the night sky. But now, what about Tezcatlipoca? We have not seen him so far as the sky.

As we open the inquiry on Tezcatlipoca, we can see at the beginning that he is the very principle of darkness. Whereas Quetzalcoatl as a deity has an obvious base in nature, first as a sky dragon, then as wind or star, Tezcatlipoca comes from the world of men, from quirks of personality, inscrutability of motivation, and the enigmas behind all decisions. The concepts "otherness" and its corollary "darkness" best describe this proclivity. In a previous work I have approached this difference, separating the two gods by connecting Ehecatl with the priest and Tezcatlipoca with the shaman.

A god modeled upon any manifestation of nature (whether vegetation, sun, star, wind, earth, fire, or whatever) suffers change over the years in only one direction, that is, in the direction of increasing personalization. This alteration in man's treatment of the supernatural is generally hesitant and slow. Contrariwise, the god who displays the power of free, arbitrary decision changes in the direction of increasing conceptualization, and he may consequently appear as a jinn or demon. In the first case a god eventuates whose boundaries of action are known; that is, he brings rain or withholds it, he shines in the heavens or is eclipsed, he lights up the darkness or dies away in the night. Tezcatlipoca illustrates the second case. He tends to be anomalous because he lacks exactly such limits in nature.

We must not make this distinction between Tezcatlipoca and Quetzalcoatl too categorical. It is useful, however, in studying the relationship between the two, a nexus that I believe to be without parallel in the rest of Mesoamerican religion. Normally it would not be too difficult to make the relationship uniting the two gods understandable to the reader, but the presence of what I have called in another book the mask pool[10] smudges the boundaries between them—so much so that in the succeeding section we shall have to consider a conjoined deification, two in one, called Yohualli Ehecatl.

We have already considered the various levels of the supernatural that Quetzalcoatl embodies, beginning with the sky dragon, down to entities within the sky (wind and the planet Venus), from which in turn we derived a deathly twin in the underworld, an imperial wandering warrior (Nacxitl) and others, the final avatar being so far removed as to appear altogether unrelated to the original numinous source. In other words the step-down tends to be from one point in nature to another related or reduplicated point—ending finally in such a deity as Nacxitl, who symbolizes not a piece of the world of nature at all but rather a piece of the world of culture.

For his part, Tezcatlipoca, through an evolution of various avatars, moves outward to meet Quetzalcoatl. Nothing is known about the early forms of Tezcatlipoca, and I am guessing here about his development in time. We assume that he began as a were-jaguar, from which he became the spirit of cavernous darkness, as seen in the god Tepeyollotli, and then from that to deceiver and mocker, to creator of discord, to juvenescent warrior, and finally to the symbolization of blind judgment and the power of the state. At this latter point he is the epitome of sovereignty and meets that particular Quetzalcoatl who is the patron of royal lineages. The whole spectrum of divinity thus covered runs from Tezcatlipoca on the one pole to Quetzalcoatl on the opposite pole. What lies between them and the way it is structured are the subjects of our present interest.

Tezcatlipoca's fundamental characteristic, as I see it, is deception and the stratagems of sorcery. As sorcerer his most significant *nahualli* was the jaguar. His other common animal disguises, such as the coyote, the turkey cock, the skunk, and the monkey, explicated several aspects of him, but his form as a jaguar was so basic that it even detached itself as an avatar of his to become a recognizable deity in its own right, Tepeyollotli, or Interior of the Mountain, perhaps best understood as Darkness.[11] Tepeyollotli, in fact, may have been the god's original configuration, as noted above.

Tepeyollotli was seen as a jaguar, whose spotted hide was an emblem of the star-flecked night (fig. 34). He was imagined as ensconced deep down in the caves of the earth, and his voice was the hollow echo that sounded out of the ravines. The echo almost became a demon figure in its own right, if indeed it did not do so in the fetish of the winged conch-shell trumpet, a receptacle wherein lay dormant, but always ready to be evoked, an eerie voice.

The jaguar thus stands for the innermost earth, thought of not as the producer of corn or flowers or flowing rain clouds but as inward-oriented and leading to Stygian blackness. Darkness to all men has meant that which at the least is unknown and at the most is impenetrable. Like an exhalation this darkness rises up out of the earth every night peppered with stars. The jaguar meant all of that.

Like many of the other gods Tezcatlipoca can appear in quadruplicate.[12] Only two of his four forms, however, are important, the red and the black, the latter being his primal form. As the black Tezcatlipoca he was the older of the two, and his statue—in at least one instance—was carved out of glistening black obsidian. The blackness of this volcanic glass was so expressive of his character that another of his avatars arose from it, Itztli, a name that refers to a knife or chip of obsidian, excessively sharp. More telling than any of these examples of the sloe-black god's affinity with obsidian was the smoking mirror from which he derived his name. This mirror was a surface of polished obsidian, a magical object out of whose ebony depths the god could summon up and command all things. Oracles were read in it, and those who peered into it could be traumatized at the horrors to be seen therein.

Blackness was merely one aspect of Tezcatlipoca's demonic nature. He afflicted men in the form of apparitions that appeared in the night, corpses wrapped in shrouds,

Figure 34

eidolons and goblins of all kinds. In his avatar as Ixpuzteque (Broken Face) he was a demon who appeared to lost travelers on the road, hopping horribly along on his single clawed foot.[13]

As a god of night and darkness he of course can be compared with Quetzalcoatl. In a previous chapter I mentioned that Quetzalcoatl's color was black, that through his Venusian avatars he was more closely connected with night than with day, and that his most common avatar was Xolotl, the sanguinary evening star and underworld denizen. This ambience by definition is congenial also to Tezcatlipoca. Standing for much the same thing, therefore, the two are obviously related. In fact on the famous Altar of Tlaxcala we see the god of the morning star, who is emerging from the maw of a dragon, intimately paired with Tezcatlipoca. But perhaps the most telling example of this affinity in demonry is the fact that Tezcatlipoca, Quetzalcoatl, and Xolotl can share the same date name, One Wind.[14]

Tezcatlipoca's love of darkness comes from his unpredictable shifts of whim and shapes. His blackness represents the concept of inscrutability and the perilous unknown, whereas Quetzalcoatl's blackness comes from his derivation out of sky, a complex of wind, air, and stars—all parts of nature.

Yohualli Ehecatl

One of Mesoamerica's most significant advances in religious formulation occurred when the divine entity Yohualli Ehecatl appeared. Yohualli Ehecatl was not a god like others who had a distinctive mask and a known jurisdiction. He seems to have been a divinized double epithet. In Nahuatl grammar there is found a rhetorical device to express a single idea with two concepts. For instance, *atl*, which means "water," joined to *tepetl*, "mountain," acquires the meaning of "community" or "homeland." In the comparison here presented *yohualli* means "night," while *ehecatl*, as we have seen, means "wind." Together the two fuse to designate "imponderable" or "invisible." One might even suggest that they carry the extended meaning "the impalpable and the energizing."

It is possible of course that the original creating pair in the earliest myth was on the one hand Yohualli and on the other Ehecatl. The two titles might have been so often recited together that jointly they formed a mask that later could be applied to either Tezcatlipoca or Quetzalcoatl.

However that may be, our objective is to determine whether the god so entitled is really a deviant from the norm of Aztec gods and whether he can thus be placed in a class apart. The double title would seem to subsume almost a totality of divinity and therefore might be the equivalent of our proper noun God as we give witness to him in such epithets as "the Omnipotent."

Important to realize is that the god Yohualli Ehecatl was invoked almost always in reference to Tezcatlipoca or Quetzalcoatl. That is not unexpected. *Yohualli* means "night," and, while Tezcatlipoca is nowhere identified as the god Night, he certainly is a lord in the night sky, and, in his avatar as Tepeyollotli, he is a lord of the darkness also.[15] He can be properly understood, therefore, in the first term of the compound. Quetzalcoatl is equally understood in the second term of the compound, for his primary avatar is the wind itself. From this one might gather that the invocation Yohualli Ehecatl is really to be translated "Tezcatlipoca *and* Quetzalcoatl." Such is not the case. Wherever used, the epithet refers to a single entity. He was a god of whom no images were made and who had no temples or organized worship, and yet a god to whom individuals could confess.

We have rejected "Tezcatlipoca *and* Quetzalcoatl" as a

translation and have stated that the divine title is given to either Quetzalcoatl *or* Tezcatlipoca and scarcely ever to other gods. In other words, either of these two gods when the occasion demanded could be raised to the level of the inscrutable and by implication to a position of exclusivity, a position, as we have already pointed out, approximating the biblical use of the word God. One of our sources undoubtedly had this in mind when describing Tezcatlipoca: "At times he appears in an aerial form under the shape of a cloud, at other times as a shadowy figure or a whirlwind. Always, however, he is hidden from human sight."[16] Such a description could be applied to Quetzalcoatl equally well.

When all the evidence is assembled, we can see in Yohualli Ehecatl a god concept modeled upon Tezcatlipoca and Quetzalcoatl as a demiurgic pair but heightened into an overarching theism, a disembodied godhead whose nature contained the unaccountability of Tezcatlipoca and the holiness of Quetzalcoatl. It was the final distillation of a unitary essence from the original pair, Tepeu and Gukumatz, Tezcatlipoca and Quetzalcoatl. Yohualli Ehecatl might almost be translated as Spirit.

But if this high god was known as Night and Air, he was also known in Tezcoco as Tloque Nahuaque, the Lord Everywhere Present, literally Owner of the Proximity and Vicinity. We know about this manifestation of the high god mainly from a very erratic source.[17] For what it is worth, this source informs us that Nezahualcoyotl, ruler of Tezcoco, experienced this new god as a result of a personal tragedy, which occurred during a war with Chalco. Nezahualcoyotl described him as "hidden and unknown" and took him as his personal god. As was said of Topiltzin of Tula in the reformed cult of Quetzalcoatl, so Nezahualcoyotl is said to have abolished human sacrifice in the cult of his unknown god. He erected a temple to him so that it rested on nine pyramid terraces, representing the number of heavens.

The shrine proper was painted black, and the exterior walls were shown covered with stars. There was no image within the cella, because by nature the god was *opu*, "invisible." For this god the great king composed over sixty hymns. The god could be called Ilhuicahua, He Who Possesses the Heavens.

How much of this can be believed is moot. The temple described was undoubtedly that of Tezcatlipoca when referred to as Tloque Nahuaque, but the statements about the absence of an image and the abolition of human sacrifice must be doubted. The truth probably was that the great king, whose genius is well attested, showed partiality to Tezcatlipoca and was instrumental in raising him to the sublimated status indicated above. In other words, the god was Tezcatlipoca, but in a new heavenly avatar in which his power to become invisible eventuated in the conception of a deity of formlessness. This apparently could be carried to the point of exclusivity, for some of the texts refer to him as "the only god." This, then, was Tloque Nahuaque, another name for Yohualli Ehecatl.

It was a not-unexpected end to the mythology of the two dragons who later became the two creators, one of them darkness, the other air and impalpability. Each going his own way, they had separated to become anthropomorphic gods assigned to different spheres. Yet having first appeared together, they could not be kept totally differentiated, and at the end of Mesoamerican history they slip together again as Yohualli Ehecatl. It is a history of the slow refining of the concept of the divine.

Of interest to us finally is that Tezcatlipoca gave slightly more to the final depiction of Yohualli Ehecatl than did Quetzalcoatl. That emphasis, however, is subtle. In the dimly perceived religious struggle to achieve a higher vision of God, Yohualli Ehecatl was a signally important step along the way and the last one that would be taken by the pre-Columbian Mesoamericans. It failed of full formulation, as can be seen in the Panotla myth.[18]

In the Panotla myth, as I have said, the ancestors, led by their god and his priests landed in their canoes at Panuco, and then coasted south, finally to settle in Tamoanchan. There in Tamoanchan the priests and wise men left the group and sailed away eastward, taking with them their sacred books and their wisdom. They also took with them their god Yohualli Ehecatl, but they promised before leaving that at the end of time the god would return to settle the affairs of men.

It is obvious that this is a close variant of the tale told about the expulsion of Topiltzin Quetzalcoatl from Tula. The connection with Tamoanchan, the disappearance of the books of wisdom, the embarkation eastward, the promise to return—these are also parts of the Topiltzin legend. My guess is that the story originally belonged to Quetzalcoatl and was extended, in the above Völkerwanderung version, to the deity Yohualli Ehecatl at a time when he was being developed by the priests.

The gist of the Panotla myth is the display of Yohualli Ehecatl's aniconic nature, for he is said to have disappeared completely from the stage of history, leaving behind only the prophecy of his reappearance in a final summation of all things. The myth thus states that he is in fact a "high god," uninvolved and whimsical, as witness his decision to withdraw. His return will bring historic time to an end.

One might have expected the development of a true theodicy in the person of this potentially exalted god, but the details of the Panotla myth effectively refute this. How could a god who departed, abandoning his fugitive people, embody anything like a universal goodness? So the final composition could not go much beyond a primitive spiritualization expressed as "A cuix tlacaitto ca yohualli ca ehecatl" ("How is it that he has no human form? For indeed he is as night and the wind").[19]

Tezcatlipoca and Quetzalcoatl in Tula

The preceding data on the relations existing between the two gods Tezcatlipoca and Quetzalcoatl have been drawn from mythology. There is an additional corpus of material that comes in the form of legend. It revolves around two personages prominent in Toltec history. The first was Topiltzin, the high priest of Quetzalcoatl in the city of Tula. The other was Huemac, an enigmatic ruler also in the same city. These two were intimately involved in certain religious upheavals that in the end shattered the Toltec state. The city of Tula, successor of Teotihuacán, is thought to have been the scene of these dimly perceived events. I shall assume here that it was.

The Toltec theogony must have been similar to that of the later Aztec world, except that the Toltecs worshiped Quetzalcoatl as their leading god, a commitment already very ancient. There, in his avatar as Wind or Storm, he was known by his date name Ce Acatl and was shown in art as a ravening dragon rushing through the vault of heaven. But there was another god powerfully competing with him for the allegiance of the warrior class. This was Titlacahuan, a form of Tezcatlipoca who had so identified himself with the nation that he could also be called Toltecatl, the "Toltec God." The rest of the pantheon was pretty much what one would expect. The great earth goddess was present, of course, as well as rain, water, and corn deities.[20] The vigorous Chichimec deities Mixcoatl and Itzpapalotl were venerated, the latter in the avatar Nine Monkey. The conceptual apex of this cluster of deities was formed by the two high gods in Omeyocan. We should not pretend that we see this religious picture clearly; the most we can say is that it appears to have been the same mix of religions that we find later in Tenochtitlán.

The legend of Topiltzin was told in a dozen different

ways, and some imprecision in the reporting is therefore inevitable. I begin with the assumption that one particular statement in the legend was indeed a fact. This statement had it that a certain famous thaumaturge was called in by the inhabitants of Tula to become the high priest of their god Quetzalcoatl. What led them to extend this invitation was probably the success that the holy man had already had in Huaxtec lands, and in nearby Tulantzinco, in the promulgation of his new religious doctrine. This man is generally referred to in our sources as Topiltzin, Our Prince, and I shall so refer to him.[21]

Nor can we be exact in describing the full range of Topiltzin's new preaching except to say that, when viewed from a Mesoamerican stance, it must have been seen as a radical challenge to the established cult. Most exceptional to our way of thinking is that it was carried abroad as a missionary effort by peripatetic priests (a curious body called the *tlanquacemilhuitime*) preaching from high places.[22] From his intimate association with the god Quetzalcoatl we may deduce that Topiltzin inculcated a reforming sky religion. It also could be that the modified god whom he presented was an avatar of Quetzalcoatl imported from Huaxtec lands—indeed, this new avatar of Quetzalcoatl is stated in one source to have been Yohualli Ehecatl.[23] The new doctrine was an aspect of the sky religion, if we may extrapolate from the fact that the celestial gods Citlallatonac and Citlalinicue were at the top of Topiltzin's pantheon. The Topiltzin story in fact can be read as a late wave of coastal religious influence on the highlands.

Topiltzin called for a new holiness that could be achieved only by an increased emphasis on autosacrifice and other penitential exercises. He forbade the sacrifice of human victims on the *techcatl*, substituting for it the offering of birds, butterflies, and snakes, these being symbols of air and sky.[24] The impact of this innovation along with the institution of the new priesthood in the metropolis must have been immense and sufficiently explains the tumults and dislocations that followed and that ultimately undermined the state. The cults of all the gods who had hitherto been fed on the blood and hearts of human victims were affected; one source states that these gods became angered at Quetzalcoatl and jeered at him and his ways.[25] Two deities were particularly affected by Topiltzin's negative on human sacrifice, Tlazolteotl and Xipe.[26] Both of these had already achieved grotesque levels of horror in their sacrificial cults, and both had therefore much to protest.

The new discipline must have had a profound effect also upon the old, established cult of Quetzalcoatl, who as Ce Acatl up to that time had been powerfully oriented toward war and its frightful companion, human sacrifice. The Toltec warrior's way of life was threatened by the reform, while the prestige of the new vicariously suffering priesthood must have been correspondingly enhanced. A religious polarization had occurred in the city of Tula.

Previously I have expressed my feeling that the Tula of Topiltzin was a memory of Teotihuacán in its later days. In Teotihuacán, Quetzalcoatl had been worshiped probably as a fertility-oriented Ehecatl, his importance as Ce Acatl only at that time beginning. The superimposition of one avatar on the other in those distant times makes it now almost impossible to disentangle them. Certainly by Toltec times Ce Acatl had already surged ahead. But whichever of the two cities Topiltzin belonged in, we can at least divide the matter of his corpus of legends into three parts: (1) a previous age of purity, (2) the temptation and the fall, and (3) the exile and prophecy of return. I shall comment on each in turn.

We are introduced to the age of purity when we first see Ce Acatl performing a rigorous seven-year retreat in the desert preparatory to becoming a Toltec warrior.[27] He is a young man, the son of Mixcoatl (Camaxtli) and a woman descended from one of the five Mimixcoa. In view of the fact that Mixcoatl is Venusian, the young hero has a stellar descent on both sides, and he will thus be another vision of the morning star. To us such a deity does not appear to be a logical model for the high-priesthood, but it must be remembered that the cult of Ce Acatl Quetzalcoatl, which was central in Tula, was a warrior's cult as well as a vital component of the sky religion.

The gods favored the young man, and he became, by the suffrage of the people, the first Toltec ruler and temple builder. It is stated categorically that he was the one responsible for introducing into Toltec society a savage cult of human sacrifice.[28]

The above prologue to the age of purity sets forth the basics in the legend of the Toltec Quetzalcoatl, namely, that the god was a war dragon who in turn was the emblem of the morning star. In another and more common version of the legend the Quetzalcoatl being talked about is really Topiltzin, the holy man who came in not from the desert but from the Huaxteca and Tulantzinco.[29] In this latter account the priestly rather than the warlike is stressed.

Both versions are correct, but they differ in that the god Ce Acatl Quetzalcoatl was the ancient and orthodox god of wind and storm who had been commandeered by the entire warrior class in Tula, whereas the god Topiltzin Quetzalcoatl was that deity as radically reformulated by one man.

In the age of purity the rulership of Quetzalcoatl in Tula was said to have produced wealth and contentment.[30] The gods were properly served, the laws were observed, maize grew to extravagant heights, and cotton bolls bloomed on the bush already dyed in rainbow colors and ready for the spinning. Vast treasures were accumulated by Topiltzin and stored in the holy city. This Saturnian age came to its end when corruption and factions appeared. The legends designate Tezcatlipoca as the catalytic agent in that disintegration. This introduces the story of the temptation and the fall.

Tezcatlipoca had become envious of the reverence accorded to Quetzalcoatl and laid plans to bring him down. One version presents this event as a head-on attack in which Tezcatlipoca assumed horrible and monstrous disguises in order to disrupt life in the city. He stole Quetzalcoatl's magic mirror, in which one could read the auspices of rain and drought, and in a final, flamboyant act of defiance he knocked down Quetzalcoatl's statue.[31] The more common version, however, shows him not so much a creature of violence as a subtle deceiver.

The legend of Topiltzin's fall so fascinated Mesoamericans that they were never able to settle on a canonical version. Four personages interact as a group in the legend. If one was thinking historically, Topiltzin the lawgiver and emperor in Tula came to mind, surrounded by his three great earls, each holding large territories under his aegis.[32] These three had become restive, and to prevent their rebellion Topiltzin sent them a jeweled ball court on which they could play out their hostilities. Needless to say, the appeasement did not work, and great battles finally erupted in the empire. The one fought in Morelos ended with the defeat of Topiltzin, but his line continued in the persons of two sons.

On the other hand, if one was thinking in terms of cult, the four were Topiltzin and, opposed to him, Titlacahuan (Tezcatlipoca) and two of his avatars—again four protagonists.[33] The latter three had been dismayed by the abolition of human sacrifice in Tula, and they consequently plotted to destroy Quetzalcoatl. A shortened, more brutal version of this confrontation tells of a ball game to which Tezcatlipoca challenged Quetzalcoatl, in the course of which the former suddenly took the form of a jaguar, stampeding all the spectators, who thereupon rushed into a river and drowned.[34]

Among storytellers there was a rich choice of reasons to be posited for Quetzalcoatl's failure to foresee his danger and take appropriate steps against it. The three most common reasons given were his impurity, his incredulousness, and his anxiety over the loss of his youth.

The first reason points directly to his profession of priesthood and tended to interest the Spanish friars more than the other two, wherefore it received more attention. Here Tezcatlipoca in disguise tempted Quetzalcoatl to become drunken on *octli* and then, while intoxicated, to commit fornication with his sister (or with the lovely goddess Xochiquetzal).[35] On awakening, Topiltzin realized that he had demeaned his office and rendered himself unfit to rule, wherefore he departed into self-imposed exile.

The second version points up Quetzalcoatl's gullibility, for in the confrontation with Tezcatlipoca he foolishly gave way to the most simple blandishments. From the point of view of narrative consistency this second version is not very convincing inasmuch as Quetzalcoatl was known to be the god of wisdom.

The third version has been neglected by scholars.[36] It is perhaps the most impressive of the three, for it comports with man's earliest serious literary themes beginning as far back as the Gilgamesh epic—the search for eternal life. Here Topiltzin is presented as palsied and debilitated with age. Tezcatlipoca induces him to peer into his magic mirror, wherein he is at last confronted with the facts of existence, namely the briefness and incompleteness of all life, including his own. Stricken now with open anxiety over the relentless approach of death, he agrees with Tezcatlipoca's suggestion that he should depart for Tlapallan, a never-never land where he can recover his lost youth and whence he can then return. In some versions of the story a hallucinatory potion revealing the future is substituted for the mirror, but it is invariably Tezcatlipoca's trickery that overcomes Quetzalcoatl in the end, forcing him out of office and allowing the Toltec cults to recover their original focus on human sacrifice.

The above relates a passage of pre-Aztec history of great interest and almost succeeds in translating its subject matter into universal terms. By seeing it confusedly as part of the story of the god Quetzalcoatl as well as the study of a mortal priest, the mythographers limited the possible interpretations of it to the realms of the inchoate and the future, neglecting present applications. The story told of the failure of purity or of the triumph of deception, depending on the angle of view, but it was not in any way the equivalent of the victory of evil over good. Tezcatlipoca was not the devil; he was more like Odysseus, sly, admirable, opportunist. In such a story Quetzalcoatl was simply the necessary protagonist. The Mesoamerican listener was thus asked to react to the telling of the tale, not with a sigh for the defeated good but with wonder at the clever and ineluctable designs of Tezcatlipoca.

One version of the tale makes this bias very apparent, for it says that Tezcatlipoca approached Ce Acatl in Tula, telling him that it was his fate to go to Tlapallan, where a palace had already been erected for him and where he was to live out his days.[37] When Quetzalcoatl had studied the signs in the sky, he found it indeed true that the gods had indicated that at the end of four years he must leave Tula. Tezcatlipoca was closer to destiny than was Quetzalcoatl.

The Flight

The legend of Quetzalcoatl's departure into exile is modeled on one or more of the historic treks of the Nahua peoples southeastward, a traditional route and a traditional direction for them. We are not going to try to discover here which of the migrations archaeologically recorded might be in question here or whether it was impelled outward from Teotihuacán or from Tula.

A little-noticed tale provides us with an early model of

the plot.[38] In it we see Ce Acatl, the warrior son of a warrior father, moving southward and conquering all the way down to the coast, then on to Acallan (present Tabasco), and finally, in great canoes, to Tlapallan (Yucatán). This is not a story of exile but of an organized Vikinglike raid ending with a settlement abroad.

There are other migration stories that undoubtedly contributed elements to the story of Quetzalcoatl's flight. The Quiché memory of early times is patterned in much the same way.[39] Because of the situation anciently in Tula the ancestors were finally forced to leave, taking with them their god Tohil (Storm) who was, of course, Quetzalcoatl. Before leaving, however, they performed a dawn watch with appropriate sacrifices to the gods. At the same time, and to increase the efficacy of their offerings, they performed autosacrifice. The star that they had awaited thereupon led them out on a journey that ended only after they had finally crossed the eastern waters.

An equally relevant story is about the great captain Xelhua, whom we have already met as one of Quetzalcoatl's avatars.[40] In this account the youthful Huemac, who in the tale is the *ueyo* ("councillor") of Tezcatlipoca, deliberately sows discord between two factions in Tula, the Toltec Chichimecs, who were of his own party, and the Nonohualca Chichimecs, adherents of Quetzalcoatl. From our source it appears that the *casus belli* was an instance of human sacrifice. After many vicissitudes Huemac was seized by the Nonohulacas and sacrificed by arrows at the entrance to the cave of Cincalco. The division had become so deep, however, that the Nonohualcas themselves decided to abandon the city. Led by Xelhua and carrying with them all the paraphernalia of Quetzalcoatl, they turned their faces to the southeast and departed. Theirs was a sacred journey, for they were accompanied by a special penitential priest, who interpreted for them the words of Quetzalcoatl (here invoked as the high god Ipalnemohuani). They ended in the

Tehuacán Valley, a region historically devoted to the cult of Quetzalcoatl. Although their leader, Xelhua, had died en route, the Nonohualcas settled down there in seven separate communities.

From the above we see that the tale of Topiltzin's flight involved a background of old migration tales, from several of which details were extracted to build up the completed legend. The one fact that we can insist on is that the exile eventuated from a great cult upheaval that once had moved men in the Mexican highlands to immense broils.

The cult of Tezcatlipoca, as we know from the legend, proved the stronger of the two, and the reformer was forced to withdraw.[41] The story is told in the style of a *Paradise Lost*. The beautiful birds that had caroled in the courts of Tula flew away forever, the cacao trees were changed into the wiry desert mesquite, and the wealth accumulated by Topiltzin was cast into a lake or burned. All verdure died, and harsh desert took over. Thus the environment changed to wasteland. As for Topiltzin, he left reluctantly, accompanied by a great number of retainers and harassed all along his route by Tezcatlipoca. The drought through which they advanced was solely of Tezcatlipoca's making, a clear sign of Quetzalcoatl's loss of fertilizing powers. The latter's most tragic loss is narrated in the incident in which, just before he departed from the Great Basin, demons waylaid him, seizing all his magic arts and skills.

The route followed in the flight seldom varies. The god went through the Great Basin; then to Tzapotlan, in Morelos; to Cholula and Cuauhquechollan; and finally down to the coast. There at the site of Coatzacoalcos the sea leg of his journey commenced, with passage to Acallan and ultimately to Tlapallan. For that part of the flight, which began in Cholula and ended in Tlapallan, the sources refer to him as Nacxitl. One tale even names the four sorcerer lords or priests who accompanied Nacxitl; they were Ten Flower, Monkey, Timal, and One Rabbit.[42]

The Chinampaneca people in the southern part of the basin gave a different account of the flight. According to them either Quetzalcoatl died in Culhuacan, the neo-Toltec capital city on the lake,[43] or else he disappeared into Mount Xicco nearby, where he lives forever, just as Huemac was supposed to do in Cincalco.[44] By maintaining that he died in the basin, the Chinampanecas of course precluded any follow-up settlement in Tlapallan.

Cholula, as one of the places through which Topiltzin passed, was obviously an embarrassment to the mythographers. Cholula was the god's holy city and had been so for centuries. To describe it as merely one of the several sites through which he passed obviously demeaned it. Awkward and unconvincing attempts were made to single it out as especially important in the tale. Topiltzin is said to have remained there for 20 years, or again for 160 years,[45] during which time he built the great temple. But it was difficult to work the overwhelming centrality of Quetzalcoatl's cult there into the tale of a discredited fugitive. The problem was that the flight concerned a historic high priest, a mortal, whereas Cholula was the metropolis of a god, similarly named, to be sure, but with his own mythology. The Cholula hierarchy probably had little interest in the discredited priest Topiltzin who came to them from the outside.

At one point in the tale there is a significant hiatus, an interruption that none of the Mesoamericans were able to square with the embarkation in the Gulf and the subsequent journey to Yucatán. This was Quetzalcoatl's self-immolation by fire after he arrived on the coast.

I have mentioned this event before when discussing Ce Acatl. The death by fire was only one of four versions given of his death or leave-taking on the coast.[46] The other three versions are (1) his departure eastward over the Gulf, (2) his entry into a mountain, and (3) his entry into the cleft of a tree. It is interesting that this clutch of termination tales should be centered in the very area where the Olmec culture arose, the matrix of Mesoamerican civilization.

The self-incineration legend was taken over by those who developed the story of the exile from an earlier myth of the god Quetzalcoatl as Ce Acatl, the morning star. On his arrival at the seashore Quetzalcoatl dressed himself in his regalia and, having mounded up a great pyre, cast himself into the flames. Two variants relate to his subsequent transfiguration. In the first one, which I have already mentioned, his spirit descends into the underworld for a period of eight days, equipping himself with deadly darts,[47] at the expiration of which time he arises as the new and fearsome warrior Ce Acatl, hurling his rays of light about at will. I have already interpreted this. The Quetzalcoatl who dies in the fire is Xolotl the evening star descending into the flames of the fallen sun. Eight days is the period of inferior conjunction of the planet Venus when it is invisible, that is, the period between the disappearance of the planet as the evening star and its first rising as the herald of the morning. That is the exact number of days alloted by the mythographers for the transfiguration of Quetzalcoatl into Ce Acatl.

In the second version the god's ashes spiral upward into the dawn to become birds of rich scarlets, of pinks, and of lemon yellows—the chromatic display of a typical morning. The god's heart, like a great spark, flies up among them to become a new and splendid divinity, the morning star.[48]

When we contrast this sacrifice in the fire of Quetzalcoatl with that of his son Nanahuatl, we can see that they are almost exactly equivalent stories. Quetzalcoatl is central in both, even though in the second he acts as an avatar. In both the pyre is the red glow of dawn, the only difference being that in one story the hero is the planet Venus, in the other Tonatiuh. The main difference between the two—and it is a minor one—is that the Topiltzin tale is anthropocentric while the Tonatiuh version is theocentric. One was astronomic and inspired by the discovery of periodicity of the Venusian disappearance and return, while the other was inspired by the less complicated but still wonderful periodicity of the rising and setting of the sun. Which tale served as the model for the other is moot, and may indeed be of little importance, for the intimate connection between the sun and the planet Venus must have made speculation about the one include automatically speculation about the other.

Two dates were given for Quetzalcoatl's transfiguration, the year 1-reed and the day 4-movement. Both fit accurately into the scenario, for One Reed is the date name of Quetzalcoatl who rises as the morning star, while Four Movement is the date name of the god's avatar Xolotl, the evening star. On the day 4-movement Quetzalcoatl was said to have "disappeared into the Red Sea," in other words, to have dropped down as the planet Venus into oceanic waters.[49] An accurate astronomical synopsis of planetary events was here transformed into one of the world's most famous myths, that of death followed by resurrection on the Gulf Coast.

Out of these two dates came the prophecies that Topiltzin was said to have given his followers just before his demise: (1) that in some year named 1-reed he or his sons would return to reclaim his imperial rights and all his authority and/or (2) that the world would end on the day 4-movement. This latter day was one of thirteen days included in the *tonalpohualli* set patronized by Quetzalcoatl and was thus under his jurisdiction.

The god's self-sacrifice in Tlatlayan, the Place of Burning, rationally should have ended the story of the flight. Adding the account of a further flight over the Gulf to Tlapallan would seem to be gratuitous but actually was not. Tlatlayan, where the god cast himself into the fire, is simply a synonym for Tlapallan, the Red Land,—the east, in other words, or the dawn. The event was thus not a contradiction that the ancients had inserted into the tale of the flight but the logical conclusion of a well-contrived myth that lay behind the legend of Topiltzin. The legend of Topiltzin's flight thus becomes for us the vehicle for the validation of Ce Acatl as a true avatar of Ehecatl Quetzalcoatl. In the Museo Nacional there is a Huaxtec statue that in a most vivid fashion refers to this final episode relating to the heart of Quetzalcoatl.[50] The stone figure is somber, crude, and powerful. The god's face is severe. He wears the pointed cap but with a death's-head emblem on it. Around his neck hangs a heavy pectoral made up of Venus glyphs. The viewer's eye is caught first by the deep cavity in the body in which is exposed the divine heart. It is a classic example of the ability of the arts to evoke an entire story (fig. 35).

Tlapallan

The land of Tlapallan figures prominently in the legend of Topiltzin, but always without detail. The Mexicans particularly remembered "when they (the Toltecs) went away, when Topiltzin Quetzalcoatl entered the water, when he went to settle in the place of red color, the place of burning."[51] We have seen that Tlapallan was the symbol of the dawn and, therefore, of the east. Thought of geographically, therefore, Tlapallan could mean Yucatán, and there can be little doubt that the Tollan Tlapallan mentioned by Sahagún was indeed that "Metropolis of the Red Land,"[52] the city known to us as Chichén Itzá.

Besides these various shades of meaning (the dawn, the east, or Yucatán) there was another. Sahagún tells us that the full name of the place was Tlillan Tlapallan. Literally this means the Land of the Black and the Red [Ink], or the land of picture writing. The reference, therefore, is to an overseas area on the east to which were attributed the arts of computation and learning, a not-unexpected folk mem-

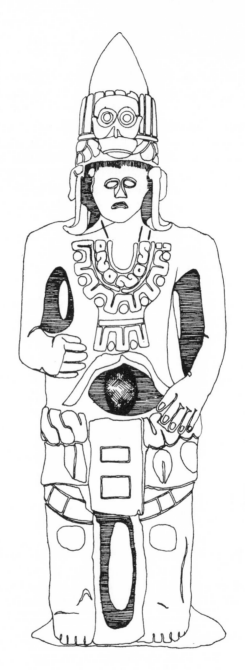

Figure 35

ory of the Maya area. It could also be described as the City of the Sun,[53] where Quetzalcoatl lived forever with his resplendent younger brother.

The direction taken by Topiltzin into exile is thus clear, but the chronology is hopelessly muddled. What follows, therefore, is speculation and not fact. We can see three possible Quetzalcoatls who are said to have been in Yucatán. In the order of their probability they are. (1) the god Quetzalcoatl, or, as his name was rendered by the Mayas, Kukulcan, (2) a title designating Toltec captains or kings who had established themselves there, and (3) the Toltec priest and exile Topiltzin. The first is certainly true, the second is probable, while the third is wholly improbable.

I have previously given my opinion that the exiled priest-ruler probably died on reaching the coast, or even before that. His death would have settled the religious controversy in Tula and would have allowed the situation to lapse back into its prereformation pattern. If that is true, it would entail an interpretation of the rest of the flight tale (that is, to Yucatán) as an armed raid from central Mexico of warriors who carried with them the Quetzalcoatl cult while their captains acted as the god's vicars. Among the Quiché Mayas, for instance rulers did take the name of the god Gukumatz, an exact equivalent of Kukulcan, the Feathered Serpent.[54]

Such raids toward the southeast had begun in Teotihuacán times, and it is probable that the trading state Acallan, a mixture of Mayas and Nahuas midway between the two areas, was already existent and served as a staging area for such excursions. From Acallan radiated influences not only along the coastal waterways but upcountry into the Maya heartland. In the Usumacinta drainage at Bonampak, a Kukulcan who wears the buccal mask appears as the patron of traffic in cacao, the currency of the area (fig. 36). We know also that the ruler in the capital city of Acallan possessed

Figure 36

Kukulcan as his family god and mascot.[55] It is certainly correct that the several waves of Nahuas moving southeast along the so-called Nonohualco coast, past Xicalanco, past Acallan, past Champotón, and all the way to Chichén Itzá, carried the standard of Quetzalcoatl—and this may have begun early, perhaps as early as the seventh century A.D. Translated into Kukulcan for further voyages toward the sunrise, the god was carried along the coasts, eventually rounding Cape Catoche and coming to rest in landings along the eastern shores of Yucatán. The splendid site of Tulum—one among others—speaks vividly to the preeminence of the god's cult there as the morning star. From that blufftop, looking eastward into the long reaches of the Caribbean Sea, the priests obtained and measured unobstructed viewings of the predawn rising of that planet. Indeed, one can think of Tulum as a particularly sacred shrine—a Mecca perhaps—for those who worshiped the warrior god of the dawn. In his avatar as god of merchants Kukulcan also sat astride the busiest route pioneered by those movers of salt, cacao, feathers, and the rest. And that these Yucatecan ports ended by projecting the god across the Gulf of Honduras and farther cannot be doubted.

The coastal raiders penetrated inland at two places in particular, one up the Usumacinta and Pasión rivers to Seibal, the other coasting north to a landing from which they made their way inland to Chichén Itzá. Seibal and Chichén Itzá are quite different in character, and one of the important differences is that the former shows Quetzalcoatl as Ehecatl with the buccal mask while at the latter only the Feathered Serpent is depicted. At this stage of our archaeological knowledge it is impossible to say why this should be so. Superficially it would appear that two groups of people are involved. The Seibal group may have been Putun Mayas who came up from coastal settlements about A.D. 850. The Chichén Itzá settlers moved up country in at least two waves, the first a partly Mexicanized group (A.D. 780?), the second no doubt heavily Toltec and patently devoted to Kukulcan as the Feathered Serpent. At Seibal there is a remarkable stela depicting Ehecatl or his priest wearing the buccal mask (see fig. 9).[56] This would mean that the cult of Ehecatl had continued at full strength in the coastal cultures while the cult of Quetzalcoatl Ce Acatl shown as a war dragon had become specialized in the Mexican highlands and was introduced into Chichén Itzá by the second wave of intruders. Again, all of this is speculation.

Thus we cannot be sure which of these errant peoples brought in Quetzalcoatl as a warrior god and a god connected with successful military lineages. The legends from Yucatán speak of a Kukulcan who introduced idolatry and heart sacrifice and who acted as an emperor in Chichén Itzá, dispensing thrones and powers and policing the legitimacy of subordinate rulers with esoteric examinations. All of this sounds very much like the Aztec conception of the god.[57] Kukulcan's annual feast was celebrated everywhere in Yucatán.

The Kukulcan people also imported into Yucatán the story of a fall into moral turpitude as adumbrating the end of the empire. The Maya legend has it that three priest-rulers, who were brothers, inherited the cloak of Kukulcan.[58] At first chaste and responsive to the needs of the gods, they ruled a prosperous land, but they finally became negligent and corrupt. Accordingly they were put to death, and soon after that the great capital of Chichén Itzá collapsed. Because of the brevity of our sources we cannot make out whether these three brothers were simply emanations of Topiltzin—they do seem to fill much the same role. Other Mayas told this legend in slightly different terms. They said that the leader Nacxit Xuchit (that is, Nacxitl) with his foreign companions introduced into Yucatán sin and the diseases that go with it.

There is a problem here. How much of the cult of Kukulcan was imported from central Mexico, how much came from the coastal area, and how much was indigenous Mayan? At the moment we cannot say. More important for our present interest, we note that Tezcatlipoca does not appear in the scraps of Quetzalcoatl mythology that we have from the Maya area. This strengthens the hypothesis that the Topiltzin legend concerned a cult confrontation in Tula alone that was not exported with the exile itself. It does not signify, however, that no opposition to Quetzalcoatl existed. He was an old god, and his clientele was elite. It would be surprising if he were without enemies everywhere.

Hueymac

Like Quetzalcoatl, Hueymac is said to have been a ruler in Tula, but his chronology also varies wildly. He is said to have been the leader under whom the first Toltecs entered Tula.[59] Again he is the leader of a Chichimec group that conquered Tula in the early days.[60] Or he is the celebrated sorcerer who early compiled the *Teoamoxtli*, or Divine Book.[61] Some said that it was he who prophesied the coming, and the later fall, of Quetzalcoatl. Or he is said to have been the third lord and ruler of the Culhuas, one of the important nations making up the Toltec people.[62] Or again he ruled at the time when Topiltzin was exercising the office of highpriest of Quetzalcoatl.[63] More often he is reported to have ruled after the departure of Topiltzin and as the state was declining to its end. One source says that he was descended from Topiltzin.[64] Several sources agree that he was the last ruler of Tula and that, after the battles that destroyed the state, he fled south and met his end at Chapultepec.[65]

Hueymac can thus be placed almost anywhere in Toltec history, depending on the source used, which leads us to believe that he may have been an important Toltec god. When we are further informed that his queen was named

Coacueye (Snake Skirt)—she is also described as *cuauhnene* ("wooden idol")[66]—we realize that Hueymac was indeed a state god who, like Huitzilopochtli later, was married to, or was the child of, the monstrous Earth Mother, Coatlicue, a name also meaning Snake Skirt. We need no special perspicacity to see that the god being pointed to is connected in some fashion with Tezcatlipoca in spite of the fact that Durán positively identified him as Quetzalcoatl.[67] We are told that the knights of central Mexico carried Hueymac's statue into battle. Indeed the name Tezcatlipoca at times has the explicative Hueymac added to it.[68]

Literally Hueymac means In a Great Hand, which probably scans as [He Who Holds Us] in a Great Hand. We recall here that fascinating description of Tezcatlipoca given by Sahagún: "He is arbitrary, capricious, he mocks. He wills in the manner he desires. He places us in the palm of his hand; he makes us round. We roll, we become as pellets. He casts us from side to side. We make him laugh."[69] Hueymac appears, however, only in tales associated with Tula, Chapultepec, and the region of Cholula. The story of his end was well known. He had succeeded Topiltzin as ruler of Tula but to no avail, for the Toltecs were locked in an endless drought. Hueymac went down to the Rock of Chapultepec, where there was a sacred spring, to see what could be done about the situation. While there he recklessly played a game of *tlachtli* against the rain gods, wagering turquoise and precious quetzal feathers while spurning green ears of corn as stakes.[70] His greed thus prevented the breaking of the drought. Yet we are told that inside that holy mountain he now presides as a god over eternal feasting and perpetual delights. The entrance to that wonderful world of Cincalco is well guarded.[71]

From the above we can deduce the double nature of Hueymac. As the mountain king in Cincalco, he is one of the rain gods. He is also an avatar of the drought god Tezcatlipoca. This snippet of mythology indeed tells the same

story as does Tezcatlipoca's subversion of Quetzalcoatl in
Tula, which on one of its levels is the story of the coming of
drought and the failure of abundance.
We now come to a puzzling contradiction. One of our
sources tells how it was Hueymac who persecuted Topiltzin, even to following him into the Cholula country, where
he immediately set himself up as a god and brought all the
neighboring cities into subjection.[72] One would think that
Hueymac, plainly an avatar of Tezcatlipoca, would always
play a role antithetical to Quetzalcoatl, as in this incident.
Such however, is not the case. At least three of our sources
give us the surprising information that Hueymac was a
transfiguration not of Tezcatlipoca but of Quetzalcoatl[73]—
or, what amounts to the same thing, that Topiltzin was his
son. We have noticed a similar contradiction in the case of
Mixcoatl, who was Quetzalcoatl's father on the one hand
and an avatar of Tezcatlipoca on the other.
To grasp the meaning of this ambiguity, we must understand that Hueymac is merely a special Toltec personification of the bloodline of the rulers, a Caesarian formulation, as it were.[74] We can state it another way—that he
was the genius of Toltec kingship, by which definition
he stands both as a god and as an office carrying the legitimacy. For this reason he is connected, at the end of Toltec
history, with the tragic failure of abundance in a catastrophic drought. Kings are always accountable. Hueymac
weakened.
It is no accident that he occurs in the sources as the first
ruler of Tula and the last as well. He represents the con-
tinuity of rule. The Mexicas, settled on some islands in
Lake Texcoco, as a newly emergent people needed before
all things a solid claim to legitimacy—and at that time this
could only mean Toltec legitimacy.[75] For that reason the
rock of Chapultepec, to which Hueymac's genius was attached, was transformed by them into a visual statement of
their Tula-derived descent. On that rock the early Mexican

rulers erected the image of the god of royal lineage, Quetzalcoatl, and from that point on each ruler had his own image carved there as a sign of his derived prerogative.[76] This emblematic nature of the headland of Chapultepec accounts for that amazing tale concerning Moteuczoma II, who, when faced with the impending entry of the Spaniards, sought to enter the rock by magical means and find there a refuge.[77] It is a tale of panic, but it is far from meaningless.

When we see Hueymac as a Toltec conceptualization of the elite class, we can understand why in our sources he appears now as Tezcatlipoca, now as Quetzalcoatl. He was understood as an avatar of Quetzalcoatl because that god was a universal and powerful patron of lineage. He was understood as a *tlachichihual*,[78] or apparition, of Tezcatlipoca—or even as his son—because that god was the giver of command and authority, exclusively royal qualities.

Now that we are aware that Hueymac can be an avatar of either Quetzalcoatl or Tezcatlipoca, we can take the final step and recognize him as a form of the god Mixcoatl, whom we have earlier discovered to be such a halfway god standing between Tezcatlipoca and Quetzalcoatl, now one, now the other, never, however, losing himself as the original "cloud dragon." Hueymac's offspring, or retainers, are the "cloud children,"[79] and this can only be the equivalent of "cloud serpents," the *mimixcoa*. The invading Spaniards, who were thought to be the sons of Quetzalcoatl, are referred to in a standard source as "the sons of Hueymac."[80] Generally, Hueymac seems to partake more of the Tezcatlipoca than of the Quetzalcoatl personality, but at any time he can shift in the direction of the latter.

Hueymac is thus our best example of the fluidity that characterizes much of the Mesoamerican pantheon. In the sky religion the masks of Tezcatlipoca and Quetzalcoatl were switched about subtly and with ease. At any critical point in the Tezcatlipoca-Quetzalcoatl axis the "numinous" had a preferred salient intruding into the sphere of particularization. Hueymac was logically drawn into that salient. There is more to it than this background of religious conceptualization that I have just sketched in. The historic element is also important. We know that the name Quetzalcoatl designates both the god and his high priest as well. Similarly in Tula there appears to have been a leader whose office was that of a *hueymac*, and we gather that, in contrast to the sacerdotal *quetzalcoatl*, he was a war leader.[81] At a certain point in Toltec history hostility broke out between the incumbents of the two offices, the one an alien holy man with abrasive ideas concerning cult, the other a personage who may have borne the name Atecpanecatl.[82] Outside his appearance as the unfortunate last dynast of Tula, Hueymac is known as the Toltec ruler who on his accession sent away for a new high priest of Quetzalcoatl.[83] It is remembered that the choice devolved upon a man called Cuauhtli, who was, however, quickly dismissed. Hueymac then had himself declared the *quetzalcoatl*.

In other words both Topiltzin the *quetzalcoatl* and Hueymac were memorable magnates and rulers in Tula, and anything told of one inevitably brought in the other. It is not surprising that later generations could have confused them on a historical as well as a religious level.

The Cults of the Two Gods

The outcome of the confrontation between Tezcatlipoca and Quetzalcoatl was a victory for the former. In this book I have eschewed the use of the term *dualism* to define the theoretical structure of this confrontation. What, then, is the meaning of the victory of the god of war and deceit over the god of culture, wisdom, and the prerogatives of blood? If it describes a purely historic passage as between men, then the question has little relevance. But we have seen that there is a powerful mythic background as well, and that does make the question meaningful. I am inclined to look for the answer not in the realm of the conceptual but in cult.

We are already aware of a spectrum of comparability between these two gods. Both are lords who can appear in the sky, both are demiurges associated in the same acts of creation, both are warriors, both are concerned with sex and increase (or its opposite, dearth), and both are givers of wealth. What do their respective cults look like? And is there an affinity there also?

The cults of the two gods are probably not equally old. Quetzalcoatl's cult surely goes back to the beginnings of priesthood in Mesoamerica. Tezcatlipoca's cult was probably diffuse and less rigorously monitored. When some of the Mesoamerican peoples finally redefined their cultures as war-oriented, then Quetzalcoatl's cult, moving strongly in the ways of priestly purity even while geared to human sacrifice, was forced to react to the presence of Tezcatlipoca's rival cult. This took place, I would guess, toward the end of Teotihuacán times; the legend of Topiltzin inherited by the Aztecs would seem to support this. By the time of the Spanish entry, however, the cult of Tezcatlipoca was centered in the Basin of Mexico, while that of Quetzalcoatl was particularly strong in the Tlalteputzco, the land on the east just over the mountains. The reasons for this regionalism are obscure.

In the solar calendar we have Tezcatlipoca's great festival celebrated in Toxcatl, the fifth month.[84] This celebration was unique in the list of eighteen, for in it the god's *ixiptla*, who had wandered freely among the people throughout the year, was sacrificed and disposed of while another was being inducted in his place. Toxcatl was thus a seam in the vaster web of the whole year and could only be read as a statement of the superiority of Tezcatlipoca over all the other gods. It indicates a feeling that there loomed behind him a cosmic numen. All levels of Aztec society from poor to rich took part in the festival: everyone acknowledged dependence on Tezcatlipoca as the god of providence and divine whim, and every four years the festival was celebrated with special éclat, for it included a plenary remission of sins. At that time penitents, weighed down by their secret sins, flagellated each other with thorny maguey leaves in order to deserve Tezcatlipoca's forgiveness. This might seem at first glance to duplicate Quetzalcoatl's strong penitential orientation, but actually it differs in the sense that it is here a voluntary, popular, and not in any sense priestly act.

Tezcatlipoca was honored secondarily as the god of drought, famine, and barrenness. All through the Toxcatl rites ran the theme of plenty and banqueting—the opposite of his usual dispensations. The famous garlands of popped corn worn by the young people taking part in the rituals represented clouds heavy with rain—again the opposite of his common gifts to mankind. Toxcatl not only was a month spent in propitiating an undependable god but also was a series of cult actions intended to circumvent him. Tezcatlipoca was the deity in whom were displayed both omnipotence and caprice, the most dangerous of all possible combinations. Men therefore needed many approaches to him.

Tezcatlipoca was a god of ultimate power. Toxcatl was thus a ceremony designed to exalt the nobility, for only the ruling classes could claim the rights of arbitrary and freakish will, the god's earmark. In the Toxcatl set of rituals no gods other than Tezcatlipoca were honored—for the duration of the month all divinity was concentrated in him. Only noblemen could participate in Dance of Toxcatl, and only they had access to courtesans and loose women brought out in that season to perform with them. Thus laid over the seasonal character of that Aztec month was the statement of

277

noble prerogative as a clear reflection of the god's own slanted nature.

Quetzalcoatl had no such calendrical ceremony devoted exclusively to him, and this in spite of the fact that he was the patron of lineages. In his holy city, Cholula, he was honored in the first month of that city's solar year, Quahui-tlehua, and that of course carried great distinction.[85] Yet Quetzalcoatl's *ixiptla* was selected only forty days before his eventual sacrifice, a custom in no sense comparable to the year-long tenure of the corresponding *ixiptla* of Tezcatlipoca. All the indications are that Quetzalcoatl was preeminently a form of the morning star in Cholula, for the *ixiptla* there was sacrificed at midnight and eaten only as the dawn appeared, while merchants and nobles danced beside a blazing fire. Yet he still appears in Cholula as a city god rather than as a god universally sovereign.

The feast of the eighth month was the before-mentioned Hueytecuilhuitl, a ritual of solemn splendor.[86] It was also curiously ambivalent. For us its importance lies in the fact that, while it honored Quetzalcoatl, the main action took place not in that god's shrine but in the Temple of Tezcatlipoca. This no doubt reflected the historical confrontation that had resulted in the defeat of the former god back in Toltec times. The initial feast of the Cholula year had been pointed to the merchants, but this one in Tenochtitlán and surrounding cities belonged to the royal lineages. We know this from the presence in the rites of a special idol representing lordship and the privileges of rule. Once again public women and concubines appeared in the festivities to demonstrate the perquisites of nobility.

Quetzalcoatl thus appears here as a patron of lineages and of privilege. The ambivalence of the ceremony lay in the fact that the Aztecs had two gods, Tezcatlipoca and Quetzalcoatl, either of whom could stand for social status and rule. Nonetheless a pronounced gap separated them. Tezcatlipoca symbolized the exercise of arbitrary power in the present; Quetzalcoatl stood for the ancestral rights that belonged to the various lineages. The Tula legends set forth clearly the regal authority of Tezcatlipoca, and the state perforce observed it in its calendar of festivals. For this reason the *ixiptla* of Quetzalcoatl was sacrificed in one of the temples of the former god.

The above three festivals have been excerpted from the solar year of invariable months. Tezcatlipoca and Quetzalcoatl appear also, however, in the series of movable feasts in the *tonalpohualli*, each honored on the day of his birth sign, Quetzalcoatl on 1-reed, Tezcatlipoca on 1-death.[87] These two essentially repeat the meanings we have derived from the rituals of the solar calendar just mentioned. Ce Acatl (One Reed) was venerated in the *calmecac* by the nobility alone, the *calmecac* being the university in which the secrets of rule and the priesthood were taught. Ce Miquiztli (One Death) was venerated by commoners and nobles alike. All levels of society were terrified of Tezcatlipoca.

There were two other pertinent movable feasts.[88] Tezcatlipoca was also honored on 2-reed, Quetzalcoatl on the day 4-wind. Both festivals focused on wealth and luxury. We have already seen that Four Wind was Quetzalcoatl's name as the second sun and as a god of storms. It was an unlucky day for merchants and, therefore, was important to them. Omacatl (Two Reed) was the name of that avatar of Tezcatlipoca who presided over banqueting and other signs of status.

Perhaps I can summarize the above. Ritually the two gods tended to come together, but Tezcatlipoca always retained his distinctiveness as a universal force, a providential dispenser or withholder feared by all. In cult Quetzalcoatl remained straitly tied to commerce and to ancestry and so did not elicit a powerful devotion from the common people. But his cult was the richer of the two and was strongly entrenched at the time of the Spanish entry.

There are, of course, many other aspects of the cults of

these two gods that I have passed over. Here I have wanted only to explore relationships. Quetzalcoatl's worship as a sky dragon, as a god of battle, or as the wind has not been in question here.

The Two Religions

In the *Popol Vuh* is a passage that I have already briefly noted regarding Quiché tribal origins. It needs more extended comment. Here is what the Quichés told of their past:[89] Before their dispersion men prayed to the gods who had created them, Gukumatz and Tepeu, and in connection with these orisons they watched the east for the first rising of the morning star, whom they knew as Sun Passer. Four ancestors, wise men and sages, comforted the people as they awaited the event that was to usher in the first day and bring light to the world. After the sun had appeared, the four led the people to the land of Chicomoztoc and then to the city of Tula. When they arrived in Tula, they found that the gods had also assembled there. Of those divine beings the first to come were Storm (Tohil) and Lord Jaguar (Avilix). Storm was the tutelary deity of most of the peoples of the earth. It was he who first gave them fire. Of him the book says: "Storm was the name of the god of the Mexican people. Yolcatl [Rattlesnake] Quetzalcoatl was his name."[90] He was the god whom the people had thanked for the coming of the dawn. From Tula all the peoples dispersed, though by that time they had lost the gift of a common speech. Now the great god Storm demanded of them heart sacrifice, which thus first appeared on earth. So they went away across the sea, taking with them their gods.

Quetzalcoatl appears here on two levels, as demiurge (Gukumatz) and as ancestor (Tohil-Ehecatl). Similarly, Tezcatlipoca appears as Tepeu and as the deity Lord Jaguar. In this sense of being able to operate on two supernatural levels, the two were almost indistinguishable to their worshipers. In myth they consistently act together. Clearly, among the Quiché Mayas the relations between the two were not dualistic—if by dualism we mean extremes of polarity dividing two beings or powers—yet they are consistently paired.

We could draw up a long list of items attesting to the easy access the two gods had to each other's regalia in the mask pool. A selected few of such items follows:

1. Tepeyollotli can be called Ce Acatl.[91]
2. Sky was created in 2-reed, one of Tezcatlipoca's names.[92]
3. A feathered coyote (Tezcatlipoca's *nahualli*) is associated with the date name 1-reed.[93]
4. Tezcatlipoca becomes Xolotl when he carries off the goddess Xochiquetzal.[94]
5. The designs on Tezcatlipoca's and Quetzalcoatl's cloaks are reversed: the latter's shows the pectoral ring; the former's, the wind jewel.[95]
6. The two change masks in the underworld.[96]

There is only one way to explain this slippage of one god into the other, and that is by positing for both a very early telling of their joint participation in acts of creation and, therefore, a lasting affinity in subsequent mythic episodes. Yet in the sky religion only Quetzalcoatl is involved in the key events of the cosmos, the fall of the sun into night, his demise there, and his subsequent revival—for the Mesoamerican these were among the greatest of all themes. Tezcatlipoca plays no part in those events.

Sahagún insisted that there were two religions—that of Tezcatlipoca and that of Quetzalcoatl—and he identified them correctly as institutionally centering respectively on the *telpochcalli* and the *calmecac*, each a center for training.[97] Those who attended the former were known popularly as "the youth"[98] because, in stressing the pristine quality of their god, the young people of both sexes enrolled in these cadres dressed and painted to resemble him. The emphasis on Dionysian energy in his cult was distinctive, setting it apart from the cult in the *calmecac*, which stressed age. In fact the annual feast of Tezcatlipoca saw these young men and women engaging in beautifully staged and costumed dances that allowed and even promoted sexual adventures.[99]

There can be no doubt that Sahagún was right—and this in spite of the close association of the two gods. In cult they differed in that Quetzalcoatl was the god who controlled priestly functions, prophecy, and learning. They differed in myth in that Tezcatlipoca evinced unquestioned superiority whereas Quetzalcoatl's roles were specifically defined and limited.

A more diagnostic difference can be seen in their respective powers as *nahualli* sorcerers. Earlier in this book we saw that, in spite of the fact that Quetzalcoatl is referred to as a *huey nahualli*, his skills as a shape shifter are in no sense clearly documented. The only common animal brought into connection with him is the monkey,[100] but it is used only as an emblem—it is not an exchange body for the god. On the contrary, Tezcatlipoca passed easily into many forms, animal and apparition. In terms of his orientation toward vitalism and lawlessness, Tezcatlipoca is also a god who can be easily grasped, but his homogeneity does not prevent him from having an iridescence of forms. He divides as swiftly as does the amoeba. In fact, as a director of many avatars Tezcatlipoca matched Quetzalcoatl; as a *nahualli* sorcerer he far surpassed him. Briefly, it was the shaman in the god Tezcatlipoca that created the difference in their two cults.

It is, in fact, revealing that what was said about Tezcatlipoca—that he was a mocker and a deceiver—was never said about Quetzalcoatl. As finally developed, Quetzalcoatl was not a vague numen but a deity at whom one could point. Quetzalcoatl's definition, however, was not so explicit that it closed off many avenues of possible development. The difference between him and most of the other gods was in the wide extent of his jurisdictions, in which respect he was equaled only by Tezcatlipoca.

A significant contrast between the two gods is that while Tezcatlipoca can and does affect each man's life as an individual, changing it indiscriminately for better or for worse, the effects that Quetzalcoatl has had on men have been in the main historical—in other words, he is the divine as it is needed to "explain" how the present came to be the way it is and how the future will be. Tezcatlipoca is a god who is active only in the present.

The relationship between the two gods is complementary. The Mesoamericans perceived this when they paired the two as the creator brothers. If, instead of this pairing, Quetzalcoatl had absorbed Tezcatlipoca as his nearest avatar, then a transcendent god might have eventuated, a god to whose law would thus have been added omnipotence—a first step toward monotheism.

What we have, then, in the interaction of these two gods is an inchoate theodicy that never succeeded in adequately formulating itself because the two religions were at bottom so disparate. Whether the two cults in Aztec days were actively competitive we do not know. Almost certainly they were even then complementary to each other. Tezcatlipoca's religion was universal, depressive, simple, and intuitively understood by everyone everywhere. That of Quetzalcoatl was elite, labyrinthine, and at times occult. Quetzalcoatl's voice ran the gamut—it could be the hoarse voice of the wind rushing through the sky or the scarcely audible breeze; Tezcatlipoca's was the idiot echo in the deep gorges, hollow and sinister. Even their voices were discrepant.

Perhaps the real reason, however, why the religion of

Quetzalcoatl never became the overriding Mesoamerican world view was just because of this many-faceted character of the god. He had no one integrating personality that might have imposed itself upon the others. Air could have been such a major emphasis if the priests had so wished; or sacrifice or generative power could have become dominant. None of them, in fact, did become dominant in Quetzalcoatl. Tezcatlipoca had an umbilical self, a singleness at his core—he was the untrammeled one who provoked discord.

Sometime in the year 1519 or just before, we hear of a powerful shaman-priest of Tezcatlipoca active on the southern incline of Popocatepetl.[101] He was known as Telpochtli (Youth), which was the name of Tezcatlipoca's avatar on those wooded slopes; additionally he was given the title Jaguar, the god's *nahualli* animal. In other words, this personage could change at will into the sacred animal, thus becoming for a time wholly privy to the god. Oracles given by Tezcatlipoca through the seer Telpochtli were accompanied by the use of hallucinogens. By means of these oracles the seer's reputation had grown so that he accepted worship on his own as the god Tezcatlipoca.

It was later attested in a Spanish court proceeding that when Moteuczoma was frantically engaged in trying to secure favorable oracles concerning the coming of Cortés and his men he turned for help to this seer, who could be depended on not to be in Quetzalcoatl's camp, inasmuch as the Spaniards were thought to be the sons of Quetzalcoatl. It was further said that this shaman-priest was arrested by Moteuczoma when it became apparent to the ruler that his association with the god Tezcatlipoca could not block the Spanish approach to the Mexican capital.

Later, under the Spaniards, Telpochtli, now christened Martín Ocelotl, illegally continued his shamanistic practices, along with his brother Andrés, who claimed to be an incarnation of Mixcoatl (who as a god was himself an avatar of both Tezcatlipoca and Quetzalcoatl). The two brothers pursued their underground professions until finally, in 1536, Telpochtli was apprehended and tried by the Spanish authorities for having preached revolt and for having celebrated certain rites of Camaxtli (brother of Tezcatlipoca) to ward off an impending drought. Telpochtli was transported to Spain and was heard of no more.

This incident is consistent with all that we know about the god Tezcatlipoca and fittingly closes this discussion. The point to be emphasized is that we have no records of similar stubbornness among the devotees of Quetzalcoatl, for those devotees were priests, not shamans. The legend of Quetzalcoatl's return was everywhere, but that only meant that the god was not present among men, for he was resting in a never-never land. For a few years after the Conquest the voice of Tezcatlipoca could be heard in the marketplace and hidden away in homes, still fomenting—as he always had—division, drought, and war.

SEVEN
A RECAPITULATION

It is now time to look back over the body of Quetzalcoatl
myths to see whether this god is indeed unique, as I have so
far contended—whether in fact he is the hinge upon which
the sky religion turned. I need hardly tell my readers that
the myths that we do have represent only the wreckage of a
once-abundant corpus now forever lost to us, and for that
reason I must caution against assuming that this reconstruction equals fact. The remarks that I shall be making, however, do advance insights that may be important.

Most of the surviving myths concerning Quetzalcoatl
have been reviewed in the preceding pages. Below I draw
the most representative—and sometimes contradictory—
ones together under five general headings. Legends relating
to Topiltzin the high priest are omitted.

1. Origins of the God

Descends from the sky
Engendering by Mixcoatl on Chimalma
Creation by Tezcatlipoca
Creation by the breath of Tonacateuctli
Appearance in the abyss as Gukumatz

2. Ordering of the Cosmos:

Creation by the two demiurges

Seating of the second sun
Invention of the *tonalpohualli*

3. Conflict Within the Ordering of the Cosmos

Arrival of Nanahuatl and the fifth sun
Translation into the morning star
Appearance as one of the Mimixcoa
Game played by the gods in the *tlachco*

4. Activities Connected with Man and His Culture

Generating of men
Discovery of maize
Introduction of maguey
Introduction of music and dance
Creation of flowers

5. Ancestral Activities

Landing in Panuco
The god in Chicomoztoc
Derivation of Quichés from Tula
Return of the god

The first rubric demonstrates that the Mesoamericans possessed a variety of insights concerning the origins of Quetzalcoatl, depending upon which of his avatars they were concerned with at the time. The most primitive of these concepts may have had to do with a god like Gukumatz, a feathered dragon living in celestial or abyssal waters along with his demiurgic counterpart. This was during the precreative time, and he can accordingly be seen to have been an undifferentiated sky-and-water numen. When perceived more energetically as one of the phases of Ce Acatl, the planet Venus, he is born of the union of Mixcoatl, the hunter in the sky, and the Earth Mother. Both of the above are simple nature myths. The priests, however, moved away from such graphic statements to develop more spiritualized concepts. They reasoned either that Quetzalcoatl was created by Tezcatlipoca (an act that would move the latter into a role of undisputed absolutism) or that the high god created Quetzalcoatl by his breath. The latter was an attempt to derive out of a numinous first principle an active property of a god that could stand for the whole, namely "breath" as standing for "spirit." There appears to have been little support for this view.

The most widely accepted myth appears to have been that of Quetzalcoatl's descent from the sky. Certainly it was the controlling version. In this myth the god can be depicted as Nine Wind, who is given the charge to bring civilization to mankind and to arrange his customs and institutions. He is in fact created just for this mission. The two high gods in Omeyocan equip him with his writ to perform great things and send him down to earth. The effect of this myth and its sequel is to switch the god's aboriginal atmospheric function to a cultural one. This may be the point where the depiction of Quetzalcoatl as a dragon is replaced or supplemented by the depiction of him as anthropomorphic and wearing the buccal mask. We might have expected the dissembler Tezcatlipoca to appear in the two last-mentioned myths, to account for the undesirable in man's culture and ecology, but he does not. The statement found in one source that Tezcatlipoca was the god who created Quetzalcoatl has the effect of making the latter's origins contingent, and it prohibits the view of Quetzalcoatl as a high god.

Yet we note that Quetzalcoatl is the only Mesoamerican god in whose origins such great interest is shown. That is indeed the salient fact to be derived from this part of the list. Sky was more changeable, more permeable than earth. It raised more questions and therefore could more easily create avatars. What it lacked in the sense of being solid and undivided it made up for in extension and variety.

Under the second rubric three distinct categories of order are introduced, in each of which both Tezcatlipoca and Quetzalcoatl appear. The three categories are space, fate, and time. The myths consider Quetzalcoatl's role in the installation of each. We know that, after changing into dragons, Tezcatlipoca and Quetzalcoatl cooperated as coequal deities in the separation of earth and sky. This act determined the dyadic shape of space. In another myth the two gods become respectively the first and the second suns in a series of five—the series determining the full extent and nature of time. But here instead of cooperation there is hostility, each in the end being undone by the other. In a third myth, which concerns fate, Quetzalcoatl, under the aegis of Oxomoco and Cipactonal, invents the *tonalpohualli*, a fluctuating system of good and ill fortune. While this work is attributable to Quetzalcoatl alone, we note in the *Codex Borgia* that Tezcatlipoca has some sort of regulatory effect over the twenty day signs—in addition to which we know that he was the only god who could mitigate, if he so willed, the worst effects of a person's fate. Tezcatlipoca was a personification of providence under whim, and as such he was an alter ego of Quetzalcoatl, who was the establisher of the fixed *tonalpohualli*. In other words, the ordering of the universe has a complementary aspect—Quetzalcoatl could not do it alone. Tezcatlipoca must also be present.

In the third rubric the adversary relationship is stepped up to become crucial. In fact here the cosmic order is the result of a serious encounter, a battle, a game, or sacrifice. And always the locus of action, which is also a point in time, is either night or the dawn. As does the preceding rubric, this one also talks about the ordering of the cosmos, but only as told by and for the warrior hero and the duelist.

It is noteworthy that none of the myths in this category presents Quetzalcoatl as Ehecatl, but only in the persons of his night-sky avatars, Nanahuatl, Xolotl, or Ce Acatl. In other words, conflict in the sky religion is seen as properly occurring in the night sky or at its edges.

The fourth rubric portrays Quetzalcoatl as that god most closely associated with man, for not only is he the officiant presiding over the resurrection of the bones of men but also he provides man thus re-created with all the elements of his culture. He is appropriately given to us here under his most comprehensive avatar, Ehecatl, though Xolotl and Nanahuatl also appear because of their connections with the underworld, from which men, maize, and flowers come. This set of myths has the god tied into the very web of man's living, yet curiously enough he does not thereby become a god of corn or maguey or jade or music and dance. He stands out rather as the rational principle behind them, providing them with an important validation.

The tale of the descent into the underworld to recover the bones of men is neither a creation myth nor an ancestor myth. Quetzalcoatl is the hero in the myth simply because he is wise and also because, as Xolotl, he is a familiar "down" god in the darkness. He does not thereby become the god of man *qua* man. Such a role more truly belongs to Tezcatlipoca, and this perception reveals to us one of the fateful non sequiturs in Mesoamerican religion. Had Quetzalcoatl been cast not only as the restorer of men and the originator of their cultures but also as the present guide and the legislator of their activities, then the over-all religious picture in Mesoamerica would have been profoundly altered.

The fifth and last rubric includes those myths wherein Mesoamerican man described the actualities of his historic situation and his destiny. The previous categories revealed to him the cosmos that he inhabited and gave assent to the structure of his culture, but they did not touch upon his historical incompleteness or the rule of contraries in his life. It is obvious that man's life on earth can be best presented in terms of expectations and longings rather than confirmed accomplishments. The myths in this category did just that; they described tribal beginnings, paradises that had been lost, life as a wandering, and present settlement as emptied of the god. The future was seen as a returning of the divinity presently lost, a kind of vague messianism. But for the Mesoamerican this return was almost devoid of moral definition. It was never stated in the prophecy that paradise would be regained when the god returned.

As I have noted previously, the above corpus of myths is unique in Mesoamerican religion in the extent of its interests and the ambiguities of its final meaning. We can, in fact, summarize its ambiguity here. The myths take Quetzalcoatl to be God as a creative spirit positively oriented toward men, but they do not attach hope to his worship. His presence in the sky religion does not even raise the religion to the crude level of a cargo cult. Looked at this way, the sky religion lays the groundwork for an impressive religious structure but fails to complete it.

Topiltzin's legends were never put together around the theme of the search for eternal life, as was the Gilgamesh epic, or as a canonical series of heroic chores, as in the twelve labors of Hercules. All the elements were present, but they remained scattered. The raw material for an exalted vision was there, but no Homeric genius ever took them in hand, pruned them here, embellished them there, to produce a fiction of man's dilemma. Such a poet in the centuries of the priesthood of Quetzalcoatl might well have appeared, but he did not.

The statements just made have been suggested by Quetzalcoatl's mythology. Yet a god can be worshiped in ways that seem incompatible with the purport of his mythology. This is only to say that myth at times may be at variance with ritual. Quetzalcoatl may have been closer to people than the above would lead us to believe. The laborer in field, forest, and quarry called on him for strength; the curer needed his image in his practice; the priest knew him as a model; one with a disease of the skin prayed to him; the stargazer consulted the god's books; and the ruler granted that as a mere placeholder he owed everything to the god.

Quetzalcoatl did affect Mesoamerican life in many of its workaday ways. Yet his importance in mythology is something else. The unknown but still apprehended possibilities of divinity are always difficult to present. The Mesoamerican was attempting this, however lamely, through the curious figure of Quetzalcoatl that he placed in the sky.

DESCRIPTIONS OF ILLUSTRATIONS

The line drawings in this book are taken from various Mesoamerican sources. For reasons of clarity, details of the originals have occasionally been deleted. In the frontispiece a small piece of design not shown has been re-created. The source of each drawing is noted so that the reader who wishes may compare it with its original.

Frontispiece

Sarcophagus lid from Palenque, A Maya view of the universe clearly depicting the role of the sky. The structure of the world is here conceived as dendroidal. Within the jaws of the earth dragon is seen the front-facing Cauac monster. Out of this motif sprouts the world tree, which is composed of several dragons (the world tree also appears in fig. 6). The tip of the tree reaching into the sky is the upturned snout of the tree dragon, and on this is perched the Moan bird, a sky symbol here shown as a quetzal bird. The branches of the tree are also dragons, in this instance two-headed. The whole structure of earth, underearth, air, and sky is encased within four borders, the two sides bearing astronomical symbols, the upper and lower ones showing the heads of named deities, three in each. Most of the dynastic implications in this scene as well as certain other symbols have been omitted. The central human figure in the original has been erased, and the lower part of the decorative pattern of the tree has been imagined by the artist.

Figure 1

Statue of Quetzalcoatl, Huaxtec culture, front view. Brooklyn Museum. All of the body tattooing has been omitted, as well as the intricate low-relief dragon pattern shown on the aureole and headband. The huge back-curved eardrops rest against the shoulders. A jade plug was probably inserted into the hole in the abdomen. The highly stylized design on the apron has been retained. The back of the same statue is shown as figure 3.

Figure 2

Monument 19, La Venta, Olmec culture. The dragon here is plainly modeled on the rattlesnake, but has a bird's beak and crest. He has surrounded or ingested a priest belonging to his cult. Above the priest is a ritual apron decorated with Saint Andrew's Crosses to indicate the celestial nature of the cult.

Figure 3

Stela 23, Izapan. The sky seen as a two-headed dragon arching over the ocean. The dragon heads are identified by the symbol over them, which is associated with the sky. Waves are seen below, foaming between two headlands depicted as the heads of earth dragons.

Figure 4

From the Sanctuary Tablet, Temple of the Cross, Palenque. The earth monster is here depicted front face and with skeletal jaws. He wears on his head the *kin* sign symbolizing the sun, which equates him with the sun beneath the earth. The sky band extends on both sides of him, the segments of which are marked with celestial glyphs.

Figure 5

From a fresco uncovered by Eduardo Contreras, Teotihuacán. It depicts a descending sky bird.

Figure 6

Stela 2, Izapan. A divine bird-man descends through a hole in the sky apparently to take up his position on the summit of the world tree, which is here shown bearing fruit. The base of the tree and its roots are shown as the earth dragon. The bird-man wears a dragon helmet and back-curved ear-drops, while each of his outstretched wings shows the Saint Andrew's Cross—he is thus the animation of the sky. Two guardians of the tree greet him.

Figure 7

Fragment of a stone box from Tres Zapotes, Olmec period. The god of the air is shown at the top as a front-facing mask. From him great winds issue. These are swirling above the waves of the Gulf of Mexico. Two warriors and a part of a third are shown toppled over and carried away in the hurricane.

Figure 8

Engraved plaque from the Teotihuacán period. It depicts the god of the air in his avatar as Seven Serpent Eye (Seven Wind). He is dressed as a priest. The hieroglyph for his date name is worn as a large pectoral. His hands are raised to the sky, and he wears the dragon casque. The frame in which he stands is ornamented with curious tassels, which are probably to be read as the dripping of rain.

Figure 9

Stela 19, Seibal. The god Ehecatl Quetzalcoatl spreading grain. He is shown wearing the buccal mask, while words issue from his lips. On his head is the dragon helmet, and he wears a back-of-the-head fan made of feathers. He also wears the skirt of a priest and a heavy belt marked with "Saint Andrew's Crosses." A band of glyphs and symbols under his feet has been omitted from this drawing.

Figure 10

Detail from Panel 6, South Ball Court, Tajín. A sacrificial scene somehow connected with the maguey plant and the intoxicating drink brewed from it. Above the shrine and presumably seated in the sky near the mountain on the right sit two gods, Tlaloc and Quetzalcoatl behind him. A priest holds a jug in his arms and points to a prone sacrificial victim. Over the whole scene the god of the air is shown with two bodies and one face distinguished by a duck bill buccal mask. Thus two forms of Quetzalcoatl appear in the same relief.

Figure 11

A petroglyph from Santa Cruz Acalpixcan. The *xonecuilli* is here obviously divinized. The curving blade of stars is shown as an extension of the upper part of a skull. From the handle, tied round with sacred paper ribbons, hang the two banded tassels characteristic of Quetzalcoatl.

Figure 12

Codex Nuttall, plate 9. A typical temple of Quetzalcoatl showing the conical thatched roof topped with a conch shell. The deity inside is presented as a sacred bundle. The temple's base is ornamented with dragon's heads. A descending quetzal-bird further identifies the god.

Figure 13

Selden Roll. Detail showing an ancestral suppliant, bearing a penitential bough, approaching a shrine of Quetzalcoatl. The god here is in one of his common forms as a bundle. His shrine is ornamented in a pronounced fashion with *olin* signs. Adjoining and in the back is an annex to which is attached a ball court. In the annex and presiding over the ball court are two individuals (priests or deities), one of whom is given Xolotl's date name Four Movement; the other is Four Wind. Both wear curious buccal masks.

Figure 14

Selden Roll. Detail showing the Mountain of Mixcoatl, described in the text.

Figure 15

Detail from a stone box of Aztec provenience. Quetzalcoatl is shown descending between two of his important date names: One Reed and Seven Reed.

Figure 16

A pot from Teotihuacán decorated in bas-relief. It shows a priest wearing a dragon helmet and greeting the morning star as it rises on the left. His orisons issue from his mouth in rolling volutes. The forms in the bottom frieze are enigmatic.

Figure 17

Codex Nuttal, plate 22. A shrine on a Mixtec mountain top dedicated to the god Itztli, the sacrificial knife. The temple is identified with the sky by a small strip of stars along the thatching. In the open area in front of the shrine is placed the Venus staff.

Figure 18

Codex Borbonicus, plate 18. The wadded mound of grass with the two maguey thorns thrust into it specify the scene as one of autosacrifice. The disheveled ball with the star eye in the center is a hieroglyph for night. The penitent is a naked warrior. In one hand he is carrying a maguey thorn and an incense bag, while in the other he wields a rasping implement ending in a knife point. Flowers are attached to the instrument to indicate the beauty of the act, which is performed before the war goddess Chantico. Certain items have been omitted from this drawing, including the date name One Crocodile (generally associated with Ce Acatl).

Figure 19

Codex Vaticanus 3773, plate 29. The Xolotl dog monster is shown with a sun disk around his neck indicating his connection with the night sun. A cannibal meal is being prepared above him, and adjoining it is his sign, *olin*.

Figure 20

A mural strip from the Painted Patio, Atetelco, Teotihuacán. This strip shows the Feathered Serpent with a body made of alternating segments of quetzal plumes and symbols of the morning star. From the dragon's mouth water pours down on the earth. Below him are two Venus monsters, which, because of the signs in their headbands, and their frontal facing, are to be identified with the evening star.

Figure 21

Detail from *Codex Becker I*. The basic vision of the sky formed by artists in the Postclassic period. It shows large stars, or constellations, alternating with knives, which are dripping blood. The chevron pattern at the top equates the sky with the warpath. The hole in the middle of the sky is the passageway through which the gods descend to earth. Hanging from the bottom of the sky are the multitudes of stars, here understood as ancestral eyes.

Figure 22

Detail from Disk H, the Cenote at Chichén Itzá. Around the rim of the disk the heads of four directional sky gods are shown (only one is included here). In the air hovers a Feathered Serpent from whose maw an armed Toltec-type warrior emerges. The scrolls along the dragon's body are to be interpreted as storm clouds.

Figure 23

Detail from a Teotihuacán vase. Quetzalcoatl as the morning star and wearing a dragon helmet is seen emerging above the eastern mountains. Within the mountain is the underworld, and below it is a frieze symbolizing the sky of the underworld.

Figure 24

Stela 1, Xochicalco, front side. The god is identified by name in the top register as Seven Serpent's Eye, generally thought to translate as Seven Wind in the Aztec system. Below the date name is the god, a dragon with a face gazing out of the maw. The bottom register can be interpreted as the sky held up by the god's two hands, but the mouth above them is enigmatic.

Figure 25

Codex Borgia, plate 40. Nanahuatl, the sun in the underworld, is shown being sacrificed by Quetzalcoatl, who is wearing a hummingbird casque, symbolizing regeneration.

Eight other avatars of Quetzalcoatl who are also involved in this sun sacrifice are not shown here, and the figure of Nanahuatl has been simplified. Taken together, the nine Quetzalcoatls correspond to the nine levels of the underworld. Below the main figure the theme of regeneration is interpreted in terms of another myth, one in which the Red Tezcatlipoca (the sun) and Tlazolteotl (the moon) play a game in the *tlachco*, death being the end of the game, followed by rebirth.

Figure 26

Codex Vaticanus 3773, plate 64. Xolotl is here a bundle image, but still wearing most of the regalia belonging to Quetzalcoatl. His date name, Four Movement, can be seen above his head.

Figures 27 and 28

Codex Borgia, plates 33 and 34. These two plates are described in the text. In the original they are filled with detail, most of which has been omitted here. Only the essentials of these plates have been retained.

Figure 29

Stela 3, Xochicalco, front side. The god's date name, Four Movement, is seen in the top register, while at the bottom is a sky band with an enclosed date, which may be 4-rain.

Figure 30

Codex Vaticanus 3773, plate 76. Quetzalcoatl and the Lord of the Underworld are here projected as a single deity, assembled in Siamese twin fashion. The conflate deity is squatting over an entrance into the earth that has an earthquake sign (*olin*) as an identification. Far under the earth is to be seen the sky of the underworld hanging down like a fringe.

Figure 31

The back of the statue of Quetzalcoatl shown in figure 1.

Figure 32

Codex Borbonicus, plate 22. A scene connected with the ending of the sacred fifty-two-year century, when both the solar year and the *tonalpohualli* cease and a new cycle starts. Quetzalcoatl and another god are shown in a ritual confrontation, possibly a dance. Quetzalcoatl wears his complete regalia and waves a smoldering censer whose handle ends in a serpent's head. The facing god is not positively identified, but he wears the pectoral ring and the star cap of Titlacahuan (that is, Tezcatlipoca) and the fire-dragon backpiece of Xiuhteuctli. He can thus be interpreted as an avatar of Tezcatlipoca who appears at the end of the Calendar Round.

Figure 33

Codex Vaticanus 3773, plate 26. The scene is the ocean, and the time, indicated by the figure in the upper right, is the

half-light of dusk. A young god who is a form of the planet
Venus is shown holding a *chicahuaztli* staff. There has been
an encounter between him and a leviathan in which he has
lost a leg. Visually the victory is not adjudged to either of
the two figures and is thus ambivalent.

Figure 34

Codex Borbonicus, plate 3. This detail shows Tezcatlipoca in
his avatar as Tepeyollotli, the jaguar god. The smoking
mirror that replaces his torn-off foot is plainly visible; another version of the mirror is attached to his temple. His
voice, which is the echo off the mountainside, is depicted as
a speech scroll.

Figure 35

Huaxtec statue in the Museo Nacional, Mexico City. The
pointed cap and the back-curved eardrops clearly identify
the figure as Quetzalcoatl. Additionally he wears an elaborate pectoral made up of Venus designs. The cynosure of
the statue is the heart, which can be seen in the cavity opened in the god's body by the sacrificial knife. This casts
him as the evening star (see also the death's head in the cap),
whose death brings about regeneration.

Figure 36

Detail from a Bonampak mural (Room 2) as restored by
Agustín Villagra. The overarching sky is fringed with rays.
A line of glyphs decorates the sky above, while astronomi-
cal symbols fill the two sides. The two sky pillars rest on

the earth, which is a stylized dragon's maw. Kukulcan emerges from these open jaws. He is spreading largesse over the land, cacao pods and cacao beans. In one hand he holds a sprouting plant, in the other a bowl of unidentified objects. He is probably Quetzalcoatl as a god of commerce and wealth (cacao beans were used as currency).

NOTES

Part One

1. Thelma Sullivan, personal communication.
2. There is one pointer in the wind suggesting a deity called Sky; the word is found as a personal name, Ilhuicatl. The naming of persons after gods and their avatars was common in Nahuatl, and this may be such a case.
3. Sahagún 1950, 2:165.
4. Seler 1960. 3:387.
5. Granata (1980) has most recently addressed himself to the problem of serpent identification in the codices. This work, long needed, has been freely drawn on for specific information regarding species classification, habitats, and so on.
6. Ibid., pp. 59–77.
7. Gay 1972, fig. 15.
8. Ibid., fig. 25.
9. Illustrations of these dragons in Izapan art can be found in Quirarte 1976 and in Wauchope 1964–76, 2:237–75.
10. Siméon 1965, p. 247.
11. I assume that when we see a dragon depicted in Tula or in Chichén Itzá we are to read it as Mixcoatl rather than as Quetzalcoatl. The knights fighting under the dragon therefore are the *mimixcoa*.
12. For illustrations of the turtle dragon see Caso 1964, fig. 4.
13. *Codex Borgia* 1976, p. 72.
14. Olmos 1965, p. 32.
15. Thompson 1970, pp. 262–65.
16. Sahagún 1950, 11:85; Sahagún 1956, 3:269 et seq.; Torquemada 1969, 2:48.
17. Motolinía 1951, p. 270.
18. Herrera 1944–47, 3:213–14. For other examples of man-eating dragons see *Tlalocan* 2, pp. 89–90.
19. *Codex Telleriano-Remensis*, 1964, 3:29.
20. Seler 1963, 2:216. Undoubtedly the Quetzalcoatl present at the Rock of Chapultepec was thought to live in the sacred spring there. See Alvarado Tezozó-moc 1944, pp. 170–71.
21. *Codex Nuttall*, 1975, plate 75.
22. My material on Itzamná comes from Thompson 1970, pp. 209–33.
23. Muñoz Camargo 1966, p. 155.

24. Among the Tlalhuicas adolescents were introduced to sex during a festival of Xochiquetzal. *Codex Magliabecchiano*, 1970, p. 41.
25. *Codex Telleriano-Remensis*, 1964, 2:22, 23.
26. Ibid., 1:11.
27. She may have descended as a demonic form of the goddess, perhaps as Tlazolteotl or Itzpapalotl. Ibid., 1:5.
28. Muñoz Camargo (1966, p. 155) has Tezcatlipoca steal the goddess from her husband Tlaloc and install her in the topmost heaven. Alarcón (*Estudios de cultura nahuatl* 6:107.) has Tezcatlipoca carry her off into the underworld. The latter seems more authentic inasmuch as Sahagún (1950, 2:210) states that the goddess descended into the land of corruption from Tamoanchan.
29. *Codex Telleriano-Remensis*, 1964, 2:30.
30. There is a detailed drawing of the Palenque bird in *Mesa Redonda de Palenque*, 1974, pt. 1, p. 82, fig. 10.
31. For references to the Moan bird, see Thompson 1960, pp. 114–15; *Mesa Redonda de Palenque*, 1978, pt. 4, pp. 105–106.
32. Mendieta 1945, 1:86; Sahagún 1956, 2:111.
33. This was particularly true in Totonac mythology. Las Casas 1966, p. 100.
34. Sahagún 1950, 6:203.
35. Castillo 1966, pp. 66, 89.
36. Ibid.
37. *Codex Laud* 1966, p. 14. In the night sky the sun is carried on the back of Xolotl. This is depicted on the Stuttgart statue.
38. Castillo 1966, pp. 66, 89.
39. *Mesa Redonda de Palenque*, 1976, pt. 3, p. 11.
40. Krickeberg 1966, p. 221.
41. The ancestors are the same as the warriors of the past who have been killed in war or sacrificed. Seler 1963, 1:196.
42. *Codex Telleriano-Remensis*, 1964, p. 8.
43. Olmos 1965, p. 32.
44. Seler 1960, 4:150.
45. *Codex Vaticanus Latinus 3738*, 1964, p. 17.
46. Ibid., p. 8.
47. Olmos 1965, p. 32.
48. Ibid., p. 33.
49. For Yohualteuctli as the sun in the underworld, see Sahagún 1950, 2:202.
50. Di Peso 1974, 2:410–17, 548; Wauchope 1964–76, 4:21ff.
51. Wauchope 1964–76, 4:104.
52. Ibid., p. 109.
53. Tyler 1964, pp. 98–103, 245.
54. Sahagún 1950, 10:189ff.
55. *Histoyre du Méchique*, 1905, p. 35; *Anales de Cuauhtitlan*, 1945, p. 7.
56. *Codex Mendocino*, 1964, pp. 54–55.
57. Olmos 1965, p. 32.
58. Sahagún 1950, 7:11, 60–61; *Histoyre du Méchique*, 1905. p. 26. We note that Yohualteuctli lives in one of the levels of heaven adjoining the abodes of Quetzalcoatl, Tezcatlipoca, and Tlahuizcalpanteuctli, a not-unexpected conjunction of

related deities—all with nocturnal associations. *Histoyre du Méchique*, 1905, pp. 22–23.

59. *Codex Vaticanus Latinus 3738*, 1964, p. 5.

60. *Leyenda de los Soles*,1945, p. 120.

61. Edmonson 1971, pp. 9–10, 12–13.

62. Furst 1978, p. 58.

63. *Codex Vaticanus Latinus 3738*, 1964, pp. 8, 17.

64. *Codex Telleriano-Remensis*, 1964, 1:8, 2:22–23. The list is as follows: Quetzalcoatl (Ce Acatl), Huitzilopochtli (garbled), Tezcatlipoca, Tonacateuctli (!), Yohualteuctli, Tlahuizcalpanteuctli, Itzpapalotl, Tzontemoc, Mixcoatl, Yacateuctli, and Mictlanteuctli. Inasmuch as all these were the children of Citlallatonac and Citlalinicue, they were necessarily also stars (they fell from the sky on the day 1-eagle). Ibid., p. 30. Every one of these gods has connections with Quetzalcoatl either in myth or in iconography.

65. Ixtlilxochitl, 1965*b*, p. 38f.

66. Serna 1953, pp. 124, 247.

67. *Codex Vaticanus Latinus 3738*, 1964, p. 15.

68. Ibid., pp. 15, 17.

69. Olmos 1965, pp. 69–70; *Codex Vaticanus Latinus 3738*, 1964, pp 1, 2.

70. Ibid., p. 3.

71. *Histoyre du Méchique*, 1905, p. 27.

72. *Codex Magliabecchiano*, 1970, p. 76.

73. *Leyenda de los Soles*, 1945, pp. 122–25.

74. Sahagún 1950, 2:209.

75. Ibid., 9:10.

76. Ibid., 6:203; 10:169.

77. The fact that the new sun was said to stop in the sign 4-movement would seem to imply a zodiac. *Leyenda de los Soles*, 1945, p. 122.

78. For the names of the five constellations see Alvarado Tezozómoc 1944, p. 396. Tezozómoc seemingly calls the Little Bear the Citlallachco, or Stellar Ball Court. Other star names and identifications are found in Sahagún 1950, 7:60–66; but, with the exception of the Pleiades, all remain doubtful. Aveni (1980, pp. 30–38) has an excellent summary of Mesoamerican stars and constellations and their possible present-day equivalents.

79. Mendieta 1945, 1:106; Sahagún 1950, 4:4 (and page opposite plate 20 in vol. 7); Serna 1953, p. 122

80. Sahagún 1956, 1:315. Olmos, however, states that Quetzalcoatl could read the meaning of the sky and of the stars. Olmos 1965, p. 38.

81. *Codex Telleriano-Remensis*, 1964, 2:33.

Part Two

1. *Codex Vaticanus Latinus 3738*, 1964, p. 17.

2. *Codex Vindobonensis Mexicanus I*, 24, 28ff., 32–36, 47–52. The recent commentary on this codex by Jill Furst should be consulted where needed.

3. The concept of Ehecatl supporting the sky is very old. See the Kaminaljuyú material reproduced in Benson 1968, p. 125.

4. Izapa Stela no. 23, reproduced in Wauchope 1964–76, 2:253.

5. Stela no. 19, Kaminaljuyú, reproduced as fig. 4 in Proskouriakoff 1968.

6. Covarrubias 1957, fig. 73.

7. Durán 1967, 1:170.

8. Seler 1960, 5:490–91.

9. Sahagún 1950, 4:101.

10. Brundage 1979, pp. 4 ff., 24–25.

11. Sahagún 1950, 1:9, rev. ed.

12. Codex Borgia 1976, p. 29.

13. We note in the *Codex Hall* (1947) the use of fans, which are being waved by five women officiants in front of a temple of the Feathered Serpent.

14. Seler 1963, 2:240.

15. Each of the four has a wind name, *Codex Vindobonensis Mexicanus I*, n.d., p. 51.

16. The revised version scarcely changes the translation. Sahagún 1950, 3:13, rev. ed.

17. This floral forehead decoration is also found in Maya representations of the Classic period in which the God K is in question. See Robicsek 1978, fig. 4. In God K we are probably talking about Bolon Dz'acab, the Maya lineage deity and a form of Itzamná. Thompson 1970, p. 225.

18. See Xolotl wearing the head fan and bearing the sun's name Seven Flower in *Codex Nuttall*, 1975, plate 76.

19. Klein 1976, pp. 199–203.

20. Otherwise referred to as the "wind jewel." Among others see Wauchope 1964–76, 11:591, 597; Thompson 1960, p. 278. At Tajín the wind jewel appears as a Venus glyph imposed on a star-shaped shell. Kampen 1972, figs. 24, 25.

21. Durán 1967, 1:62.

22. *Codex Magliabecchiano*, 1970, p. 61.

23. Alvarado Tezozómoc 1944, p. 241.

24. Wauchope 1964–76, 3:751ff.

25. Kampen 1972, fig. 24.

26. Stela no 19, Seibal.

27. Coe 1967, p. 57.

28. Wauchope 1964–76, 3:882.

29. Sahagún 1950, 7:66–67.

30. *Codex Borbonicus*, 1974, p. 26.

31. *Codex Magliabecchiano*, 1970, p. 61.

32. Muñoz Camargo 1966, p. 43.

33. See the dragon backpiece worn by Xiuhteuctli in *Codex Borbonicus*, 1974, p. 9.

34. *Codex Vindobonensis Mexicanus I*, n.d., p. 48; *Selden Roll*, 1955.

35. *Codex Vaticanus Latinus 3738*, 1964.

36. Kubler 1962, p. 80. For the prevalence of round structures in the Huaxteca see Weaver 1972, pp. 215–16.

37. Alvarado Tezozómoc 1944, p. 154; *Codex Nuttall* 1975, p. 15.

38. Klein (1976, p. 147) identifies the dragon-maw entrance as that of an earth dragon. This is undeniable, yet I feel that it also represented the dragon as a night-sky creature. There is really no incompatibility between the two interpretations.

39. Mendieta 1945, 1:92; Motolinía 1951, pp. 104–105. The distinction made by the latter between two types of round temples, high and low, is worthless, since he does not clearly indicate whether both types belonged to Quetzalcoatl. The Malinalco complex of buildings (three of them circular in ground plan) show that a great elaboration of meaning had taken place by the late period.

40. Di Peso 1974, 2:548–49.

41. Pollock (1936) believes that there is probably a circular temple buried inside the great pyramid of Cholula.

42. Edmonson 1971, passim.

43. *Leyenda de los Soles*, pp. 120–21; *Histoyre du Méchique*, 1905, pp. 26–27.

44. Torquemada 1969, 2:76.

45. *Anales de Cuauhtitlan*, 1945, p. 5.

46. *Codex Vindobonensis Mexicanus I*, n.d., pp. 10, 23–26, 29, 33, 43. There is a picture of Tonacateuctli in *Codex Vaticanus Latinus 3738*, 1964, p. 1.

47. *Selden Roll*, 1955; *Codex Vindobonensis Mexicanus I*, n.d., pp. 47–48. There is a difficult variant of this in *Codex Nuttall* 1975, pp. 18–21. See also Furst 1978, p. 107.

48. Sahagún 1950, 3:34ff. Cogulludo (quoted in Tozzer 1957, p. 113), referring to Yucatán, mentions Quetzalcoatl as the god who named all the features of the land, but he unaccountably calls him Zamna.

49. *Histoyre du Méchique*, 1905, pp. 31–32. Mythical mountains filled with corn go as far back as Teotihuacán, as we can see from the murals.

50. *Leyenda de los Soles*, 1945, p. 121. There is a later translation in Garibay K. 1961, p. 223.

51. *Codex Borgia* 1976, p. 43.

52. Edmonson 1971, p. 147.

53. Olmos 1965, p. 33.

54. Ibid., p. 37.

55. *Codex Magliabecchiano*, 1970, p. 53.

56. *Histoyre du Méchique*, 1905, p. 27.

57. Sahagún 1950, 3:35. The statement (Olmos 1965, p. 37) that it was Camaxtli (i.e., Mixcoatl) who invented *octli* in no wise contradicts Ehecatl's claims. See chapter 4 of this book for the interchangeability of the two gods.

58. Alvarado Tezozómoc 1944, p. 272.

59. *Histoyre du Méchique*, 1965, pp. 32–33. This myth casts Ehecatl as the priest or devotee of Tezcatlipoca, doing that god's bidding in bringing song and dance into the world.

60. Sahagún 1956, 3:186.

61. *Codex Magliabecchiano*, 1970, p. 78; Cervantes de Salazar 1914, p. 41. One of Quetzalcoatl's avatars, Nanahuatl, was a god of skin diseases. Torquemada 1969, 2:152.

62. Durán 1967, 1:65–66. The specific ailments ascribed to Quetzalcoatl are easily explained. Blindness is to be connected with the often-seen depiction of the god with the buccal mask and the extruded eye, the latter meaning blindness

sacrificially induced. The skin afflictions are connected with Nanahuatl, whose name was the word for an eruptive skin condition referred to as "the Indian disease" and possibly venereal in character. Hernandez 1964, p. 49. Coughs are simple references to Quetzalcoatl as the god of the winds.

63. Roys 1967, p. 83.

64. Scholes and Roys 1968, p. 57.

65. Garibay K. 1958, p. 118.

66. *Codex Borbonicus*, 1974, p. 30.

67. *Codex Magliabecchiano*, 1970, p. 34; Veytia 1944, 2:341.

68. Serna 1953, p. 181.

69. Clavijero 1958, 2:69; Torquemada 1969, 2:52.

70. Sahagún 1950, 11:80.

71. Sahagún 1950, 3:35. As far as I am aware male genitalia were sacrificed only to Quetzalcoatl. See Cervantes de Salazar 1914, p. 37.

72. *Codex Hall* 1947.

73. Thompson 1960, p. 73.

74. Sahagún 1950, 6:203.

75. Sahagún 1956, 2:212.

76. *Codex Telleriano-Remensis*, 1964, 2:2.

77. Ibid., 1:3. Of course, the very opposite omen could be attributed to the date 9-wind. Sahagun (1950 4:7ff.) tells us that the date was unfortunate. Whatever the man born on that date contrived would, like wind or water, vanish or be turned away.

78. *Codex Vaticanus Latinus 3738*, 1964, p. 5.

79. Durán 1967, 1:265.

80. Sahagún 1956, 2:118. See Merle Robertson's statement that "possibly all of Middle America claimed ancestral kinship to the serpent," *Mesa Redonda de Palenque*, 1974, 1:79.

81. Durán 1967, 1:265.

82. *Codex Vaticanus Latinus 3738*, 1964, p. 5.

83. Alvarado Tezozómoc 1944, p. 490.

84. *Anales de Cuauhtitlan 1945*, p. 3. The *Selden Roll* graphically displays how the tribes departed from the Seven Caves, taking with them the god Quetzalcoatl as a bundle. The first two plates in the Durán *Atlas* show Quetzalcoatl closely connected with Chicomoztoc.

85. Garibay K. 1958, p. 118.

86. Alvarado Tezozómoc 1949, pp. 43–44.

87. With the Mexicans it could be direct descent from the god in Chicomoztoc or through their connections with the Culhuas, whose ancestral founder had been Quetzalcoatl. Motolinía 1951, p. 82. Another version of the founding of Mexico describes how the god first sat on a red-and-black rock, which thus became the omphalos of later Tenochtitlán. The rock was called the *tepetlatl*. Alvarado Tezozómoc 1949, pp. 43–44.

88. Scholes and Roys 1968, pp. 56–57.

89. Kukulcan here is probably the god Bolon Dz'acab. *Mesa Redonda de Palenque*, 1974, 3:12.

90. Recinos and Goetz 1953, p. 64.

91. Ibid., pp. 59, 76.
92. Edmonson 1971, p. 247.
93. Roys 1967, pp. 67, 88–98, 192–95; Edmonson 1971, pp. 215, 217.
94. It is probable that Cholula was the grand exemplar for all of Aztec cult. The information is limited, however, most of it coming from Gabriel Rojas, the *corregidor* of Cholula in the latter part of the sixteenth century. For a summary of the limited Cholula material see Marqina 1970, pp. 212–17.
95. At the end of every lustrum rulers looked for the return of Quetzalcoatl. Serna 1953, p. 123.
96. Sahagún 1950, 3:36.
97. Sahagún 1969, pp. 120–21. Quetzalcoatl's connection with the *coapetlatl* may be as old as Teotihuacán. Séjourné 1962, fig. 38. The god also appears as the first Aztec ruler seated on the serpent mat in the Durán *Atlas*, plate 1.
98. The date of the exit from Chicomoztoc is also given as 1-reed. *Anales de Cuauhtitlan*, 1945, p. 3.
99. Cervantes de Salazar 1914, p. 43.
100. Olmos 1965, p. 38.
101. Alvarado Tezozómoc 1944, pp. 170–71.
102. *Historia Tolteca-Chichimeca*, 1976, passim.
103. *Codex Vaticanus Latinus 3738*, 1964, pp. 5, 14.
104. Caso seems to identify this god One Jaguar with the fire serpent. Caso 1964, fig. 4. There is some doubt about this.
105. The full name may be translated as the Mountain Made by Man in the Metropolis of Cholula. The correct spelling shows the double *l*, but I use the modern equivalent.
106. The Maya god corresponding to Yacateuctli is Ek Chuah (who is probably the God M of the codices), a black god with a long nose. Kelley 1965, p. 102.
107. Sahagún 1950, 2:119–20.
108. Torquemada 1969, 2:57.
109. Ibid.; Sahagún 1950, 9:51. We know also that Quetzalcoatl had as another avatar the god Amimitl, who was the deified wand or staff of Mixcoatl. Olmos 1965, p. 40. When we remember that, among the Pipil, Mixcoatl was a god of merchants, we realize that we have a parallel instance to the above.
110. Gómara 1964, pp. 128, 130–31; Olmos 1965, p. 38; Las Casas 1966, p. 5.
111. Motolinía 1951, p. 123.
112. Motolinía 1967, p. 68.
113. Torquemada 1969, 1:56; 2:350–51; see also note 94 above.
114. Quetzalcoatl was known in Cholula as Ce Acatl (*Códice Xolotl*, 1951, p. 1); as Ehecatl (Durán 1967, 1:170); and as Nacxitl Tepeuhqui (*Historia Tolteca-Chichimeca* 1976, p. 143). He could also be invoked there as Ipalnemoani Tloque Nahuaque (ibid.).
115. Marquina 1970, pp. 102–103. Could this altar have been the *coamomoztli* (*Historia Tolteca-Chichimeca* 1976, p. 110)?
116. Marquina 1970, p. 36.
117. Durán 1967, 1:166.
118. Ixtlilxochitl 1965*b*, p. 21; 1965*a*, p. 24.
119. Ixtlilxochitl 1965*b*, pp. 20, 470; 1965*a*, p. 24.

120. Ixtlilxochitl 1965*b*, p. 20; 1965*a*, pp. 3, 69. This tree was symbolized in a cross made of *pochotl* wood. Sahagún 1956, 1:291. The early friars immediately equated this with the Christian cross (Ixtlilxochitl 1965*a*, p. 369), thus deepening their conviction that Quetzalcoatl was Saint Thomas.

121. Also in *Codex Borgia*, 1976, p. 53.

122. Ixtlilxochitl 1965*a*, p. 23f.

123. The leaves and buds of the Green Willow tree (*quetzaluexotl*) were used medicinally to cure fevers and pustules, both of them diseases sent by Quetzalcoatl. Sahagún 1950, 11:169.

124. Garibay K. 1964, 2:21ff.

125. Hernández 1964, p. 179; Torquemada 1969, 2:290; Las Casas 1966, pp. 90–91.

126. Torquemada 1969, 2:50–51, 350–51.

127. *Codex Vaticanus Latinus 3738*, 1964, p. 20; *Codex Telleriano-Remensis*, 1964, 2:5. The Lienzo Antonio de León gives the date year 7-reed, day 7-reed for the appearance out of Chicomoztoc of the first Aztecs, who were presumably carrying with them their god Quetzalcoatl. It is certainly no accident that Ahuitzotl chose it as the date of the inauguration of the great temple in Tenochtitlán. The date also appears on the Acuecuexatl Stone in the main hall of the Museo Nacional.

128. Torquemada 1969, 2:574–75; Sahagún 1950, 4:29; Sahagún 1956, 1:330.

129. Durán 1967, 1:63–64.

130. *Codex Telleriano-Remensis*, 1964, 2:5.

131. Marquina 1970, p. 213.

132. A full description of the Cholula idol is to be found in Durán 1967, 1:62.

133. Durán 1967, 1:65–66.

Part Three

1. Sahagún 1950, 3:15, rev. ed.

2. By giving birth to the deified knife of sacrifice, the goddess Citlalinicue can be said to have originated heart sacrifice. Mendieta 1945, 1:83.

3. *Anales de Cuauhtitlan*, 1945, p. 14.

4. *Leyenda de los Soles*, 1945, p. 123; Olmos 1965, p. 36f.

5. *Codex Telleriano-Remensis*, 1964, 2:28.

6. Torquemada 1969, 2:115.

7. Mendieta 1945, 1:85, 87.

8. *Codex Vindobonensis Mexicanus I*, n.d., p. 49.

9. Ibid., p. 48.

10. *Codex Nuttall* 1975, plates 21, 22.

11. *Codex Borgia*, 1976, p. 40.

12. Torquemada 1969, 2:177; Pomar 22; Sahagún 1956, 1:307.

13. Sahagún 1950, 6:210.

14. Sahagún 1950, 2:161; Durán 1967, 2:159.

15. The priesthood of Quetzalcoatl excelled all others in the rigor of its discipline. Torquemada 1969, 2:221–22.

16. Seler 1960, 3:517, 519. This rite has often been described, see among others Motolinía 1951, pp. 129ff.; Mendieta 1945, 1:112.

17. One Jaguar is a name usually applied to Xipe. In the *Selden Roll* he is a penitential and sacrificial god whose promptings in Chicomoztoc send the ancestors forth carrying with them their god Quetzalcoatl.

18. León-Portilla 1958, p. 91; Alvarado Tezozómoc 1944, 289, 304. For the presence of Tlilpotonqui as Nine Wind in Mexican cult, see Sahagún 1950, 2:194.

19. Torquemada 1969, 2:182-83; Las Casas 1966, pp. 69-70, 93; Motolinía 1951, 126; Mendieta 1945, 1:114-15.

20. Durán 1967, 1:55, 170; Las Casas 1966, pp. 93-94.

21. *Leyenda de los Soles*, 1945, p. 121.

22. *Codex Vaticanus Latinus 3738*, 1964, p. 9.

23. Sahagún 1950, 3:13.

24. Ruiz de Alarcón 1953, p. 67.

25. Edmonson 1971, pp. 233-34.

26. *Leyenda de los Soles*, 1945, p. 120-21.

27. Beyer 1965, p. 457.

28. Durán 1967, 1:207.

29. Herrera 1944-47, 3:194.

30. Durán 1967, 1:73. The statue of a dancing monkey wearing a buccal mask was recently found in the metro excavations at Pino Suárez Street in Mexico City. This is the area of the small, round shrine of Ehecatl. See *National Geographic* 158 (December, 1980):706ff.

31. *Codex Borgia*, 1970, p. 72.

32. This scene is depicted in *Codex Vaticanus Latinus 3738*, 1964, p. 6.

33. Ibid., p. 9; *Codex Telleriano-Remensis*, 1964, p. 24.

34. Torquemada 1969, 2:52.

35. The *tonalamatl* can be fitted loosely into the category of sorcery (*nahuallotl*) because it belonged to the *nahualtin*. Sahagún 1950, 4:1.

36. Serna (1953, p. 120) mentions Cipactli as the first man created.

37. *Codex Telleriano-Remensis*, 1964, 2:14, 16.

38. Ibid.

39. Mendieta 1945, 1:106.

40. Thompson 1971, p. 115.

41. Tamoanchan is once used in parallelism with Yohualichan. Garibay K. 1964, "The House of Night," 1:2, 29, 30.

42. Sáenz 1967, *passim*.

43. Sahagún 1956, 2:172; Durán 1967, 1:228.

44. Olmos 1965, p. 25.

45. All of this calendrical learning was centered in the *calmecac*, of which Quetzalcoatl was the patron god. Sahagún 1950, 2:36-37; 3:59, 65; Hernández 1964, pp. 24ff.

46. Thompson (1972, p. 112) puts the 260-day sacred almanac at the center of the Maya universe.

47. Edmonson 1971, p. 9.

48. Ibid, pp. 10-13. This high god (who interestingly is single, not double) is called Kux Kah, and his calendrical name is One Leg (a day name in Yucatec Mayan; Ibid., p. 11).

49. For these items of measurement of the Castillo, see Cahodas 1978, pp. 254–55.
50. Kampen, South Ball Court Panel 6.
51. Sahagún 1956, 1:109; Hernández 1964, p. 145.
52. *Codex Telleriano-Remensis*, 1964, 2:12; *Codex Vaticanus Latinus 3738*, 1964, p. 27. We also see that Tlaloc can assume the regalia of Quetzalcoatl. *Codex Vaticanus Latinus 3773*, 46.
53. Sahagún 1950, 10:168–69.
54. From Teotihuacán comes a representation of a Tlaloc head supported by twin dragons (Kubler 1967, fig. 32) that points to the same close relationship between the two gods as do the heads adorning the Quetzalcoatl temple in that city.
55. Soustelle 1967, p. 38.
56. Pasztory 1974, passim.
57. For the presence of Xolotl in Teotihuacán, see Kubler 1967, fig. 25.
58. One can hardly fail to feel the warlike bias of this avatar of Quetzalcoatl.
59. Durán 1967, 2:292.
60. For Quetzalcoatl as one of the Tlalocs, see León-Portilla 1967, pp. 152–55.
61. A Quetzalcoatl priest at Teotihuacán wears a buccal mask, but it is not like the later Aztec Ehecatl mask. Séjourné 1969, p. 278. The typical Ehecatl buccal mask is not found in Teotihuacán.
62. Sahagún 1950, 2:23, 29. The best depiction of the winds is in *Codex Borgia*, 1976, p. 29. The winds inhabited the sixth heaven. Olmos 1965, p. 69. Winds were considered noxious. *Codex Vaticanus Latinus 3738*, 1964, p. 2.

Part Four

1. Ponce de León, 1965, p. 131; Muñoz Camargo 1966, p. 6.
2. Olmos 1965, p. 33.
3. *Anales de Cuauhtitlan*, 1945, p. 3.
4. Corona Nuñez 1957, p. 18.
5. I am not including the myth of Mixcoatl and his three descendants (*Anales de Cuauhtitlan*, 1945, pp. 61–62), since it is basically an early genealogy of Cuitlahuac.
6. *Leyenda de los Soles*, 1945, pp. 122–23.
7. Olmos 1965, pp. 36–37.
8. *Anales de Cuauhtitlan*, 1945, p. 3; Muñoz Camargo, 1966, pp. 39–40.
9. *Leyenda de los Soles*, 1945, pp. 123–24.
10. Ibid., p. 124. The two-headed deer is the sky, that Camaxtli—i.e., Mixcoatl—is said to have carried about on his back. Olmos 1965, p. 37. The passage cited also confirms that the Feast of Quecholli, which celebrated sky with many fires, was established by Camaxtli. The two-headed deer thus competes with the Feathered Serpent as a personification of the sky.
11. *Leyenda de los Soles*, 1945, p. 124.
12. Olmos 1965, pp. 112–13.

13. *Leyenda de los Soles*, 1945, p. 125.
14. *Codex Telleriano-Remensis*, 1964, 2:33.
15. *Anales de Cuauhtitlan*, 1945, p. 30.
16. Tozzer 1957, fig. 392.
17. Ibid., fig. 126. Representations of the Feathered Serpent in Teotihuacán with the Venus symbol on his body are also found.
18. An easily accessible reproduction of this can be found in Morley and Brainerd 1946, fig. 42.
19. The best-known depictions of this god are in *Codex Borgia*, 1976, pp. 16, 19, 53, 54, 69, 76.
20. *Anales de Cuauhtitlan*, 1945, p. 11.
21. Sahagún 1950, 7:62.
22. This is perhaps the most widespread of all the functions of the morning star and the one most graphically depicted. See *Anales de Cuauhtitlan*, 1945, pp. 11–12; plates 46–50; *Codex Cospi* 1968, pp. 9–11.
23. Thompson 1970, pp. 302–303.
24. Nowotny 1976, fig. 5.
25. Seler 1960, 3:443.
26. Medellín Zenil 1976, p. 223.
27. Wauchope 1964–76, 2:244.
28. Sahagún 1956, I, 237; Torquemada II, 152.
29. Wauchope 1964–76, 2:13, 18.
30. The myth specifies four sisters as being present, but inasmuch as they are essentially four aspects of Tlazolteotl, I have substituted her name. Sahagún 1950, 7:7.
31. Huitzilopochtli is a form of the sun god who destroys all his enemies, the stars and the moon. This is the matter of the myth of the gigantomachy, and it is the "alternative telling" I am referring to above.
32. Thompson 1960, p. 220; 1972, p. 69. Ixquimilli is a god of darkness, of cold, and of blind fate. His name refers to his characteristic of wearing a blindfold and can be translated as the Heedless One. Specifically, he would seem to be that fate active on the battlefield which selected warriors out of the melée for capture and sacrifice. This Ixquimilli was an avatar of Tezcatlipoca, as well as a form of Venus. Ixquimilli had an avatar who was a god of sexual sin (*Codex Telleriano-Remensis*, 1964, p. 18), which explains why he was the patron of the *trecena* beginning with 1-lizard. In this avatar he is called Itztlacoliuhqui. In any case, he was a star in the heavens who walked backward, was blindfolded, and gave auguries of war and births.
33. Durán 1967, 1:98.
34. It is possible that there is a connection between this officiant and the depiction of Ce Acatl as a feathered coyote (or wolf?), see *Smithsonian*, May, 1978, p. 58.
35. Durán 1967, 1:175–76.
36. *Codex Vaticanus Latinus 3738*, 1964, pp. 10, 12, 41, 42; *Codex Borbonicus*, 1974, p. 14; *Codex Borgia*, 1976, p. 67.
37. Seler 1960, 3:337; 4:113–14.
38. Durán 1967, 1:95.

39. Sahagún 1950, 2:172.
40. *Leyenda de los Soles*, 1945, p. 122.
41. This is attested both from the Sun Stone and from the *Historia de los mexicanos por sus pinturas*. Caso 1967, p. 196.
42. The reader must be warned that this name is based on a textual emendation, Sahagún 1950, 2:214; Garibay K. 1958, p. 222.
43. Olmos 1965, p. 69.
44. This is the sun as Huitzilopochtli.
45. *Codex Vaticanus Latinus 3738*, 1964, p. 15.
46. Sahagún 1956, 1:253.
47. *Codex Borgia*, 1976, p. 40.
48. Sahagún 1950, 6:206.
49. *Codex Borgia*, 1976, p. 40.

Part Five

1. Among the Mayans, Xolotl is a deformed dog whose name was Lahun Chan, Ten Sky. Thompson 1960, pp. 77, 218–19.
2. Sandford 1966, p. 150; Swadesh and Sancho, 1966, p. 75. The word had a strong pejorative sense. Andrews 1975, p. 485.
3. Sahagún 1958a, p. 177.
4. Edmonson 1971, pp. 4, 125.
5. Xolotl appears to be represented, paired with the Feathered Serpent, on a Teotihuacán mural. Kubler 1967, fig. 25.
6. *Codex Vaticanus Latinus 3738*, 1964, p. 45.
7. *Codex Vindobonensis Mexicanus I*, n.d., pp. 49, 50. On plate 50 the twinned Xolotl appears twice in his form as a stone creature. On plate 49 he appears in his dog-faced form. The birth of Nine Wind (Quetzalcoatl) is shown as subsequent to the above appearances.
8. Torquemada 1969, 2:77; Mendieta 1945, 1:85.
9. The Mixtec codices *Nuttall*, *Selden*, and *Vindobonensis* present this stone form of Xolotl.
10. *Estudios de cultura nahuatl*, 6:107.
11. *Codex Telleriano-Remensis*, 1964, 2:28.
12. Torquemada 1969, 2:151.
13. *Codex Borgia*, 1976, pp. 33–34.
14. Durán 1967, 1:65–66. The *curanderos* traditionally used images of Quetzalcoatl in the practice of their art. *Codex Magliabecchiano*, 1970, p. 78.
15. *Codex Telleriano-Remensis*, 1964, 2:24.
16. *Codex Vindobonensis Mexicanus I*, n.d., p. 49; Furst 1978, p. 103.
17. Sahagún 1950, 8:8. An interesting popular ceremony took place on the finding of a double ear of maize. Ponce de León 1965, p. 376.
18. Wauchope 1964–76, 10:144, 11:497.
19. The Cuilapa myth is reproduced and thoroughly analyzed in Furst 1978, pp. 60–67.

20. Wauchope 1964–76, 3:697, fig. 13.
21. Durán 1967, *Atlas*, plate 1.
22. Marquina 1970, p. 103, photos 44–47.
23. Wauchope 1964–76, 4:104.
24. Tyler 1964, pp. 213–14.
25. *Codex Borbonicus*, 1974, p. 16.
26. *Codex Vindobonensis Mexicanus I*, n.d., p. 28; *Codex Telleriano-Remensis* 1964, p. 26; see also Furst (1978, pp. 168–69) for One Crocodile.
27. Miller 1973, fig. 346.
28. Four Movement and four of his avatars here preside over a cult scene in a *tlachco*. *Codex Vindobonensis Mexicanus I*, n.d., p. 20. See also Furst 1978, pp. 163–64.
29. *Codex Vindobonensis Mexicanus I*, n.d., p. 30.
30. Furst (1978, pp. 240–41) says that Four Motion was the divine guardian to the entrances of the underworld.
31. *Codex Vaticanus Latinus 3738*, 1964, p. 25. The two stone Xolotl figures in *Codex Vindobonensis Mexicanus I* (n.d., p. 50) support this.
32. Durán 1967, 1:240. The verb *olini* means simply "to move."
33. *Codex Borgia*, 1976, p. 10.
34. Kampen, South Ball Court Panels 4 and 5.
35. *Codex Borgia*, 1976, p. 65.
36. *Codex Vaticanus Latinus 3738*, 1964, p. 17.
37. Xipe, who is also a sun god, bears among other names that of Four Movement. *Codex Borbonicus*, 1974, p. 14.
38. See Navarrete and Heyden 1975, who identify the god as Tlalteuctli.
39. Sahagún 1950, 2:202. Yohualteuctli's other name was Yacahuitztli (Sharp Nose), which almost duplicates the other names of Yacateuctas as the god of travelers. These names are Yacapitzahuac (Pointed Nose) and Yacacoliuhqui (Aquiline Nose), both names referring to sagacity in the opening of routes. Thus the night sun, Yohualteuctli, was probably thought of as an astral body (sun and/or the planet Venus) seeking its way through the sky of the underworld.
40. Xolotl's stone nature is shown in the Mixtec sources.
41. For the *tlachco*, see Brundage 1979, *passim*.
42. A sacred game was played in the *tlachco* during the summer solstice, the so-called Little Feast of the Lords. *Codex Borbonicus* 1974, p. 27.
43. The center line with the stone marker in the middle was the *tlecotl*. Sahagún 1950, 3:35; Sahagún 1956, 1:291. The word undoubtedly refers to ascent rather than to descent (from *tlehco*, "to ascend"?). It could also be called *itzompan*, meaning "summit" and referring to the zenith of the night sky, i.e., to the nadir. Brundage, 1979, p. 11.
44. *Chronicles of Michoacan*, 1970, pp. 63–64; Corona Nuñez 1957, pp. 20–21.
45. *Codex Borbonicus*, 1974, p. 27.
46. There are competing translations of the hymn. Sahagún 1950, 2:212; Sahagún 1958a, pp. 152–53.
47. Quetzalcoatl's connections with the *tlachco* through his avatar Xolotl are clear. The month of Etzalcualiztli runs into the Tecuilhuitontli. In the first, images of Quetzalcoatl and Xolotl were placed in the *tlachco*, and the *motepulizo*, the

drawing of blood from the penis, was performed. *Codex Magliabecchiano*, 1970, p. 34. The god's temple adjoins a *tlachco* in the *Selden Roll* and is attended by two avatars as priests, one of whom is Four Movement, i.e, Xolotl. This close connection is again shown in *Codex Vindobonensis Mexicanus I*, n.d., p. 20; see also Furst 1978, p. 240. In Tajin, Xolotl is shown as one of the two proprietary gods of the *tlachco*. Kampen 1972, fig. 22.

48. Edmonson 1971, *passim*.

49. The ball could be painted with the face of a deity. Cahodas 1978, pp. 112, 117.

50. The *nahuallachco* see note 42 above. For a ball game played by an exiled prince and certain sorcerers, see Chimalpahin 1965, p. 96. The *nahuallachco* is also connected with Chicomoztoc and the installation of princes. *Historia Tolteca-Chichimeca* 1976, pp. 172, 221.

51. Alvarado Tezozómoc 1944, p. 396.

52. Edmonson 1971, p. 159.

53. See, among others, Serna 1953, p. 198.

54. The connection between Nanahuatl and the underground corn can be clearly seen in *Codex Borgia*, 1976, p. 43.

55. *Histoyre du Méchique*, 1905, p. 30.

56. Ibid., pp. 31–32.

57. Ibid., p. 30.

58. Olmos 1965, p. 35.

59. Muñoz Camargo 1966, pp. 131–32.

60. The sources of the myth of the appearance of the fifth sun are so well known they have not been cited here. See Brundage 1979, *passim*. The presence of a natural cave in the rocks under the temple of the sun at Teotihuacán suggests that at that early time the sun as an underworld figure (Nanahuatl?) was being linked through sacrificial rites to the daytime sun on the pyramid above. See Heyden, 1973.

61. *Codex Borgia*, 1976, p. 42.

62. We know that Nanahuatl had an *ixiptla* who was sacrificed and flayed. Sahagún 1950, 2:172.

63. Muñoz Camargo 1966, p. 131. He is the patron god of the movement sign in *Codex Borgia* 1976, p. 10.

64. *Leyenda de los Soles*, 1945, p. 121.

65. For Nanahuatl's diseases see Sahagún 1956, 1:297; Muñoz Camargo 1966, p. 131.

66. Torquemada 1969, 2:152.

67. *Codex Magliabecchiano* 1970, p. 61; Ixtlilxochitl 1965a, p. 103r.

68. *Codex Borgia* 1976, pp. 56, 73; *Codex Vaticanus Latinus 3773*, pp. 75–76; *Codex Laud*, 1966, p. 1.

69. This sculpture has been mentioned at the end of the Introduction.

70. *Codex Magliabecchiano*, 1970, p. 62.

71. Sahagún 1950, 3:35.

72. Ruiz de Alarcón 1953, p. 121.

73. *Codex Borgia*, 1976, p. 40.

Part Six

1. Sahagún 1956, 1:37.
2. *Codex Borgia*, 1976, p. 32; *Codex Vaticanus Latinus 3773*, p. 26; *Codex Fejérváry-Mayer*, 1971, p. 42v.
3. Olmos 1965, p. 25.
4. Ibid., p. 30.
5. Ibid., p. 69.
6. Edmonson 1971, pp. 32–39.
7. Ibid., p. 4 *et passim*.
8. *Histoyre du Méchique* 1905, pp. 28–29, 31. In this reference Tezcatlipoca is called One Wind, a name that he shares with Quetzalcoatl. Sahagún 1950, 4:101–102, 7:14; Durán 1967, 1:170. This is a particularly significant case of the joining of two gods.
9. Olmos 1965, p. 32.
10. Brundage 1979, pp. 50–53.
11. Tepeyollotli was one of the nine Lords of the Night, all of whom had underworld connections. His connections with Quetzalcoatl are evident. He shares the patronage of the third week of the *tonalpohualli* with Quetzalcoatl. *Codex Borbonicus*, 1974, p. 2; *Codex Telleriano-Remensis*, 1964, 2:4–5; *Codex Vaticanus Latinus 3738*, 1964, p. 19. His temple is of peaked thatch, and, like Quetzalcoatl, he is involved in autosacrifice.
12. On the nature and forms of Tezcatlipoca see Brundage 1979, chap. 4.
13. *Codex Vaticanus Latinus 3738*, 1964, p. 3.
14. One Wind was a sinister avatar, generally associated with Quetzalcoatl. Sahagún 1956, 1:357–58; Sahagún 1950, 4:102. For the other references see Caso 1967, p. 190.
15. Tezcatlipoca could be called Tlayohualli (Darkness). Sahagún 1950, 1:68.
16. Hernández 1964, p. 133.
17. Ixtlilxochitl 1965a, pp. 21, 227–28; 1965b, pp. 11, 247ff, 253, 324, 496. More solid sources are Sahagún 1950, 6:34; 9:13–14; Muñoz Camargo 1966, pp. 129–30, 222; Pomar 1891, pp. 23–24.
18. Sahagún 1950, 10:190–91; Sahagún 1956 1:30; Muñoz Camargo 1966, p. 41.
19. Sahagún 1950, 6:50.
20. For the gods worshiped in Tula see *Anales de Cuauhtitlan*, 1945, pp. 8f. We can assume that the gods listed in the *Leyenda de los Soles* (1945, p. 121) also refer to an early (i.e., Toltec) pantheon. The three deities mentioned as native to Culhuacán (one of whom was Nine Monkey) must also refer back to Tula, *Anales de Cuauhtitlan* (1945, p. 29). The three first rulers of Tula (mentioned in Torquemada (1969, 1:254) are divine names, avatars of both Tezcatlipoca and Quetzalcoatl.
21. Topiltzin would seem to have been the name of an avatar of Quetzalcoatl connected with lineage.
22. Sahagún 1956, 1:278; Sahagún 1950, 10:169–70.
23. Sahagún 1950, 10:190.

24. Ibid., p. 169.
25. *Anales de Cuauhtitlan*, 1945, p. 8.
26. Ibid., pp. 13–14.
27. Olmos 1965, pp. 37–38.
28. *Histoyre du Méchique*, 1905, p. 35.
29. This is the legend in Sahagún 1950, *passim*.
30. See, among many other sources, Sahagún 1956, 1:278–79.
31. *Histoyre du Méchique*, 1905, pp. 36–37.
32. Ixtlilxochitl 1965a, pp. 32–33; 1965b, pp. 47–54.
33. In one version the tempters are Tezcatlipoca, Ihuimecatl, and Toltecatl. *Anales de Cuauhtitlan*, 1945, pp. 8–9. In another version they are Titlacahuan, Huitzilopochtli, and Tlacahuepan. Sahagún 1950, 3:15. We may consider all of them as roughly the same deity.
34. Alvarado Tezozómoc 1944, 2:79.
35. There are several versions of this event. See among others *Anales de Cuauhtitlan*, 1945, pp. 9–10.
36. Alvarado Tezozómoc 1944, 2:48–49; Sahagún 1950, 3:15–16, 31; Sahagún 1956, 1:280.
37. Olmos 1965, p. 38.
38. *Leyenda de los Soles*, 1945, pp. 124–25.
39. Edmonson 1971, pp. 163–73.
40. *Historia Tolteca-Chichimeca*, 1976, pp. 132–36.
41. There are many accounts of the flight of Quetzalcoatl. The most detailed are Sahagún 1950, 3:31–36, 10:170; Sahagún 1956, 1:288–91; *Histoyre du Méchique*, 1905, pp. 37–38; Torquemada 1969, 2:49ff. The same tale, but told as an emigration legend of the Quiché people, is found in Edmonson 1971.
42. Alvarado Tezozómoc 1944, p. 514. See, however, Garibay 1964, 3:1ff., where Ten Flower is a knight left behind in Tula and Topiltzin is additionally referred to as Ihuitimal (or Timal). Ten Flower is said to be Topiltzin's successor in the rule of Tula. *Anales de Cuauhtitlan*, 1945, p. 8.
43. *Anales de Cuauhtitlan*, 1945, p. 8.
44. Ixtlilxochitl 1965b, p. 55.
45. *Histoyre du Méchique*, 1905, p. 37.
46. For a summary of these tales and their sources, see Sahagún 1950, 3:36, n. 7. Anderson and Dibble, however, omit the tales of entry into a mountain and into a tree. For these see Durán 1967, 1:12; *Histoyre du Méchique*, 1905, p. 38. There is another difficult reference to the god's demise (Garibay K. 1958, pp. 202–203) where he is reduced to cinders in a "jeweled container." We note that the places on the coast associated with the end of Quetzalcoatl (Tlapallan and Tlatlayan), which we have interpreted mythically, are also found as actual settlements in the Tuxtlas and Coatzacoalcos areas. Coe and Diehl, 2:13.
47. *Anales de Cuauhtitlan*, 1945, p. 11; Alvarado Tezozómoc 1944, p. 524. Almost certainly the famous myth of Quetzalcoatl's cremation and rise as Ce Acatl is depicted twice in Chichén Itzá. Cahodas 1978, figs. 16, 28.
48. *Anales de Cuauhtitlan*, 1945, p. 11; Torquemada 1969, 2:79–80.
49. *Codex Vaticanus Latinus 3738*, 1964, p. 17. Strictly speaking, the ocean into which Quetzalcoatl as Xolotl disappears must be the Pacific rather than the Gulf

of Mexico. Knowledge of both bodies of water, however, must have existed everywhere in Mesoamerica. The tale therefore makes sense in this larger context.

50. Illustration 102 in Bernal n.d.
51. Sahagún 1950, 10·175–76.
52. Ibid., 3:16.
53. Sahagún 1956, 2:282.
54. Edmonson 1971, p. 233.
55. Wauchope 1964–76, 3:678.
56. Seibal Stela 19.
57. Roys 1967, pp. 88–98.
58. Landa 1941, pp. 19–23, 177; Tozzer 1957, pp. 31, 37.
59. Ixtlilxochitl 1965b, pp. 23–24, 29.
60. Hernández 1964, p. 122.
61. Ixtlilxochitl 1965b, pp. 31–32, 48; Veytia 1944, 1:168–70.
62. Origen de los mexicanos, 1891, pp. 262–63.
63. Torquemada 1969, 2:48.
64. Relación de la genealogía . . . , 1941, p. 245.
65. Anales de Cuauhtitlan, 1945, p. 15; Leyenda de los Soles, 1945, p. 127.
66. Anales de Cuauhtitlan, 1945, pp. 12, 14.
67. Durán 1967, 1:15.
68. Torquemada 1969, 1:255–56; Muñoz Camargo 1966, p. 5.
69. Sahagún 1950, 6:51.
70. Leyenda de los Soles, 1945, p. 126.
71. Durán 1967, 2:493–94; Alvarado Tezozómoc 1944, pp. 503, 505ff. Another name for the rock of Chapultepec was Hueymacco (the Place of Hueymac). Chimalpahín 1965, p. 69.
72. Torquemada 1969, 2:255–56.
73. Durán 1967, 1:14–15; Ixtlilxochitl 1965a, p. 23; 1965b, pp. 20–21, 470; Veytia I, 115.
74. Lehmann 1958, p. 76.
75. The royal blood of the Toltec rulers came from Hueymac, who was a descendant of Topiltzin and the founder of the second dynasty. Relación de la genealogía . . . , 1941, p. 243. This bloodline in the Basin of Mexico and elsewhere represented an unimpeachable legitimacy. It came to the Mexicas through the Culhuas (ibid., p. 245) whose leader had been Hueymac. Histoyre du Méchique, 1905, p. 19.
76. Alvarado Tezozómoc 1944, pp. 170–71.
77. Durán 1967, vol. 2, chap. 67.
78. Historia Tolteca-Chichimeca, 1976, p. 133.
79. Durán 1967, 1:14–15.
80. Ibid.
81. Torquemada 1969, 2:48.
82. Anales de Cuauhtitlan, 1945, p. 12.
83. Ibid.
84. It was called the Easter of the Aztec calendar. Sahagún 1950, 2:9. Descriptions of it can be found in Sahagún 1950, 2:9–10, 64–73; Sahagún 1956, 1:114–15, 152–60; Sahagún 1974, pp. 31–34; Durán 1967, 1:39–45.

85. For Quetzalcoatl's festivals in Cholula, see Durán 1967, 1:63–64, 170; *Codex Telleriano-Remensis*, 1964, 2:5; *Codex Vaticanus Latinus 3738*, 1964, pp. 20, 23.
86. Sahagún 1950, 2:14–15, 91–100; Sahagún 1956, 1:118–19, 174–82; Durán 1967, 1:265ff. It is expressly stated that during the feast the nobles displayed their devices and told tales of the deeds and honors of their ancestors. Torquemada 1969, 1:297–98.
87. Sahagún 1950, 2:36–37; Sahagún 1956, 1:134.
88. Sahagún 1950, 2:37–38; Sahagún 1956, 1:135–36.
89. Edmonson 1971, pp. 161–73.
90. Ibid., p. 183.
91. Caso 1967, p. 195.
92. Ibid., p. 196. The more usual and contrasting date was 1-reed. Tezcatlipoca changed his name to Mixcoatl in the year 2-reed. Olmos 1965, p. 33.
93. Statue in the Museo Nacional.
94. *Estudios de cultura nahuatl*, 1959–76, 6:107.
95. *Codex Magliabecchiano*, 1970, pp. 3, 5.
96. *Codex Borgia*, 1976, p. 35.
97. Sahagún 1956, 2:212–13.
98. Telpochtiliztli. Torquemada 1969, 2:220.
99. Durán 1967, pp. 43, 257. See also the passage on the Toxcatl festival in the *Codex Tudela*.
100. *Histoyre du Méchique*, 1905, p. 33.
101. The story of Martin Ocelotl is summarized in Lafaye 1976 pp. 20–23. I have been unable to check Lafaye's source.

BIBLIOGRAPHY

Alvarado Tezozómoc, Hernando
1944   *Crónica mexicana.* Mexico City: Fondo de Cultura Económica.
1949   *Crónica mexicayotl.* Translated by Adrián León. Mexico City: Imprenta Universitaria.
Anales de Cuauhtitlan
1945   In *Códice Chimalpopoca.* Mexico City: Imprenta Universitaria.
Andrews, J. Richard
1975   *Introduction to Classical Nahuatl.* 2 vols. Austin: University of Texas Press.
Aveni, Anthony F.
1980   *Skywatchers of Ancient Mexico.* Austin: University of Texas Press.
Benson, Elizabeth B., ed.
1968   *Dumbarton Oaks Conference on the Olmec, 1967.* Washington, D.C.: Dumbarton Oaks Research Library and Collection, Trustees of Harvard University.
Bernal, Ignacio
N.d.   *3000 Years of Art and Life in Mexico, as Seen in the National Museum of Anthropology, Mexico City.* Translated by Carolyn B. Czitrom. New York: Harry Abrams.
Beyer, Hermann
1965   *Mito y simbología del México antiguo.* Mexico City: Sociedad Alemana Mexicanista.
1969   *Cien años de arqueología mexicana.* Mexico City: Sociedad Alemana Mexicanista.
The Book of Counsel: The Popol Vuh of the Quiché Maya of Guatemala.
1971   Translated by Munro S. Edmonson. Middle American Research Institute Publication no. 35, New Orleans, La.: Tulane University.

Brundage, Burr C.
  1979   *The Fifth Sun*. Austin: University of Texas Press.
Cahodas, Marvin
  1978   *The Great Ball Court at Chichén Itzá, Yucatán, Mexico*.
           New York: Garland Publishing Co.
Carmack, Robert M.
  1973   *Quichean Civilization*. Berkeley: University of California Press.
Carrasco Pizana, Pedro
  1945   "Quetzalcoatl, dios de Coatepec de los costales, Guerrero." *Tlalocán*, vol. 2 [Mexico City].
Caso, Alfonso
  1964   *Interpretación del Códice Selden*. Mexico City: Sociedad Mexicana de Antropología.
  1967   *Los calendarios prehispánicos*. Mexico City: Universidad Nacional Autónoma de México.
Castillo, Cristobal del
  1966   *Fragmentos de la obra general sobre historia de los mexicanos*. Translated by Francisco del Paso y Troncoso. Ciudad Juárez: Editorial Erandi.
Cervantes de Salazar, Francisco
  1914   *Crónica de la Nueva España*. Madrid: Hispanic Society of America.
Chimalpahin Cuauhtlehuanitzin [Francisco de San Antón Muñon]
  1965   *Relaciones originales de Chalco Amaquemecan*. Translated by Silvia Rendón. Mexico City: Fondo de Cultura Económica.
The Chronicles of Michoacán
  1970   Translated by Eugene R. Craine and Reginald C. Reindorp. Norman: University of Oklahoma Press.
Clavijero, Francisco Javier
  1958   *Historia antígua de México*. 2d ed. 4 vols. Mexico City: Editorial Porrúa.
Codex Borbonicus
  1974   Graz, Austria: Akademische Druck-u. Verlagsanstalt.
Codex Borgia
  1976   Graz, Austria: Akademische Druck-u. Verlagsanstalt.

Codex Cospi
1968   Graz, Austria: Akademische Druck-u. Verlagsanstalt.
Codex Fejérváry-Mayer
1971   Graz, Austria: Akademische Druck-u. Verlagsanstalt.
Codex Hall: An Ancient Mexican Hieroglyphic Picture Manuscript,
            by Charles E. Dibble.
1947   Monographs of the School of American Research,
            no. 11. Albuquerque: University of New Mexico
            Press.
Codex Laud
1966   Graz, Austria: Akademische Druck-u. Verlagsanstalt.
Codex Magliabecchiano
1970   Graz, Austria: Akademische Druck-u. Verlagsanstalt.
Codex Mendocino
1964   In vol. 1 of *Antigüedades de México, basadas en la re-
            copilación de Lord Kingsborough*. 4 vols. Mexico City:
            Secretaría de Hacienda y Crédito Público.
Codex Nuttall: A Picture Manuscript from Ancient Mexico . . .
1975   Introduction by Arthur G. Miller. New York: Dover
            Publications.
Codex Telleriano-Remensis
1964   In vol. 1 of *Antigüedades de México, basadas en la re-
            copilación de Lord Kingsborough*. 4 vols. Mexico City:
            Secretaría de Hacienda y Crédito Público.
Codex Vaticanus Latinus 3738 (Codex Ríos)
1964   In vol. 3 of *Antigüedades de México, basadas en la re-
            copilación de Lord Kingsborough*. 4 vols. Mexico City:
            Secretaría de Hacienda y Crédito Público.
Codex Vaticanus Latinus 3773
1972   Graz, Austria: Akademische Druck-u. Verlagsanstalt.
Codex Vindobonensis Mexicanus I
N.d.   Graz, Austria: Akademische Druck-u. Verlagsanstalt.
Códice Xolotl
1951   Translated by Charles E. Dibble. Mexico City: Pub-
            licaciones del Instituto de Historia.
Coe, Michael D., and Diehl, Richard Diehl
1980   *In the Land of the Olmec*. 2 vols. Austin: University of
            Texas Press.

Coe, William R.
  1967   *Tikal: A Handbook of the Ancient Maya Ruins.* Philadelphia: University of Pennsylvania Museum.
Corona Nuñez, José
  1957   *Mitología tarasca.* Mexico City: Fondo de Cultura Económica.
Covarrubias, Miguel
  1957   *Indian Art of Mexico and Central America.* New York: Alfred A. Knopf.
Di Peso, Charles
  1974   *Casas grandes.* 3 vols. Flagstaff, Ariz.: Northland Press.
Durán, Diego
  1967   *Historia de las Indias de Nuevo España e islas de la tierra firme.* Edited by Angel María Garibay K. 2 vols. Mexico City: Editorial Porrúa.
Edmonson, Munro S.
  1971   See *The Book of Counsel.*
Estudios de cultura nahuatl
  1959–76 Vols. 1–12. Mexico City: Instituto de Historia, Seminario de Cultura Nahuatl, Universidad Nacional Autónoma de México.
Furst, Jill L.
  1978   *Codex Vindobonensis Mexicanus I: A Commentary.* Institute for Mesoamerican Studies Publication no. 4. Albany: State University of New York at Albany.
Garibay K., Ángel María
  1953   *Historia de la literatura Nahuatl.* 2 vols. Mexico City: Editorial Porrúa.
  1958   *Veinte himnos sacros de los Nahuas.* Mexico City: Universidad Nacional Autónoma de México.
  1961   *Llave del Nahuatl.* 2d ed. Mexico City: Editorial Porrúa.
  1964–68 *Poesía Nahuatl.* 3 vols. Mexico City: Universidad Nacional Autónoma de México.
Gay, Carlo
  1972   *Chalcacingo.* Portland, Oreg.: International Scholarly Book Services.
Gómara, Francisco López de

1964   *Cortés: The Life of the Conqueror by His Secretary.* Translated by Lesley Byrd Simpson. Berkeley: University of California Press.

Granata, Joseph John
1980   "The Significance of Zoological Identification of Serpent Species in the Pictorial Manuscripts of Ancient Mexico." Ph.D. dissertation, University of Texas at Austin.

Hernández, Francisco
1964   *Antigüedades de la Nueva España.* Mexico City: Editorial Robredo.

Herrera, Antonio de
1944–47   *Historia general de los hechos de los castellanos en las islas y tierra firme de el Mar Océano.* 10 vols. Asunción, Paraguay: Editorial Guaranía.

Heyden, Doris
1976   "La diosa madre: Itzpapalotl." *Boletín,* Instituto Nacional de Antropología e Historia, vol. 2, no. 11.

1973   "Un Chicomoztoc en Teotihuacán? La cueva bajo la piramide del Sol," *Boletín INAH* 2 : 3–18.

Historia Tolteca-Chichimeca
1976   Translated by Paul Kirchhoff, Lina Odena Güemes, and Luis Reyes García. Mexico City: Instituto Nacional de Antropología e Historia.

Histoyre du Méchique
1905   Edited by M. Edouard de Jonghe. Journal de la Société des Américanistes de Paris, n.s., vol. 2, no. 1.

Ixtlilxochitl, Fernando de Alva
1965a   *Historia de la nación chichimeca.* Vol. 2 of *Obras históricas,* edited by Alfredo Chavero. Reprint. Mexico City: Editor Nacional.

1965b   *Relaciones.* Vol. 1 of *Obras históricas,* edited by Alfredo Chavero. Reprint. Mexico City: Editor Nacional.

Kelley, David H.
1965   "The Birth of the Gods At Palenque." *Estudios de cultura maya,* vol. 5 [Mexico City].

Kampen, Michael E.
1972   *The Sculptures of El Tajín, Veracruz, Mexico.* Gainesville, Fla. University of Florida Press.

Klein, Cecelia
1976   *The Face of the Earth: Frontality in Two-Dimensional Mesoamerican Art.* New York: Garland Publishing Co.
Krickeberg, Walter
1966   "El juego de pelota mesoamericano y su simbolismo religioso." In *Traducciones mesoamericanistas*, vol. 1. Mexico City: Sociedad Mexicana de Antropología.
Kubler, George
1962   *The Art and Architecture of Ancient America.* Harmondsworth, Middlesex: Penguin Books.
1967   *The Iconography of the Art of Teotihuacán.* Studies in Pre-Colombian Art and Archaeology, no. 4. Washington, D.C.: Dumbarton Oaks.
Lafaye, Jacques
1976   *Quetzalcoatl and Guadalupe: The Formation of Mexican National Consciousness.* Chicago: University of Chicago Press.
Landa, Diego de
1941   *Relación de las cosas de Yucatán.* Edited by Alfred M. Tozzer. Papers of the Peabody Museum. Cambridge, Mass.: Harvard University Press.
Las Casas, Bartolomé de
1966   *Los indios de México y Nueva España: antología.* Edited by Edmundo O'Gorman. Mexico City: Editorial Porrúa.
Lehmann, Walter, trans.
1958   *Das Memorial Breve acerca de la fundación de la ciudad de Culhuacan* [by Chimalpahin]. Stuttgart: W. Kohnhammer.
León-Portilla, Miguel
1958   *Ritos, sacerdotes, y atavíos de los dioses.* Mexico City: Instituto de Historia, Universidad Nacional Autónoma de México.
1967   *Trece poetas del mundo azteca.* Mexico City: Universidad Nacional Autónoma de México.
Leyenda de los Soles
1945   In *Códice Chimalpopoca*, translated by Primo Feliciano

Velázquez. Mexico City: Universidad Nacional Autónoma de México.

Marquina, Ignacio
1970   *Proyecto Cholula*. Mexico City: Instituto Nacional de Antropología e Historia.

Medellín Zenil, Alfonso
1976   *El Centro de Veracruz* In *Los Señoríos y estados militaristas*. Mexico: Panorama histórico y cultural, vol. 9, edited by Román Piña Chan. Mexico City: Instituto Nacional de Antropología e Historia.

Mendieta, Gerónimo de
1945   *Historia eclesiástica indiana*. 4 vols. Mexico City: Editorial Chávez Hayhoe.

Mesa Redonda de Palenque
1974   Parts 1 and 2. Edited by Merle Greene Robertson. Pebble Beach, Calif.: Robert Louis Stevenson School, Pre-Columbian Art Research.
1976   Part 3. Edited by Merle Greene Robertson. Pebble Beach, Calif.: Robert Louis Stevenson School, Pre-Columbian Art Research.
1978   Part 4. Edited by Merle Greene Robertson and Donnan Call Jeffers. Pebble Beach, Calif.: Robert Louis Stevenson School, Pre-Columbian Art Research.

Miller, Arthur G.
1973   *The Mural Painting of Teotihuacán*. Washington, D.C.: Dumbarton Oaks.

Molina, Alonso de
1944   *Vocabulario en lengua castellana y mexicana*. Reprint. Madrid: Ediciones Cultura Hispánica.

Morley, Sylvanus G., and Brainerd, George W.
1946   *The Ancient Maya*. 3d ed. Stanford, Calif.: Stanford University Press.

Motolinía, Toribio de
1951   *Motolinía's History of the Indians of New Spain*. Translated by Francis Borgia Steck. Washington, D.C.: Academy of American Franciscan History.
1967   *Memoriales*. Facsimile of the Pimentel edition of 1903. Edited by E. Avina Levy. Guadalajara.

Muñoz Camargo, Diego
1966 *Historia de Tlaxcala*. Facsimile edition. Guadalajara.
Navarrete, Carlos, and Heyden, Doris
1975 "La Cara Central de la Piedra del Sol: una hipótesis," *Estudios de cultura nahuatl*, vol. 9. Mexico City: Universidad Nacional Autónoma de México.
Nowatny, Karl Anton
1976 *Kommentar: Codex Borgia*. Graz, Austria: Akademische Druck-u. Verlagsanstalt.
Olmos, Andrés de
1965 *Historia de los mexicanos por sus pinturas*. In *Teogonía e historia de los mexicanos: tres opusculos del siglo 16*, edited by Ángel María Garibay K. Mexico City: Editorial Porrúa.
Origen de los mexicanos
1891 In *Relaciones de Tezcoco y de la Nueva España* Mexico City: Chávez Hayhoe.
Pasztory, E.
1974 *The Iconography of the Teotihuacán Tlaloc*. Washington, D.C.: Dumbarton Oaks.
Pollock, H. E. D.
1936 *Round Structures of Aboriginal Middle America*. Washington, D.C.: Carnegie Institute of Washington.
Pomar, Juan Bautista
1891 *Relación de Tezcoco*. In *Nueva colección de documentos para la historia de México*, edited by Joaquín García Icazbalceta. Vol. 3. Nandeln, Liechtenstein: Kraus Reprints.
Ponce de Leon, Pedro
1965 *Tratado de los dioses y ritos de la gentilidad*. In *Teogonía e historia de los mexicanos: tres opusculos del siglo 16*, edited by Ángel María Garibay K. Mexico City: Editorial Porrúa.
Proskouriakoff, Tatiana
1968 "Olmec and Maya Art: Problems of Their Stylistic Relation." In *Dumbarton Oaks Conference on the Olmec*, edited by Elizabeth Benson, pp. 119–34. Washington, D.C.: Dumbarton Oaks.
Quirarte, Jacinto

1976   "The Relationship of Izapan-Style Art to Olmec and Maya Art: A Review." In *Origins of Religious Art and Iconography in Preclassic Mesoamerica*, edited by H. B. Nicholson. Los Angeles: UCLA Latin American Center Publications.

Recinos, Adrián and Goetz, Delia, trans.

1953   *The Annals of the Cakchiquels* and *Title of the Lords of Totonicapán.* Norman: University of Oklahoma Press.

Relación de la genealogía y linaje de los señores que han señoreado esta tierra de la Nueva España

1941   Facsimile edition. Mexico City: Chávez Hayhoe.

Robicsek, Francis

1978   "The Mythological Identity of God K." In *Tercera Mesa Redonda de Palenque.* Vol. 4. Palenque, Chiapas, Mexico: Pre-Columbian Art Research Center.

Roys, Ralph L., trans. and ed.

1967   *The Book of Chilam Balam of Chumayel.* Norman: University of Oklahoma Press.

Ruiz de Alarcón, H.

1953   *Tratado de las supersticiones y costumbres gentílicas.* In *Tratados de las idolatrías, supersticiones, dioses, ritos, . . . ,* edited by Francisco del Paso y Troncoso. 2d ed. 2 vols. Mexico City: Librería Navarro.

Sáenz, César A.

1967   *El fuego nuevo.* Mexico City: Universidad Nacional Autónoma de México.

Sahagún, Bernardino de

1950–76   *General History of the Things of New Spain (Florentine Codex).* Translated by Arthur Anderson and Charles Dibble. 12 vols. (vols. 1 and 12 revised). Sante Fe, N. Mex.: School of American Research.

1956   *Historia general de las cosas de Nueva España.* Edited by Ángel María Garibay K. 4 vols. Mexico City: Editorial Porrúa.

1958*a*   *Veinte himnos sacros de los nahuas.* Translated by Ángel María Garibay K. Mexico City: Universidad Nacional Autónoma de México.

1958*b*   *Ritos, sacerdotes, y atavios de los dioses.* Translated by

Miguel León Portilla. Mexico City: Universidad Nacional Autónoma de México.

1969   *Augurios y abusiones*. Translated by Alfredo López Austin. Mexico City: Universidad Nacional Autónoma de México.

1974   *Primeros memoriales*. Translated by Wigberto Jiménez Moreno. Mexico City: Consejo de Historia, Instituto Nacional de Antropología e Historia.

Scholes, France V., and Roys, Ralph L.

1968   *The Maya Chontal Indians of Acalan-Tixchel: A Contribution to the History and Ethnography of the Yucatán Peninsula*. Norman: University of Oklahoma Press.

Séjourné, Laurette

1954   "El Quetzalcoatl en Teotihuacán." *Cuadernos americanos*, no. 3.

1962   *El universo de Quetzalcoatl*. Mexico City: Fondo de Cultura Económica.

1969   *Teotihuacán, métropole de l'Amérique*. Paris: François Maspero.

Selden Roll [*Codex Selden*]

1955   Edited by Cottie A. Burland. Berlin: Verlag Gerb. Mann.

Seler, Eduard

1960   *Gesammelte Abhandlungen*. 5 vols. and index vol. Graz, Austria: Akademische Druck-u. Verlagsanstalt.

1963   *Comentarios al Códice Borgia*. 2 vols. Mexico City: Fondo de Cultura Económica.

Serna, Jacinto de la

1953   *Manual de ministros de indios para el conocimiento de sus idolatrías*. In *Tratados de las idolatrías, supersticiones, dioses, ritos . . .* , edited by Francisco del Paso y Troncoso. 2d ed. 2 vols. Mexico City: Ediciones Fuente Cultural.

Siméon, Rémi

1965   *Dictionnaire de la langue nahuatl ou mexicaine*. Graz, Austria: Akademische Druck-u. Verlagsanstalt.

Soustelle, Jacques

1967   *Arts of Ancient Mexico*. London: Thames and Hudson.

Stanford, Thomas

1966 *Linguistic Analysis of Music and Dance Terms.* Offprint Studies, no. 76. Austin: University of Texas.

Swadesh, Mauricio, and Sancho, Madalena
1966 *Los mil elementos de mexicano clásico.* Mexico City: Universidad Nacional Autónoma de México.

Thompson, Sir J. Eric S.
1960 *Maya Hieroglyph Writing.* Norman: University of Oklahoma Press.
1970 *Maya History and Religion.* Norman: University of Oklahoma Press.
1972 *A Commentary on the Dresden Codex.* Philadelphia: American Philosophical Society.

Torquemada, Juan de
1969 *Monarquía indiana.* 3 vols. Mexico City: Editorial Leyenda.

Tozzer, Alfred M.
1957 *Chichén Itzá and Its Cenote of Sacrifice.* Memoirs of the Peabody Museum, vol. 12. Cambridge, Mass.: Peabody Museum.

Tyler, Hamilton A.
1964 *Pueblo Gods and Myths.* Norman: University of Oklahoma Press.

Underhill, Ruth M.
1965 *Red Man's Religion.* Chicago: University of Chicago Press.

Veytia, Mariano
1944 *Historia antigua de México,* 2 vols. Mexico City: Editorial Leyenda.

Wauchope, Robert, ed.
1964–76 *Handbook of Middle American Indians.* 16 vols. Austin: University of Texas Press.

Weaver, Muriel P.
1972 *The Aztecs, Maya, and Their Predecessors.* New York: Seminar Press.

Zorita, Alonso de
1963 *Life and Labor in Ancient Mexico: Brief and Summary Relation of the Lands of New Spain.* Translated by Benjamin Keen. New Brunswick, N.J.: Rutgers University Press.

INDEX